A FORCE FOR GOOD

A FORCE FOR GOOD

HOW ENLIGHTENED FINANCE CAN RESTORE FAITH IN CAPITALISM

EDITED BY

JOHN G. TAFT

palgrave
macmillan

To Laura

CONTENTS

PREFACE

John G. Taft

CEO, RBC Wealth Management—U.S.

In the seven years since the world was plunged into chaos by the financial crisis of 2008–09, I have traveled extensively across the country: speaking at conferences and business schools; appearing on financial shows, from *Bloomberg Surveillance* to CNBC's *Squawk Box*; writing *Stewardship: Lessons Learned from the Lost Culture of Wall Street* (Wiley, 2012); and posting blogs like "10 New Year's Resolutions for Wall Street." I was driven by my deep belief that there is no more important undertaking than to help build the foundation for what I call enlightened finance: finance in the service of society. Finance based on the core premise of stewardship. Finance as a means to greater ends, namely, making the world a better place.

The central idea of this book is that the financial services system has an opportunity to move past the damage of the past several years and become, in fact, an agent of positive social change. To stand for "goodness" rather than "badness" (as Judge Smails, of the cult movie classic *Caddyshack*, would say). To forge what the *Economist*'s Matthew Bishop terms "the road from ruin," and to walk the path back to respectability, crawl out from underneath an increasingly suffocating pile of recent regulation and rule making.[1] To contribute to constructive change at a time when most political leaders, and the system they serve, have all but abdicated their responsibilities.

So what needs to happen in order for finance to become a force for good in the world? A force for enhancing our collective standard of living? The answer is threefold: the financial industry must stop contributing to the extreme volatility in markets that periodically destabilizes the world economy. Next, financial market participants must foster and engage in a conversation about what outcomes society wants and needs from its economic system.

Finally, we must work to realign the financial system so it supports the economic model that best achieves those outcomes.

In financial capitalism, which is the dominant socioeconomic construct in the world today, there exists a metaphorical contract between society and business. Call it the corporate social compact. This compact isn't written down. It isn't explicit or static. Instead, it evolves and morphs over time. The corporate social compact represents the public's expectations of the role an individual business, industry or entire economic sector will play in society. In return for living up to those expectations, businesses are granted a "license to operate"— metaphorically and literally—to pay their employees and profit their owners.

What we witnessed in the financial sector over the past decade was, in essence, a wholesale breach of contract. We saw the financial services industry failing to live up to its end of the bargain. ("One more scandal and we're going to end up like the tobacco industry," a colleague accurately lamented to me.) Predictably, society's reaction has been punitive. This punishment consists not only of investigations, fines and settlements equaling tens of billions of dollars, but also the most extensive new set of regulations ever promulgated for a single industry.

In the absence of what Warren Buffett calls an "inner scorecard," society has imposed an "outer scorecard" on the financial system.[2] No one yet knows what the cumulative effect of this punitive activity will be on financial firms, markets or the economy as a whole. But one thing is clear: Unless and until we can quantify that effect, the chances of achieving an optimal balance between economic growth and stability are remote.

What is also clear is that if the financial services industry wants to "stand for goodness"—if it wants to do a better job of delivering what society expects and needs—then asset management firms, consumer banks, investment banks, wealth management firms, mutual funds, insurance companies, hedge funds and private equity investors are going to have to do a much better job listening to, interpreting and understanding the needs of society—and then responsibly living up to the terms of the compact.

This is not a trivial undertaking, especially since not everything society wants is healthy—in the short or the long term. Also what society wants is changing, and will continue to change over time.

A Force for Good owes a considerable debt to the CFA Institute's Future of Finance Initiative, a multiyear project that is working through the question of how financial market participants can act "for the ultimate benefit of society."[3] Those words were added a few years ago to the CFA Institute's mission statement. I was invited by former CFA Institute president and CEO John Rogers to serve on the Future of Finance Initiative's advisory committee. Through that assignment, and as a member of the board of directors of the Securities Industry and Financial Markets Association (SIFMA), I have been privileged to meet and interview many people who are passionate about forging a constructive future for finance. Several of them contributed chapters to this book. Some, like me, are or have been executives operating financial services firms. Others served as regulators. Still others come from academia. There is a Nobel laureate and even a politician (albeit a retired one).

This book is, in effect, an effort to pick their brains at a time when many of the quasi-axiomatic assumptions underlying modern capitalism are being called into question, which is prompting a parallel and far-reaching examination of how the financial system that supports capitalism will have to evolve.

What are some of those assumptions?

- Economic growth will continue at an average rate of 2 percent to 3 percent annually, as has been the case since the industrial revolution.
- Capital markets will generate nominal returns for patient investors of 7 percent to 8 percent (5 percent in real terms) over long periods of time.
- "Financial deepening" and the growth of the financial sector relative to GDP has been and will continue to be a net positive contributor to economic growth and to rising standards of living.
- Instability can be engineered away through increasingly sophisticated and complex regulatory structures.
- Resource inputs are infinite and negative side effects need not be explicitly accounted for.
- Faster is better.

As U.K. regulator Adair Turner suggests in "What Do Banks Do?," "We need to ask fundamental questions about the optimal size and functions of the financial system and about its value within the economy, and about whether and under what conditions the financial system tends to generate economic growth or stability."[4]

Each day on my way home from the office, I pass by the Walker Art Center, Minneapolis's contemporary art museum. Stenciled on the Walker's brick walls are these words from a work by conceptual artist Larry Weiner: "bits and pieces put together to present a semblance of a whole." That's what this book represents—a curated collection of bits and pieces that explores a number of common themes. Like these, for example:

- We in the financial services industry need to return to first principles, to articulate and remind ourselves of the purpose of finance.
- The post–financial crisis contract between society and finance expects finance to "serve a public utility function" and "have a fundamental and higher responsibility to serve the real economy."[5]
- The age-old problem of conflicts between principals and agents persists today, and continues to lead to suboptimal outcomes in which the needs and goals of users of the financial system are sometimes undermined by the interests of participants in the financial system.
- We need to accept the possibility that low-growth or no-growth may be the nature of the economic landscape for decades to come. If so, lower-than-historical returns on investment portfolios may pose challenges to individuals and institutions of all kinds.
- We still have a long way to go when it comes to restoring trust in the integrity of financial firms, the authenticity of industry leaders and rebuilding confidence in financial markets.
- Short-term thinking and speculative activity needs to be replaced by long-term thinking and activity that benefits real players in real markets in the real world.
- While growth remains the key to improving social well-being, sustainable growth is replacing growth at all costs and leverage-driven growth as the ultimate goal of capitalism.

What makes this book different from the others in the postcrisis literature? These contributors were not asked to comment on what went wrong in 2008–09, but rather on what needs to be done in the future to adapt to tectonic shifts going on beneath the surface of capitalism. They explore how the goals of finance could be more closely aligned with those of society at large.

Here are just a few highlights of the game plan these all-stars have put into place.

REFRAME AND RESTATE THE COVENANT
BETWEEN SOCIETY AND FINANCE

The financial crisis caused many to question the assumptions underpinning our system of financial capitalism. It's a system where finance is "as much . . . an ordering principle in our lives as the rising and setting sun, the seasons and the tides" in the words of Robert J. Shiller, Sterling Professor of Economics at Yale University. But an intense international debate is raging about the role, benefits, costs and risks of finance, with no consensus yet emerging as to what society expects from our financial system. Until we can state these expectations clearly, and until there is some degree of consensus, efforts to give us the financial system we deserve are destined to fail.

COMPLETE AND SIMPLIFY REFORM OF
FINANCIAL REGULATORY INFRASTRUCTURE

Seven years after the financial crisis, we're only two-thirds or so of the way through implementation of the Dodd-Frank Wall Street Reform and Consumer Protection Act, the principle legislative and regulatory response in the United States to the financial crisis. Much has been done to make the financial system safer, sounder and more secure, thanks mainly to requirements for more capital and less leverage on the balance sheets of major financial institutions.

But, as former Federal Deposit Insurance Corporation (FDIC) chair Sheila C. Bair writes, "many essential reforms remain incomplete and significant structural weaknesses remain" when it comes to mitigating the kind of systemic risk that nearly brought the global economy to its knees in 2008–09. While we try to squeeze risk out of regulated financial institutions, we need to be careful that we don't squeeze it into unregulated institutions and into less transparent corners of the economy where imbalances and excesses could build up and catch us, once again, by surprise, as banking expert Karen Shaw Petrou explains.

RESTORE ETHICS, INTEGRITY AND CLIENT FOCUS
TO THE FINANCIAL SERVICES INDUSTRY

Trust, the lifeblood of finance and of financial capitalism, was severely damaged by the financial crisis and, as PIMCO CEO Douglas M. Hodge points out, "once lost, financial trust—like any other kind of trust—is hard to restore." Financial services organizations need to focus on their core purpose, which is to mediate between investors, who are sources of capital, and organizations that can productively deploy capital. The goal is to manage the risks inherent in that mediation so we boost the economy and enhance our collective standard of living.

Finance needs to deliver on what Charles D. Ellis, a highly regarded investment expert, calls "the iconic statement: 'the needs of our clients always come first.'"

A return to fiduciary principles, as John C. Bogle has been urging throughout his career, is certainly part of the answer. But financial services providers need to move beyond a minimum legalistic standard to what 3ethos founder Donald B. Trone describes as the "intersection between leadership, stewardship and governance."

For until we reconnect financial institutions to their mission and purpose—helping real clients achieve their goals and objectives—no amount of legislation or regulation or rule making will enable the financial system to be a consistent, stable provider of societal benefits.

RESTORE INVESTOR TRUST AND CONFIDENCE IN FINANCIAL MARKETS

Along with trust in financial institutions, investor confidence in the fairness of financial markets was also damaged by the financial crisis. Michael Lewis's incendiary allegation that "the markets are rigged" confirmed the worst fears of many individual investors, as have a litany of technology glitches like the 2010 "Flash Crash," America's debt-ceiling brinksmanship and the never-ending drumbeat of regulatory fines and enforcement actions against financial institutions. As long as investors don't trust the financial markets, they will remain overallocated to the "safety" of cash while inflation eats away at zero percent returns. They will also shy away from providing the long-term patient equity capital on which, says former Securities and Exchange Commission chair Mary Schapiro, "the success of all nations depends." As Roger L. Martin, former dean of the Rotman School of Management, puts it, finance needs to focus on the "real market" rather than the "expectations market."

CORRECT UNSUSTAINABLE IMBALANCES IN FISCAL AND MONETARY POLICY

Just as human life exists within strict environmental parameters, financial capitalism can function constructively only within a relatively narrow range of fiscal and monetary conditions. We currently find ourselves way outside that range. How skillfully and smoothly we can unwind the enormous amounts of debt incurred by developed nations—euphemistically known as managing the exit—is the single biggest factor in whether developed economies grow and whether stock and bond markets deliver positive returns over the coming decades. As money manager Brian Walsh puts it, "We are living through a real-time experiment in central bank policy." Eventually, and inevitably, it will come time to pay the piper—but how? And over what time period? At what cost to whom?

The stakes are enormous. Warns former U.S. Senator Judd Gregg: "Every generation in the history of our nation has passed on to the next generation a stronger and more prosperous country. We are on the verge of reversing this history."

RESTRUCTURE OUR RETIREMENT SAVINGS AND HOUSING FINANCE SYSTEMS

We all expect to accumulate enough savings to live on for the rest of our lives and be able to purchase housing on an affordable basis. Yet significant gaps remain between society's expectations and the financial system's ability to meet those expectations.

As BlackRock vice chairman Barbara G. Novick points out, the current patchwork quilt of retirement savings vehicles—Social Security, defined benefit pension plans and defined contribution vehicles (401(k) and 403(b) plans)—is woefully inadequate when it comes to fully funding the retirement liabilities of aging baby boomers. Financial firms will need to do a better job of educating savers and delivering product innovations to help individual retirees who are living longer than ever before in human history.

As for the U.S. system of housing finance, remarkably little serious work has yet been done to restructure the single most important contributor to the last financial crisis. Today, almost every new mortgage loan involves some kind of support and participation from the U.S. government. Private capital is not yet ready to support one of society's most important policy objectives—access to affordable mortgages to support middle class housing—and won't be until the housing finance system of the future is more clearly defined, writes Jeremy Diamond.

USHER IN AN ERA OF LONG-TERM INVESTING AND "REAL" OWNERSHIP

So-called short-termism is like an ever-present virus in the financial system that flares up whenever the system is subjected to stress or excesses. The *Economist*'s Matthew Bishop writes that "American capitalism remains hooked on superficial, short-term financial success rather than on building long-term, sustainable prosperity."[6]

Three of our contributors—Dominic Barton, Mark Wiseman and John Rogers—write hopefully of signs that asset owners with long-term objectives—Rogers calls them "super-fiduciaries"—may be getting large enough and influential enough to start driving salutary changes through the financial system.

These "universal owners," Rogers explains, "serve today's and tomorrow's generations, possibly in perpetuity." They generate "income and returns" that "support human life and society" and have as their mandate long-term prosperity for their constituents.

RETOOL THE FINANCIAL SYSTEM FOR SUSTAINABILITY

The ethical legitimacy of an economic system driven by growth without regard to the long-term costs to our life-sustaining ecosystem is being called into question by financiers like David Blood. Long-term efficiency and financial market stability are also at stake. Blood calls for a paradigm shift to Sustainable Capitalism: "While the present form of capitalism has proven its superiority, it is nevertheless abundantly clear that some of its manifestations do not incorporate sufficient regard for its impact on people and the planet."

Some of the biggest flows of investment money are going today to strategies that reward responsible corporate behavior and enlightened environmental, social and governance practices. The financial system supporting Blood's Sustainable Capitalism or John Fullerton's "Regenerative Capitalism" will necessarily look a lot different than it looked throughout the post–World War II era of financial capitalism.

EVOLVE FROM RESPONSIBLE FINANCE
TO ENLIGHTENED FINANCE

Few would argue with this 2012 assertion in *Harvard Business Review*: "In general, finance does serve a crucial economic purpose."[7] But it is a long way from there to Yale professor Shiller's vision for a financial system that advances the goals of a "good society." Given the complexity of the modern financial system, getting there will require that we return to the core principles in which finance should be grounded. It requires, as a first step, that we stop engaging in the irresponsible practices that contributed to the financial crisis. It requires, further, that we model the do-no-harm ethics and principles of responsible finance that Vikram Mansharamani describes in his closing essay. These include honesty and authenticity, respect for the priority of client interests, transparency around conflicts of interest and alignment between what clients want and the capabilities of the financial services providers.

But it will also require that we move beyond responsible finance to an even more elevated paradigm, which I call enlightened finance. In enlightened finance, the financial sector is engaged in a constructive partnership with society, helping intuit and deliver what society really wants. Today, this would appear to be a balance between economic growth and other considerations: more sustainable environmental impact; less income inequality; fewer destabilizing and less frequent financial crises; and reduced debt and entitlement burdens on our children and grandchildren.

On the pages that follow, these all-stars each contribute an intellectual flagstone on the path we must follow toward realizing the potential of enlightened finance as a consistent and positive force for social good.

NOTES

1. Matthew Bishop and Michael Green, *The Road from Ruin: How to Revive Capitalism and Put America Back on Top* (New York: Crown Business, 2010, 2011).
2. Alice Schroeder, *The Snowball: Warren Buffett and the Business of Life* (New York: Bantam Books, 2008, 2009), 32.
3. "Mission and Vision," 2014 *CFA Institute*, accessed June 2014, http://www.cfainstitute.org/about/vision/Pages/index.aspx.
4. Adair Turner, Andrew Haldane, Paul Woolley, et al., in *The Future of Finance: The LSE Report* (London: London School of Economics and Political Science, 2010), 5.
5. "Ed Miliband calls for bank reforms: speech in full" *The Telegraph*, July 9, 2012, http://www.telegraph.co.uk/finance/newsbysector/banksandfinance/9386288/Ed-Miliband-calls-for-bank-reforms-speech-in-full.html.
6. Bishop and Green, *Road from Ruin*, preface xvi.
7. Robin Greenwood and David S. Scharfstein, "How to Make Finance Work," *Harvard Business Review*, March 2012, http://hbr.org/2012/03/how-to-make-finance-work/ar/1.

CONTRIBUTOR BIOGRAPHIES

(IN ALPHABETICAL ORDER)

Sheila C. Bair
Former FDIC Chair; Senior Advisor, Pew Charitable
Trusts; Chair, Systemic Risk Council
Sheila C. Bair served as the nineteenth chair of the Federal Deposit Insurance Corporation for a five-year term, from June 2006 through July 2011. Bair currently chairs the Systemic Risk Council, an independent body of former regulators and financial policy experts committed to addressing regulatory and structural issues relating to systemic risk in the United States. Bair has an extensive background in banking and finance in a career that has taken her from Capitol Hill to academia and to the highest levels of government. Before joining the FDIC in 2006, she was the Dean's Professor of Financial Regulatory Policy for the Isenberg School of Management at the University of Massachusetts Amherst since 2002. Other career experience includes serving as assistant secretary for financial institutions at the U.S. Department of the Treasury (2001 to 2002), senior vice president for government relations of the New York Stock Exchange (1995 to 2000), a commissioner of the Commodity Futures Trading Commission (1991 to 1995), and research director, deputy counsel and counsel to Senate Majority Leader Robert Dole (1981 to 1988).

Dominic Barton
Global Managing Director, McKinsey & Company
Since joining the McKinsey firm in 1986, Barton has advised clients in a range of industries, including banking, consumer goods, high tech and industrial. Barton also leads McKinsey's work on the future of capitalism, long-term value creation and the role of business leadership in society. In 2011 and 2012, he co-led a task force on inclusive capitalism sponsored by the Henry Jackson Society, a London-based think tank, which developed new approaches for engaging and scaling business actions to address issues

that create both social and economic value. Before becoming global managing director, Barton served as McKinsey's chair in Asia from 2004 to 2009, based in Shanghai, and led McKinsey's office in Korea from 2000 to 2004.

David Blood
Cofounder and Senior Partner, Generation Investment Management
David Blood is cofounder and senior partner of Generation Investment Management. Previously, he spent 18 years at Goldman Sachs including serving as co-CEO and CEO of Goldman Sachs Asset Management from 1999 to 2003. Blood received a BA from Hamilton College and an MBA from the Harvard Graduate School of Business. He is on the board of New Forests, SHINE, Social Finance US and The Nature Conservancy.

John C. Bogle
Founder, The Vanguard Group
John C. Bogle is founder and former chief executive of Vanguard and president of its Bogle Financial Markets Research Center. The organization he created in 1974 is now the largest mutual fund organization in the world, and manages assets totaling over $3 trillion. In 1975, Bogle founded the first index mutual fund. He was chairman of the Investment Company Institute in 1969 and 1970.

Bogle graduated from Princeton University, magna cum laude in Economics, in 1951. In 1999, Princeton awarded him the Woodrow Wilson Award, and in May 2005, it awarded him an honorary Doctor of Laws degree.

In 2004, *Time* magazine named him as one of "the world's 100 most powerful and influential people," and in 1999, *Fortune* magazine named Bogle as one of the investment industry's four "Giants of the 20th Century." His numerous awards include the Award for Professional Excellence by CFA (Chartered Financial Analyst) Institute and the Legends of Leadership Award by the Yale School of Management. A prolific writer and speaker, the most recent of Bogle's ten books are: *The Clash of the Cultures: Investment vs. Speculation* (2012), *Don't Count on It!* (2011), *Enough* (2008) and *The Little Book of Common Sense Investing* (2007).

Ricardo R. Delfin
Former Executive Director, Systemic Risk Council
At the time of authorship, Ricardo Delfin was the executive director of the Systemic Risk Council. Before joining the SRC, Delfin was special counsel to the chair of the Securities and Exchange Commission (Mary Schapiro). In that role he advised the chair on a wide range of postcrisis financial reforms, including the implementation of the Dodd-Frank Act and the formation of

the Financial Stability Oversight Council. He was a member of several FSOC committees and was a point person on a variety of intergovernmental efforts, particularly those related to systemic risk. Delfin was also senior counsel to the House Committee on Financial Services (Barney Frank, chair). There he worked on emergency legislation to respond to the financial crisis as well as a wide variety of banking and other financial services legislation to reform mortgage finance, consumer credit and corporate governance. Before going into public service, Delfin was an associate with Wilmer, Cutler & Pickering in Washington, D.C.

Jeremy Diamond
Former Managing Director, Annaly Capital Management
Jeremy Diamond served as managing director and member of the Executive Committee at Annaly Capital Management (NYSE: NLY), the largest residential mortgage real estate investment trust (REIT) in the country, where he was head of research and head of government policy relations. Annaly invests primarily in various types of Agency mortgage-backed securities and related derivatives to hedge these investments. He also served as a member of the board of directors of an affiliated mortgage REIT, Chimera Investment Corporation (NYSE: CIM), which invests in residential mortgage loans, non-Agency and Agency mortgage-backed securities and various other real estate-related assets. Prior to joining Annaly in 2002, Diamond was president and publisher of Grant's Financial Publishing, a financial research company, and its flagship publication, *Grant's Interest Rate Observer*. Diamond began his career as an investment banking analyst at Lehman Brothers, where he worked on a wide range of mergers and acquisitions and financing transactions. He serves on the Advisory Council for the Bendheim Center for Finance at Princeton University, and is a commissioner on the Fiscal and Budget Policy Commission in Bellport, NY.

Charles D. Ellis
Author of Winning the Loser's Game
Charles D. Ellis serves as a consultant to large institutional investors and wealthy families and as managing partner of a pro bono partnership of nearly 100 Harvard Business School classmates and friends, Partners of '63, which commits time and treasure in support of entrepreneurial, change-oriented ventures in education, particularly those focused on children born into tough circumstances. Ellis's professional career centered on serving Greenwich Associates, the international-strategy consulting firm he founded in 1972. Services to the investment profession include: chair and two terms as governor of the profession's CFA Institute and an associate editor of both the *Journal of Portfolio Management* and the *Financial Analysts Journal*. He is one

of ten individuals honored for lifetime contributions to the investment profession by the CFA Institute, has written 16 books, mostly on investing, and has taught admired investment courses at Harvard Business School and Yale School of Management. He has served as a trustee of Yale University (where he also chaired the investment committee), trustee at Robert Wood Johnson Foundation, chairman of Whitehead Institute for Biomedical Research and trustee of Phillips Exeter Academy.

John Fullerton
Founder and President, Capital Institute
John Fullerton is the founder and president of Capital Institute. He is also an active impact investor through his Level 3 Capital Advisors.

Previously, he was a managing director of JPMorgan, where he managed multiple capital markets and derivatives businesses around the globe and then ran the venture investment activity of the JPMorgan's high-tech investment vehicle, LabMorgan, as chief investment officer until the merger with Chase Manhattan Bank in 2001. John served as JPMorgan's representative on the Long-Term Capital Management Oversight Committee in 1997-98. He is a cofounder and director of Grasslands, LLC, a holistic ranch management company with the Savory Institute, a director of New Day Farms, Inc., New Economy Coalition, Savory Institute, and an advisor to Armonia, LLC, and Richard Branson's Business Leader's initiative ("B Team"). Fullerton is a member of the Club of Rome.

Fullerton is the creator of the "Future of Finance" blog at Capital Institute.org, which is also syndicated with the *Guardian*, *Huffington Post*, *CSRWire*, the *EcoWatch* blog and the New York Society of Security Analysts' Finance Professionals' Post.

Kenneth E. Goodpaster, PhD
Senior Academic Fellow, Center for Ethical Business Cultures, and
Professor Emeritus, Opus College of Business, University of St. Thomas
Kenneth E. Goodpaster taught moral philosophy at the University of Notre Dame throughout the 1970s before joining the Harvard Business School faculty in 1980. In 1989, Goodpaster accepted the Koch Endowed Chair in Business Ethics at the University of St. Thomas—Minnesota, where he taught for 25 years before retiring as emeritus professor in 2014.

He has published numerous articles in professional journals as well as two books: *Policies and Persons: A Casebook in Business Ethics* (McGraw-Hill, 4th ed., 2006) and *Conscience and Corporate Culture* (Wiley-Blackwell, 2007). He also was executive editor of the award-winning history *Corporate Responsibility: The American Experience* (Cambridge University Press, 2012). Goodpaster is an associate editor of *Business Ethics Quarterly* and in 2014 received the Outstanding Scholarly Achievement award from the Society for Business Ethics.

Judd Gregg
Former U.S. Senator and Former CEO, the Securities
Industry and Financial Markets Association (SIFMA)

In his most recent role as CEO of SIFMA, Judd Gregg promoted the role the financial services industry plays in leading economic growth and promoting job creation to the benefit of all Americans. Gregg served as a United States senator from 1993 to 2011 and was both chair and the ranking member of the Senate Budget Committee. Prior to his tenure in the Senate, Gregg served as governor of New Hampshire (1989 to 1993) and as a U.S. representative (1981 to 1989). He is a national leader on fiscal policy, a well-known budget expert and a respected voice on economic and financial regulatory issues. He served as the chief Republican Senate negotiator on the Emergency Economic Stabilization Act of 2008 (better known as TARP) and as a member of the Senate Banking Committee. Gregg served as one of the principal negotiators working to modernize the U.S. financial regulatory system. Along with Senators Alan Simpson and Erskine Bowles and Governor Ed Rendell, he cochairs the Fix the Debt initiative, an effort to develop a comprehensive deficit reduction agreement along the lines of the Simpson-Bowles Commission, on which Gregg served. In New Hampshire, he is known as a champion of land conservation with a more than 30-year commitment to protect the state's environment. As the former chair of the Senate Health, Education, Labor and Pensions (HELP) Committee, he has also been a major force for promoting excellence in the higher-education community. In 2012, Gregg was appointed the first distinguished fellow at Dartmouth College, where he lectures on national governance and history issues.

Douglas M. Hodge
CEO and Managing Director, PIMCO

Douglas M. Hodge is chief executive officer of Pacific Investment Management Company (PIMCO) and a managing director in PIMCO's Newport Beach, California, office. He also serves on PIMCO's executive committee and on the global executive committee for Allianz Asset Management, the governing body of asset management for the Allianz Group. Earlier, Hodge led the Asia-Pacific region from the firm's Tokyo office from 2002 to 2009. He joined PIMCO in 1989 and has previously served the firm as a senior account manager responsible for client relationships worldwide and as a global product manager. Hodge currently serves on the board of the Securities Industry and Financial Markets Association (SIFMA).

Ron James
President and CEO, Center for Ethical Business Cultures
Ron James serves as president and CEO of the Center for Ethical Business Cultures (CEBC) in the Opus College of Business at the University of St. Thomas—Minnesota and teaches graduate-level business ethics. James has been recognized by Ethisphere in its 2010 list of the 100 Most Influential People in Business Ethics in the world in the thought leadership category and in 2006 by the Society for Corporate Compliance and Ethics, receiving one of several international awards for "pioneering in the field of applied business ethics through executive leadership education." A former executive in telecommunications, James was recognized in 2011 in Minnesota by the National Association of Corporate Directors as an outstanding director and for lifetime achievement in corporate governance.

Vikram Mansharamani
Lecturer, Yale University, Program on Ethics, Politics and Economics
Vikram Mansharamani is the president and founder of Kelan Advisors, a global strategic advisory firm. He is also a senior fellow at the Mossavar-Rahmani Center for Business & Government at the Harvard Kennedy School and a lecturer at Yale University in the program on Ethics, Politics, & Economics, where he teaches courses on investment management, business ethics and financial bubbles. Mansharamani is also the author of *Boombustology: Spotting Financial Bubbles Before They Burst* (Wiley, 2011) and regularly contributes to the business and financial media. He currently serves on the board of the Africa Opportunity Fund and is chairman of the Torit Language Center Montessori School. He is a former director of the US-Pakistan Business Council, Interelate Inc., ManagedOps and the Association of Yale Alumni.

Roger L. Martin
Former Dean, Rotman School of Management, University of Toronto
Roger Martin is Premier's Chair in Productivity & Competitiveness and academic director of the Martin Prosperity Institute at the Rotman School of Management. From 1998 to 2013, he served as dean. Previously, he spent 13 years as a director of Monitor Company, a global strategy consulting firm based in Cambridge, Massachusetts, where he served as cohead of the firm for two years. His research work is in integrative thinking, business design, strategy, corporate social responsibility and country competitiveness. He writes extensively and is a regular contributor to *Harvard Business Review*'s The Conversation blog, the *Financial Times*' Judgment Call column, and *Washington Post*'s On Leadership blog. He has written 19 *Harvard Business Review* articles and published eight books, most recently *Playing to Win*

(with A. G. Lafley, Harvard Business Review Press, 2013). In 2013, Martin placed third on the Thinkers50 list, a biannual ranking of the most influential global business thinkers. He serves on a number of public service boards: Skoll Foundation, Canadian Credit Management Foundation, Tennis Canada (past chair), and Ontario Task Force on Competitiveness, Productivity and Economic Progress (chair).

Barbara G. Novick
Vice Chairman, BlackRock
Barbara G. Novick is a member of BlackRock's Global Executive and Global Operating Committees and chairs the Government Relations Steering Committee. From the inception of the firm in 1988 to 2008, Novick headed the Global Client Group and oversaw global business development, marketing and client service across equity, fixed income, liquidity, alternative investment and real estate products for institutional and individual investors and their intermediaries worldwide. In her current role, Novick heads the firm's efforts globally on government relations and public policy. Prior to founding BlackRock in 1988, Novick was a vice president in the Mortgage Products Group at First Boston Corporation. Novick joined First Boston in 1985, where she became head of the Portfolio Products Team. From 1982 to 1985, Novick was with Morgan Stanley. Novick has authored numerous articles, including a series of BlackRock Special Reports and public policy *ViewPoints* and First Boston's *Mortgage-Related Securities Guide.* She is a member of the Reuters Editorial Advisory Board and CFA Institute's Future of Finance Advisory Committee. She currently serves as a trustee of Cornell University, UJA-Federation and the HCM Foundation.

Karen Shaw Petrou
Managing Partner, Federal Financial Analytics
Karen Shaw Petrou is the cofounder and managing partner of Federal Financial Analytics, a privately held company that, since 1985, has provided analytical and advisory services on legislative, regulatory and public-policy issues affecting financial services companies doing business in the United States and abroad. The firm's practice is a unique blend of strategic advice and policy analysis that does not include lobbying or any other projects that would compromise its objectivity and independence. Prior to founding her own firm in 1985, Petrou worked in Washington as an officer at Bank of America, where she began her career in 1977. She has served on numerous boards of banking organizations and sits as a director on the board of the Foundation Fighting Blindness and as an advisory member of the board of the Morin Center for Banking and Financial Law.

David H. Rodbourne
Vice President, Center for Ethical Business Cultures
David Rodbourne is vice president of the Center for Ethical Business Cultures (CEBC) at the University of St. Thomas' Opus College of Business. He plays a leading role developing the center's programs in ethics and corporate responsibility, facilitates workshops for clients, developed a management team simulation used by students and speaks to business and professional groups. He was project manager for the center's corporate responsibility research, which published *Corporate Responsibility: The American Experience*, a 200-year exploration of American business. Rodbourne co-chairs the Minnesota Business Ethics Awards.

John Rogers
Former President and CEO, CFA Institute
John Rogers joined CFA Institute in January 2009 after more than two decades of global experience as an investment practitioner and executive in the Asia-Pacific region and the United States. Rogers worked with Citibank and Cigna in Japan and Australia prior to joining Invesco. He served as president and chief investment officer of Invesco Asset Management, Japan; CEO and co-CIO of Invesco Global Asset Management, N.A.; and as CEO of Invesco's worldwide institutional division, with over $200 billion in assets under management and 2,500 employees. After leaving Invesco in 2007, he founded Jade River Capital Management. Rogers is a director of numerous boards, endowments and advisory committees in both the not-for-profit and corporate sectors.

Mary Schapiro
Former U.S. Securities and Exchange Commission (SEC) Chair
Mary Schapiro's service as the twenty-ninth SEC chair culminated decades of regulatory leadership. She was the first woman to serve as SEC chair, and the only person to have served as chair of both the SEC and the Commodity Futures Trading Commission. During four years as chair from January 2009 to December 2012, Schapiro presided over one of the busiest rule-making agendas in the SEC's history, during which time the agency also executed a comprehensive restructuring program to improve protections for investors. Before becoming SEC chair, Schapiro served as CEO of the Financial Industry Regulatory Authority, the largest nongovernmental regulator of securities firms. Earlier, she was chair of the CFTC, a commissioner of the SEC, and general counsel and senior vice president of the Futures Industry Association. She began her career at the CFTC, serving first as a trial attorney and later as counsel and executive assistant to the chair. She also serves

on the boards of Promontory Financial Group, General Electric and several not-for-profit boards.

Robert J. Shiller
Economist, Yale University

Robert J. Shiller is Sterling Professor of Economics, Department of Economics and Cowles Foundation for Research in Economics, Yale University, and professor of finance and fellow at the International Center for Finance, Yale School of Management. He received his BA from the University of Michigan in 1967 and his PhD in economics from the Massachusetts Institute of Technology in 1972. He has written on financial markets, financial innovation, behavioral economics, macroeconomics, real estate and statistical methods, as well as on public attitudes, opinions and moral judgments regarding markets. Shiller was awarded the 2013 Nobel Prize in Economic Sciences, together with Eugene Fama and Lars Peter Hansen of the University of Chicago, "for their empirical analysis of asset prices." He is president-elect of the American Economic Association.

Donald B. Trone
Chief Ethos Officer, 3ethos

Donald B. Trone has been named by numerous organizations as "one of the most influential people" in the retirement, financial planning and investment advisory industries. In 2003, he was appointed by the U.S. Secretary of Labor to represent the investment counseling industry on the ERISA Advisory Council, and in 2007 he testified before the Senate Finance Committee on fiduciary issues associated with retirement plans. Trone has authored or coauthored the following books: *The Management of Investment Decisions* (1995); *Freedom From Wealth* (2011); *Fiduciary Ethos* (2009); *401k Ethos* (2010); *Procedural Prudence* (1991); *The Prudent Investment Practices* series (2003); *Management of Native American Investment Decisions* (2008); and *LeaderMetrics* (2014).

Brian Walsh
Chair and Chief Investment Officer, Saguenay Strathmore Capital

Brian Walsh cofounded Saguenay Capital in 2002 to manage alternative portfolios for a client base of international institutions and family offices. Walsh has over 30 years' experience in investment banking, international capital markets and investment management. He had a long career at Bankers Trust that culminated in his appointment as cohead of the Global Investment Bank. Prior to that, Walsh served as chair of Bankers Trust International, where he ran the global derivatives business. After leaving Bankers Trust in 1996, Walsh focused solely on investment management for clients, including the Bass family of Fort Worth, Texas, and a major Canadian pension fund. He then founded Veritas Capital, a hedge fund largely focused on volatility strategies, prior to Saguenay Capital. Walsh serves on the board of directors of Great-West Lifeco, the Great-West Life & Annuity Insurance Company and Putnam Investments and serves on the international advisory board of HEC (Ecole des Hautes Etudes Commerciales) and on the Global Business Council of Queen's University School of Business.

Mark Wiseman
President and CEO, CPP Investment Board
Mark Wiseman assumed the role of president and CEO of the Canada Pension Plan Investment Board in July 2012 and is responsible for leading the board and its investment activities. Wiseman joined the CPP Investment Board in June 2005 as the organization's senior vice president of private investments. He was later named executive vice president of investments, responsible for managing all of the investment activities of the board: public market investments, private investments and real estate investments. Prior to joining the CPP Investment Board, Wiseman was responsible for the private equity fund and co-investment program at the Ontario Teachers' Pension Plan. Previously, Wiseman was an officer with Harrowston, a publicly traded Canadian merchant bank, and a lawyer with Sullivan & Cromwell, practicing in New York and Paris. He also served as a law clerk to Madam Justice Beverley McLachlin at the Supreme Court of Canada. From 2004 to 2007, Wiseman was chair of the Institutional Limited Partners Association, a nonprofit organization committed to serving limited partner investors in the global private equity industry.

Stephen B. Young
Author of Moral Capitalism
Stephen Young is the global executive director of the Caux Round Table and is president of Winthrop Consulting and the Minnesota Public Policy Forum. He was formerly the third dean of the Hamline University School of Law, an assistant dean of Harvard Law School, has worked with the Council on Foreign Relations and consulted to the U.S. Department of State. Young wrote the book *Moral Capitalism* to explicate the economic and moral approach of the Caux Round Table to free market capitalism. *Moral Capitalism* integrated the moral sense theory of Adam Smith with other theories of moral philosophy and economics.

ABOUT THE EDITOR

John G. Taft is CEO of RBC Wealth Management—U.S., the eighth-largest full-service retail brokerage firm in the United States, with nearly 2,000 financial advisors in 41 states and over $281 billion in assets under administration.

Taft has been active in the Securities Industry and Financial Markets Association (SIFMA), the leading securities industry trade group representing securities firms, banks and asset managers in the United States. He served as chair-elect in 2010 and chair in 2011. As a representative of SIFMA, Taft advocated for responsible financial reform and testified before Congress in support of a federal fiduciary standard of care for investment professionals who provide advice to individual clients.

Taft has worked in the financial services industry since 1981. Prior to leading RBC WM—U.S., he served as chair, president and CEO of Voyageur Asset Management; president and CEO of Dougherty Summit Securities; a member of the boards of directors of Segall Bryant & Hamill, the Clifton Group and Vintage Mutual Funds; and a managing director at Piper, Jaffray & Hopwood. He was assistant to the mayor of the City of St. Paul, Minnesota, and has worked as a journalist.

An active diversity advocate around issues of gender identity, Taft serves as executive sponsor for RBC WM—U.S.'s Proud RBC Individuals for Diversity and Equality (PRIDE) employee resource group. Under his leadership, RBC WM—U.S. received a 100 percent rating in the Human Rights Campaign's *Corporate Equality Index*. In 2010, the National Gay & Lesbian Chamber of Commerce (NGLCC) named him the "Outstanding Corporate Diversity Leader."

Taft is the author of *Stewardship: Lessons Learned from the Lost Culture of Wall Street* (2012). The book explores the importance of stewardship as a core principle: for Taft personally; for the financial services industry; for the global financial system; and for society. Readers selected the book as one of Amazon's top picks for March 2012, and it was named "best book of spring 2012" on Bloomberg radio, while Bloomberg TV cited it as an "absolute must-read book."

Taft is a frequent presenter and speaker at various events across the country, including the Securities Industry Institute at the Wharton School; the Center for Ethical Business Cultures at the University of St. Thomas; the Rotman School of Management, University of Toronto; Tuck School of Business at Dartmouth, Heider College of Business at Creighton University, and Babson College.

As a member of the board of directors and as a volunteer, Taft has served a wide range of not-for-profit and public service organizations. He is an active member of the boards of the Itasca Project, Greater Twin Cities United Way, Taft School and The Andy Warhol Foundation for the Visual Arts, and serves on the Minnesota Business Partnership Executive Committee. Previously, he served as a director of the Walker Art Center, Macalester College, Breck School, Northwest Area Foundation, Minnesota Public Radio, Twin Cities Public Television, St. Paul Chamber Orchestra, Illusion Theatre and the Minnesota Film Board. He has also served on several public sector task forces, including the Mayor's Council on Economic Development Finance, Blue Ribbon Commission on Pensions and the Mayor's Working Group on Local Government Finance.

Taft graduated magna cum laude, Phi Beta Kappa with a BA degree from Yale University and earned an MA in public and private management from the Yale School of Organization and Management.

Taft and his wife, Laura, live in Minneapolis. He has three children, Mary Allison, Lauren and Colin, and two stepchildren, Gabrielle and Liam.

A FORCE
FOR GOOD

PART I

REFRAMING SOCIETY'S CONTRACT WITH FINANCE

INTRODUCTION

John G. Taft

At the beginning of Charles Dickens's classic *A Christmas Carol*, Ebenezer Scrooge's deceased former business partner, Jacob Marley, appears before Scrooge as a ghost. Tortured by regret, dragging iron chains around the infinite wasteland of eternity, Marley bemoans his failure to contribute more to society during his life. He saw himself exclusively as a businessman, with no further obligations to humanity, when he was alive.

"You were always a good man of business, Jacob," Scrooge responds lamely.

To which the ghost of Marley thunders, "Business?! . . . Mankind was my business! The common welfare was my business; charity, mercy, forbearance, and benevolence, were all my business! The dealings of my trade were but a drop of water in the comprehensive ocean of my business!"[1]

To paraphrase Dickens, there is no more important task than getting the business of finance right, right now. There's no better time to step back from the "dealings" of markets and transactional "drops of water." These drops represent trillions of interactions every day between financial services firms and their clients and their regulators. As stewards of other people's money, we have no more important task than to articulate, to understand, to appreciate—and to respect—the "comprehensive ocean" of finance.

A necessary first step in making finance a force for good is to answer this question: To whom, and for what, is the modern financial institution responsible?

Is it anything less than "timely support for more prosperity," as suggested by Stephen B. Young, CEO of the Caux Round Table, a nonprofit that promotes ethical business practices? Is it anything less than to "promote freedom, prosperity, equality, and economic security," as Yale University economist Robert J. Shiller writes?

And once we have answered that question, how does finance better manage "the gap between society's expectations of its behavior and its actual behavior," which "dramatically affects it social legitimacy" in the words of contributors from the Center for Ethical Business Cultures (CEBC)?

The three essays by the authors in this section address different aspects of the corporate social contract (or compact). The CEBC shows how notions of corporate social responsibility have evolved for all types of American businesses. According to the CEBC, society has always had moral expectations of business, which apply no less to financial services than to anyone else. "Business must be both profitable and serve society," they write. Society expresses its expectations in terms of law and regulations. But ultimately, principled and responsible behavior must come from within organizations—specifically from leadership, which sets the "tone at the top." Leaders provide the "moral compass" that commits corporations to what General Mills CEO Ken Powell calls "doing the right thing."

Focusing more narrowly on the financial sector, Young suggests that in a world where "good social contract terms depend on good performance," financial intermediaries can improve the terms of their social contracts "by being good stewards of their customers' money." In an industry entrusted with other people's money, stewardship should be not only a core value, but also the key to good performance.

For Young, financial intermediation is a kind of public service. But it is Shiller who articulates even more expansively a vision for what finance looks like in support of a good society. "Finance, suitably configured for the future, can be the strongest force for promoting the well-being and fulfillment of an expanding global population—for achieving the greater goals of the good of society," Shiller writes. Further, he states, "At its broadest level, finance . . . is really creating the architecture for reaching a goal."

"The goals served by finance originate within us," Shiller explains. "They reflect our interests in careers, hopes for our families, ambitions for our businesses, aspirations for our culture and ideals for our society; finance in and of itself does not tell us what our goals should be. Finance does not embody a goal. Finance is not 'just about making money' per se. It is a 'functional' science in that it exists to support other goals—those of the society. The better aligned a society's financial institutions are with its goals and ideals, the stronger and more successful the society will be."

Better alignment between finance and the goals of society. That is the foundation upon which a more constructive future of finance must be built. In a world where financial capitalism remains the dominant socioeconomic model, finance must serve the goals of society. As Shiller describes, "financial institutions and financial variables are as much a source of direction and an ordering principle in our lives as the rising and setting sun, the seasons and the tides."

Welcome to the comprehensive ocean of finance.

NOTE

1.　Charles Dickens, *A Christmas Carol* (New York: Puffin Classics, 2008), 26.

CHAPTER 1

CORPORATE RESPONSIBILITY IN AMERICA

TWO CENTURIES OF EVOLUTION

Ron James

President and CEO, Center for Ethical Business Cultures

Kenneth E. Goodpaster

Senior Academic Fellow, Center for
Ethical Business Cultures

Professor Emeritus, Opus College of
Business, University of St. Thomas

David H. Rodbourne

Vice President, Center for Ethical Business Cultures

Rooted in the early nineteenth century, the corporation, as an idea and a legally constituted institution, has provoked continuous questions that challenge the purpose and role of business in American society. Among the most important is this: *"To whom, and for what, is the modern corporation responsible?"*[1]

This question elicits yet more questions. Is the sole purpose of the corporation to generate profits for its shareholders? Or does it have certain obligations to those who have—explicitly or implicitly—given it a license to operate? What are the consequences and future implications of a failure to live up to the expectations of those who have accepted, trusted, endorsed and supported business? Are there lessons to be learned from the past that may help future business leaders?

These questions framed the research for the landmark book produced by the Center for Ethical Business Cultures at the University of St. Thomas—*Corporate Responsibility: The American Experience* (hereafter *CRAE*).[2] It explored the corporate form over 200 years of American history, charting the ever-shifting roles and responsibilities of business in society.

The invention and proliferation of the corporation was crucial to the rise of the American economy. "Corporations—capitalism's dominant organizational form—are very efficient mechanisms for producing wealth, meeting consumer needs, and building industries that employ millions."[3] But with this power comes responsibility and accountability to others. Business operates not within a vacuum, but as a part of an interdependent set of systems that address societal needs. A business's license to operate, or social contract, is highly dependent on how it participates in these systems.

Over two centuries the social contract with the economic or business system evolved in relation to two other systems: the political and the moral-cultural.[4] (See figure 1.1.)

The Economic System: *The system that brings together those with capital seeking to invest for a fair return, those seeking capital to build businesses that*

FIGURE 1.1

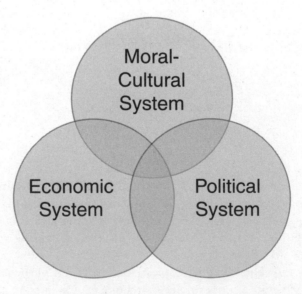

provide goods and services for a profit, and those who seek to consume the goods and services for a price. In economic life, corporations have three defining characteristics: They can raise large sums of money enabling them to meet societal and consumer needs; as limited liability entities, they can sell shares that permit investors to make investments that carry risk reward potential; and they can endure over an unlimited lifetime. Corporations also employ millions of individuals who, along with the corporations, pay taxes to sustain a way of life in the community.

The Political System: *The system that represents the citizenry and governs by establishing laws, rules and regulations intended to serve the common good.* In political life, corporations wield considerable power and influence, raising the question of whether they are used to further their own agendas or to participate in the democratic process of addressing societal needs. Numerous attempts have been made to curb corporate influence in the political process, generally falling short.

The Moral-Cultural System: *The system that shapes society's ethics, values and acceptable standards of behavior consisting of the family, formal education, media, religious traditions and nongovernmental organizations (NGOs).* In our cultural lives, the corporation plays an important role through voluntarism and philanthropy. The corporation provides financial and human volunteer resources to increase the capacity of organizations that improve the quality of life in the local communities. Corporations also lend their business expertise to enhance the ability of social organizations to provide their services. Moreover, social organizations create jobs and pay wages, both of which contribute to local communities. Whether in the arts, education, health care, social services or other areas, corporations have been a positive contributor to the cultural landscape of the community. Their contributions include supporting communities through philanthropy and employee voluntarism, and treating the environment with the respect it deserves.

Within and across these three systems, corporations also engage in the marketplace of *ideas*, taking positions in debates over values and social arrangements, advocating for ideas about economic arrangements and structures, and articulating and defending ideas about appropriate legal frameworks to sustain a free enterprise economy. For two centuries corporations have worked to persuade Americans that capitalism as a *system* and the corporation as an *institution* deserve public support. Depending on corporate behavior, this message has been met with both receptivity and rejection.

THREE PROPOSITIONS

The book's research supports three propositions that frame the evolution of corporate responsibility over the last two centuries: (1) businesses have encountered financial *and* moral expectations from society; (2) where moral expectations for corporate responsibility have not been met, society has imposed laws, regulations and nongovernmental guidelines, which may be necessary but never will be sufficient; and (3) corporate responsibility must derive from within business organizations, not from outside of them. Let's examine each proposition a little more closely.

PROPOSITION 1

Institutions making up the economic sector (corporations and smaller business entities) have all along encountered moral expectations in addition to financial expectations. Sometimes these moral expectations have been communicated through moral-cultural institutions in the public square (e.g., consumer movements, labor unions, churches and the media), and sometimes they have been communicated through laws and regulations (e.g., antitrust, civil rights and environmental protection). And while the scope of these moral expectations has been a matter of debate (minimal versus maximal), there is no question that in the American experience, an expectation of ethical responsiveness has gone hand in hand with an expectation of market responsiveness.[5] Business institutions must never lose sight of their moral foundations.

Again and again, we have witnessed this pattern: *appeals* by citizens and civic associations in the public square for business leadership and accountability, and when those fail, *appeals in legislatures and courtrooms* for curbs on business behavior and punishment for past wrongdoing. Americans presume that the corporation, despite its preoccupations with efficiency, profitability and competitiveness, and despite its need to comply with governmental imperatives, *can and should be responsive to individual rights and to the common good.*[6]

Evolving Moral Expectations of Business

Moral considerations have propelled many if not all of the challenges faced by business over the past 150 years. Battles about wage rates, working conditions, child labor, health and safety, unfair competition, fraudulent advertising, product safety, accountability to investors, corporate political power and environmental impacts were fired by moral indignation as well as the pure economics of any particular practice or activity. Very often these were not quiet intellectual debates, but rather social upheavals and violent confrontations. Some issues were crystallized for the public and for business by a catastrophic disaster such as the Triangle Shirtwaist Fire of 1911 and the Ludlow Massacre in 1914. (See box.)

EVOLVING MORAL EXPECTATIONS OF BUSINESS

- In the nineteenth century, we moved from frequent worker destitution and homelessness to the innovation of company towns, with the unintended consequence of lost civic autonomy and independence, and have since learned to lessen workers' dependency on the corporation.
- In the wake of World War II, we grew from economic depression and material sacrifice to corporate innovation in goods and services, leading to prosperity and consumerism, but also to a culture of consumption. We are now attending to the need for *sustainable* economic growth.
- We moved in the mid-twentieth century from an absence of credit to the innovations associated with the liberal credit/debt policies of modern banking, with the unintended consequences of unrestrained credit, systemic risk and eventually a loss of trust in financial institutions, and we are now seeking to discern the *appropriate* use of credit/debt.
- Our innovative business system has led us from time-consuming transportation using horses and wagons to railroads and eventually to automobiles, aircraft and space technology, with unintended consequences relating to safety and pollution, and we now are reflecting upon the true costs and true benefits of all forms of transportation.
- That same innovative business system has led us from slow communication by "pony express" and telegraph to a high-tech Internet revolution, with its unintended side effects of too much information (and *misinformation*), and we are now examining ways to protect our privacy against identity theft and our communication systems against cyber threats.[7]

Alexis de Tocqueville's 1835 observation about the proclivity of Americans to form groups and associations provides a clue to the voices that emerged early to push back against aspects of the economic system and business conduct. Abolitionists in the pre–Civil War period, labor unions in the second half of the nineteenth century, a National Consumers League founded in 1899, organizers of institutions like Hull House, politicians of various stripes, farmer-labor groups, religious groups and even business groups (e.g., the formation of the Better Business Bureau in 1912) are just a few examples in the more distant past. Echoes in the mid-twentieth century are the civil rights movement, the women's movement, the consumer protection movement (recall Ralph Nader's *Unsafe at Any Speed*) and the environmental movement (marked notably by the first Earth Day in 1970). Today we experience these voices and demands for change in the form of NGOs that address issues such as the environment, human rights, consumer protection and world peace.

Clarifying Corporate Responsibility

Two centuries of change, conflict and debate have gradually led us to a better understanding of the expectations and responsibilities of business. Over that time the nomenclature associated with these ideas has shifted frequently. In 1916, J. M. Clark called for an "economics of responsibility."[8] Since then, others have called for business leaders to assume the role of stewards or trustees. Eventually, the language of "social responsibility" emerged, then "corporate social responsibility," "business ethics," "corporate citizenship," "shared value" and "sustainability." As discussed in *CRAE*, we use the phrase *corporate responsibility* as the umbrella term that captures the essential meaning across time.

The precise content of the term *corporate responsibility* has been difficult to pin down because circumstances and expectations have been in flux. Yet some aspects have become clearer over time. In his 2008 study, Alexander Dahlsrud identified these five dimensions of corporate responsibility:

1. The *environmental dimension*, including the "natural environment," "a cleaner environment," "environmental stewardship" and "environmental concerns in business operations";
2. the *social dimension*, including "contribution to a better society," the "relationship between business and society," "integrating social concerns in business operations" and "considering the full scope of their impact on communities";
3. the *economic dimension*, including socioeconomic or financial "contribution to economic development," including "preserving profitability," CSR [corporate social responsibility] in a firm's "business operations";
4. the *stakeholder dimension*, including firms' "interactions with their stakeholder groups" or "how organizations interact with their employees, suppliers, customers and communities"; and
5. the *voluntariness dimension*, including "actions not prescribed by law," "based on ethical values" or actions "beyond legal requirements."[9]

That these dimensions compose a broadly shared view is evident from the fact that they are reflected in a wide range of international and industry frameworks, among them: the *UN Global Compact, ISO 26000 Guidelines on Corporate Social Responsibility, The Minnesota Principles,* the Caux Round Table *Principles for Business* and numerous other norms and statements of principles developed over the past two decades.

PROPOSITION 2

Compliance with laws, regulations and nongovernmental guidelines may be necessary but never will be sufficient for corporate responsibility. Rules are inevitably lagging indicators of responsible behavior. The Sarbanes-Oxley Act of 2002, the Dodd-Frank Act of 2010, the Sherman Antitrust Act of 1890 and the Securities Exchange Act of 1934 are significant pieces of legislation but were enacted subsequent to corporate scandals that most would argue *should* and *would* never have happened if businesses had been ethically responsible. "The corporation can and must develop an ethical response system, not just an economic and a legal response system."[10]

Given the challenges to corporations indicated above, two things become clear:

- The sources of the challenges have *in common* that they represent forces *external* to the corporation, for example, forces emanating from either the political sector (legislation, regulation) or the moral-cultural sector (media and NGO pressures, union activities, technological changes), and
- They are *insufficient*, even if they might be *necessary*, for achieving corporate responsibility.

Many businesses seek to respond to society's rising expectations. But they often fall short by placing their own economic interests ahead of the interests and rights of a broader set of stakeholders.

Debates about legitimacy provide important lessons for business executives and societal leaders of the twenty-first century as they discuss the role of business in society. There is an important tension between public expectations and corporate power. Sometimes this tension is resolved by economic market forces, other times by political forces. Sometimes it is resolved when business earns respect and public understanding because of how it treats its customers, employees, investors and other stakeholders. Societal expectations, given voice by various stakeholders, have had the effect (in the United States at least) of shifting the seat of corporate responsibility—the moral compass of the business—from outside to inside:

It is, of course, one thing to say that since ethics is on the agenda of those with whom a company interacts, the company had better pay attention; it is quite another to say that ethics is on the company's *own* agenda, part of the way that its management looks at the world. In both cases, attention is paid to ethics. But there is a difference in the *way* the attention is paid. In the first case, ethics is an environmental *constraint* that is only indirectly part of the decision-making process. In the second case, ethics is something that is brought *to* the environment. Making decisions that have ethical implications is not optional. What *is* optional is whether those ethical implications will be considered *outside* forces or made part of the *internal* decision process itself. It is the latter option that I believe management must undertake when I use the phrase "moral agenda."[11]

Corporations can be a force for good because certain workplace or community practices are mandated by the law; because interest groups demand good behavior; or because competitive pressures lead to changes in behavior. All of these, however, represent *external* or *systemic* pressures, which can shift and change without much warning. In "The Rock," T. S. Eliot writes that men frequently dream "of systems so perfect that no one will need to be good."[12] The only true guarantee of corporate responsibility is to internalize it.

PROPOSITION 3

Finally, in view of propositions 1 and 2 above, corporate responsibility must ultimately derive from within business organizations, not from outside of them. It is to the principle-driven leadership and the governance of the modern corporation that we must look for responsibility. The moral character of the corporation is an "inside deal" as the *Federal Sentencing Guidelines for Organizations* (FSGO 1991, revised in 2004) make clear. In November of 2004, the revised FSGO introduced explicit new requirements calling (among other things) for corporate cultures that encourage *ethical conduct*, not simply observance of law. The business scandals of 2001 and 2002 had clearly indicated the prior influence of a firm's *ethical* values on its compliance culture.

In the end, it is the tone at the top—leadership—that provides the internal moral compass of the corporation. Leaders of financial institutions must exhibit statesmanship—and lead with a vision *beyond compliance*. And they must collaborate with the public and the moral-cultural sectors when problems are present that call for multisector solutions.

Corporate Responsibility—from the Inside Out

That progress has come with responsibilities is ably expressed by General Mills CEO Ken Powell in the foreword to *CRAE*:

> Shareholders, customers, employees and host communities today increasingly demand responsible, even enlightened, engagement that goes well beyond a corporation's earnings of the last quarter. I believe this interest is driven by a yearning for principled behavior—for clear and strong values—in all American institutions including business. Stockholders still want to know about sales and earnings of course. But today they also want to know that a Corporation is committed to "doing the right thing" as we say at General Mills. They want to know how we treat our employees and how we are improving the health and safety of our products. They want to know our commitment to the sustainable use of resources in our products and about our engagement and support of the communities where we reside. They correctly see corporations as large and powerful institutions that should be engaged in the right behavior with respect to all of these issues. And they expect us to do the right thing all the time.[13]

Business leaders must answer three questions if they are to be a force for good—and if they hope to earn public trust, support and endorsement.[14]

First: "To whom is the corporation responsible?"[15] We believe the answer lies within a complex array of stakeholders, including its customers, employees, suppliers, investors and communities. And while this list represents a set of primary stakeholders, there are others who share a vested interest in the decisions that lead to the outcome of the corporation's success, including governments (local, national and international), NGOs, competitors, business partners and more. While addressing the interests of stakeholders certainly adds greater complexity, corporations can and must consider the implications of their decisions on those they impact. Sometimes these groups will have conflicting interests, and not everyone will have their needs addressed all the time. But they still need to be considered and the corporate response balanced.

Second: "For what is the modern corporation responsible?"[16] At the most basic level, corporations must build and service high-quality products and services, create meaningful work with livable wages for their employees and ensure a fair return for their investors. Corporations must invest in the communities, especially where they do business, to aid in the quality of life. A side benefit occurs as this also helps to create an environment to attract and retain qualified workers. "Sustainability—conducting activities in ways that do not jeopardize the ability of future generations to meet their needs—is predicated on the [foundation] that no person or business has a right to irreparably destroy the Earth's vital resources."[17]

Third: "How is a company to meet its responsibilities?"[18] Not only must a corporation know and establish a relationship with its stakeholders, it must establish a pattern of how it interacts with them. Corporate leadership must be focused on "honesty, disclosure and transparency."[19] Trust is built on a foundation of accountability and transparency.

When answering the questions of **to whom, for what** and **how**, it is important to remember that what gets measured receives attention, focus and management. In today's world, business "must understand and measure [its impact] in three domains: economic, environmental and social . . . a triple bottom line"[20] This triple bottom line measure provides a way for business to collect meaningful data and keep score on its progress. And it provides a meaningful way for business to communicate with its stakeholders.

Measures like triple bottom line reporting (reflected in frameworks like the Global Reporting Initiative, Sustainability Accounting Standards Board [SASB] and the International Integrated Reporting Council [IIRC]) have created ways for investors to better understand how businesses are addressing corporate responsibility to assist them in making informed investing choices. Indeed, a movement of socially responsible investors has attracted trillions of dollars of investment from pension funds, endowments and other funds from around the world. They are using their considerable assets to create leverage to encourage responsible corporate behavior.

Organizational Hurdles and Barriers

The will and aspiration to lead with a high ethical standard faces substantial hurdles because of the way organizations and organizational cultures operate. Margaret Heffernan's book *Willful Blindness* and research on the psychology of individuals and organizational dynamics underscore this point. Barriers to information sharing, complexity in large global organizations, conflicting incentives and compensation schemes, fear of retaliation, work overload, uncertainty about who has what responsibility in collaborative partnerships—all pose obstacles that require patient and discerning leadership.

Given the diverse stakeholders of the business, there is no single owner of corporate responsibility inside the corporation. Environmental health and safety managers are responsible for issues of sustainability, resource conservation and industrial health practices. Community relations managers address community development, philanthropy and local relationships. Human resources managers address the needs of the workforce, including compensation, benefits, equal opportunity and diversity. And consumer affairs, supplier relations and customer relations all provide a window into the interests and expectations of the company's stakeholders.

But ultimately, it is the CEO and board that are responsible for setting the tone for corporate behavior, establishing the moral compass and ensuring corporate policies that responsibly address the needs of its stakeholders. This moral compass of the organization requires deliberate and thoughtful consideration; it must be institutionalized throughout the organization; and it has to be evident in its processes and systems.

Where Do We Go from Here?

So where do we go from here, and what are the implications for leaders of today and tomorrow?

Corporate responsibility has emerged as capitalism has evolved over the last 200 years. From individual freedom in the colonial period to worker solidarity in the industrial era to global responsibility in the twenty-first century, the debate in the public square has shaped the social legitimacy of the corporation.

The corporation's ability to manage the gap between society's expectations of its behavior and its actual behavior dramatically affects its social legitimacy. And when business falls short, the political arena and the moral-cultural arena often challenge its legitimacy and attempt to legislate responsible behavior. And while legislation is necessary, it alone is not sufficient. One cannot legislate integrity. It must come from inside the corporation. It requires leadership with the highest ethical standards.

Business can and must affect the perceptions of its behavior by the choices it makes. Herbert Simon, a renowned twentieth-century economist, points out that every business decision has a factual component and a values component. These values include honesty, integrity and respect for others. But since people are human, they often act unethically by lying, cheating, stealing or taking advantage of others. Every society wrestles with how to address unethical behavior through some combination of legislation, education and enforcement.

Business ethics has sought to play a role through education, from the personal level to the professional level to the organizational level. Ethical leadership is concerned with both *what* is being done and *how* it is being done. Leaders must focus their organizations on both means and ends by asking, What are we trying to do and how do our actions line up with our purpose and our values?

Business leaders are key to linking business ethics and corporate responsibility. A strong sense of purpose beyond creating economic value has to be addressed at the beginning, not the end, of business strategy. And business leaders now operate in what Peter Drucker called a world of "new realities."[21] Businesses today operate globally—with size no longer providing insulation from competitive threat. Disruptive technologies, customer preferences and social media all provide opportunities for new entrants to threaten established industries and corporations. "As with individual moral character, a corporation's character takes shape by default when it is not given shape by design. It has become increasingly clear that, left unmanaged, the ethical aspects of corporate policy and practice take on a life of their own."[22]

Likewise, public expectations of how a responsible corporation will act in such a world continue to change. The corporation is expected to safeguard and increase the value of the resources it has been entrusted with; to protect the environment, not to cover it with waste, and to respond proactively in the face of natural disasters striking communities at home and abroad (e.g., Hurricane Katrina, the 2004 tsunami in Indonesia, the earthquakes in Haiti in 2010 and Japan in 2011). Whether providing training for safe practices, fair and equitable compensation or attending to the privacy rights of the individual, business is expected in ever new ways to do the right thing in the right way. Business must be both profitable and serve society.

NOTES

1. Archie B. Carroll, Kenneth J. Lipartito, James E. Post, and Patricia H. Werhane, *Corporate Responsibility: The American Experience*, ed. Kenneth E. Goodpaster (Cambridge: Cambridge University Press, 2012), 3. This quotation refers to Edwin Merrick Dodd Jr., "For Whom Are Corporate Managers Trustees?" *Harvard Law Review* 45, no. 7 (1932): 1145–63.
2. Carroll et al., *Corporate Responsibility*.
3. Ibid., 1.
4. For more on these subsystems or "sectors," see Michael Novak, *The Spirit of Democratic Capitalism* (New York: Simon and Schuster, 1982), 56; for an interpretation of Novak's tripartite view of society, see Kenneth E. Goodpaster, "Tenacity: The American Pursuit of Corporate Responsibility," *Business and Society Review* 118, no. 4 (2013): 583–84.
5. Minimalists such as Milton Friedman insisted that businesses are most responsible when they stick to their profit-making expertise, while modern stakeholder

advocates would have the corporation internalize the distinct concerns of each stakeholder group (customers, employees, vendors, local communities and the environment).

6. Goodpaster, "Tenacity," 582.
7. Ibid., 592.
8. John Maurice Clark, "The Changing Basis of Economic Responsibility," *Journal of Political Economy* 24, no. 3 (1916): 210.
9. Carroll et al., *Corporate Responsibility*, 7–8; Alexander Dahlsrud, "How Corporate Social Responsibility Is Defined: An Analysis of 37 Definitions," *Corporate Social Responsibility and Environmental Management* 15, no. 1 (2006): 4.
10. Goodpaster, "Tenacity," 582.
11. Kenneth E. Goodpaster, *Conscience and Corporate Culture* (Malden, MA: Blackwell, 2007), 112.
12. T. S. Eliot, "Choruses from 'The Rock,'" VI, 159, 1934. In *The Complete Poems and Plays of T. S. Eliot* (London: Faber, 2004).
13. Carroll et al., *Corporate Responsibility*, xiv.
14. Ibid., 22.
15. Ibid.
16. Ibid., 23.
17. Ibid.
18. Ibid., 24.
19. Ibid., 23.
20. Ibid., 24. Here, the authors refer to the role of business; in *CRAE*, the authors refer similarly to the roles of managers, writing that they must also understand and measure the effects of their activities in these three domains. For more on the triple bottom line, see John Elkington, *Cannibals with Forks: The Triple Bottom Line of Twenty-First-Century Business* (Oxford: Capstone, 1997), 22.
21. Peter F. Drucker, *The New Realities: In Government and Politics, in Economy and Business, in Society and World View* (New York: Harper and Row, 1989), ii. Please see also the introduction to *CRAE* for a discussion about leadership, organizations and responsibility relative to these realities, Carroll et al., *Corporate Responsibility*, 21.
22. Goodpaster, *Conscience and Corporate Culture*, 112.

CHAPTER 2

A BETTER SOCIAL CONTRACT FOR FINANCIAL INTERMEDIARIES

Stephen B. Young

Author of Moral Capitalism

At 6 a.m. on Wednesday, March 26, 2014, the phone rang in Michael Corbat's hotel room in Seoul, Korea. It was bad news. An official from the Federal Reserve informed Citigroup's chief executive that the Fed would not permit any increase in dividend payouts to the company's owners.[1] From Corbat's vantage point, the news meant that he had failed in his principal fiduciary duty. Now he was unable to return certain company profits to the shareholders of Citigroup. From the shareholders' vantage point, their company was burdened with a bad social contract. The public, as represented by the Fed, would not let Citigroup shareholders maximize profit from their investment in a private enterprise. Money earned by the company had to stay with the company.

In this case, Citigroup's social contract was explicit. It had been set forth in federal government regulation—specifically, in the Dodd-Frank legislation designed to prevent a repeat of the 2008 financial market collapse. The terms of this social contract had been negotiated for Citigroup by its lobbyists, in tandem with lobbyists for other financial firms and their political allies. On the other side of the negotiating table were President Obama and his senior financial advisors, the Federal Reserve System's board of governors, and congressional leaders. These public officials were society's chosen representatives, standing in for society at large. Citigroup and other large financial firms held a weak hand in the negotiations. They had tanked the global economy by issuing subprime mortgage securities that performed poorly and other speculative investment contracts that depended on the repayment of such mortgage loans. Now the banks had to pay recompense to an angry and disappointed public.

That poor performance had destroyed the previous social contract enjoyed by the finance industry: a license with the Securities and Exchange Commission that allowed Citigroup to borrow money for speculative investing. Citigroup had determined that contract by negotiating with Congress and the Clinton administration in the 1990s for repeal of the Glass-Steagall Act, which ended the separation between traditional banking and riskier investment banking. The new Dodd-Frank rules imposed on Citigroup prevented Michael Corbat from doing his duty to shareholders because he was now obligated to keep enough capital on hand to withstand any losses that might follow a severe recession. Citigroup claimed it had capital levels of 10 percent, while Federal Reserve officials estimated the levels at only 7.2 percent.[2] Corbat was unable to convince the Federal Reserve staff, so the government calculations prevailed. Citigroup didn't have enough capital to increase its dividend payments to shareholders, and if it had gone ahead with the payments, it would have been in breach of its contract and out of business. Thus it had no choice but to submit to the public interest.

The lesson here is a simple one: good social contract terms depend on good performance. The better the performance, the better the terms. Financial intermediation, because of its fundamental importance to the economy, is more than a private business. It also has aspects of public service. With economic growth so dependent on financing, society cannot afford the risk of leaving financial intermediation entirely in the hands of those who may not share its larger goals and values. Society has therefore put a "lien" on financial companies, authorizing regulators to step into these private businesses when the need arises to protect society's interests. This essay aims to clarify the specific terms of the license between society and financial intermediaries, concluding with a seven-point code of conduct for banks and other financial intermediaries.

Financial transactions have a dual nature. In one sense, they are private exchanges of value free from any social considerations. But they also must be evaluated by society to see if they contribute to the common good. In the language of economists, financial transactions come with many "externalities" that create public "goods" and public "bads." Constructive externalities—the positive, direct and indirect consequences of a financial transaction—are assimilated to public goods, while harmful or negative externalities are associated with public bads. Obviously, society wants to have more of the goods and less of the bads. Requiring financial intermediaries to operate with a license seeks to promote the production of public goods, and the eschewing of public bads, on the part of financial intermediaries.

From this perspective, financial intermediation is scrutinized by two very different judges: private ones such as Citigroup that are themselves the financial intermediary, and public judges that stand apart from the transactions but have a keen interest in their consequences, such as the Federal Reserve.

These public judges are first the regulators—and if events turn more serious, the legislators—who exercise the police power of society. Not all regulation is designed to prevent public bads from following on financial intermediation. Much of it is enacted to promote the odds of public goods being achieved, such as low interest rates, easily available liquidity, soundly priced securities, the absence of asset bubbles and market crashes.

How can financial intermediaries improve the terms of their contracts? By being good stewards of their customers' money. Good stewardship reduces the intensity and scope of negative externalities that might be caused by financial intermediaries. In addition, good stewardship practices enhance the reliability of financial contracts, drawing forth more investment from satisfied customers and expanding the volume of financial intermediation. Stewardship leads to more public goods and fewer public bads emerging from financial intermediation. In short, good stewardship practices can tip the balance of negotiating power away from regulators toward the private sector, leading to improved terms of the industry's social contract.

But stewardship also promotes the best interests of private participants in financial transactions. Stewardship is a guarantor of prudence and long-term benefits.

OTHER PEOPLE'S MONEY

Stewardship enhances the overall quality of financial intermediation because it confronts the Achilles' heel of the industry, which is its dependence on the use of "other people's money."

Financial intermediation is different than ownership. Financial intermediaries are responsible for temporary transfers and repayments, while owners have the rights of private dominion. Financial transactions involve the transfer of the use of funds from owners to others for a fee. In financing the needs of others, the owner of the funds becomes dependent on the intermediary for wise use of the funds provided, avoidance of their loss and timely return of such funds with profit.

Even the purchase of an ownership interest in a business has a return of capital aspect. The investor may at some time in the future want to sell off his or her interest in the firm—for a profit or to avoid further loss. The intermediary stands on both sides of the financial transaction between the transferor and the transferee to provide reassurance that all will turn out as intended. The intermediary is placed in a position where the parties making the exchange of funds for promises of future performance depend on his or her skill and good judgment.

This functional role of the intermediary, and of the financial industry as a whole, involves dealing with other people's money under conditions of trust and reliance if the parties are to reach agreement on the transfer of funds.

Adam Smith famously observed the potential for abuse of power with respect to other people's money. He wrote in *Wealth of Nations*: "The directors [of joint stock companies], however, being the managers rather of other people's money than of their own, it cannot be well expected, that they should watch over it with the same anxious vigilance with which the partners in a private co-partnery frequently watch over their own."[3]

The antidote to such indifference on the part of those who manage other people's money is a moral sense of responsibility. Smith described this sensibility as an inner conscience, or an "impartial spectator" capable of speaking to the self to bring to mind a context greater than mere self-interest.[4] Smith propounded the idea that duty and obligation in contracts on the part of the promisor didn't come from self-interest but from placing the promisee in a subordinate position of dependency on the promisor for attainment of the promisee's self-interest. Smith's linkage of duty to dependency is the same moral ambience binding a shepherd to his flock, and applies to all those who contract for financial performance. Those who manage the money of others are the shepherds and those who so consign their money are the flock, an idea that was invented well before Adam Smith.

THE ANCIENT ORIGINS OF STEWARDSHIP PRINCIPLES IN BUSINESS TODAY

The ancestry of stewardship as a major instrument of social well-being is ancient. Adam Smith merely drew on old learning and practice. A very early source that has resonated over the centuries in Judeo-Christian practices was the Code of Hammurabi. King Hammurabi of Babylon (1792–1750 BC) asserted that his right to issue laws or "the rules of righteousness" arose from a duty to "destroy the wicked and evildoers" and promote the welfare of those under his sway and "further the well-being of mankind."[5]

A more familiar work is the Bible, which influenced our understanding of stewardship. In the Old Testament, the book of Samuel notes that the elders of the tribes of Israel refused to follow the sons of Samuel for they had "turned aside after lucre."[6] In the New Testament, Jesus teaches that the door to the Kingdom of Heaven was open to those who considered the interests of their neighbors. This call to "love thy neighbor as thyself" leads directly to good stewardship practices and contributes to making decisions that benefit the self and others.

Later John Calvin made service and ministry the road to overcome sinful alienation from God. By directing the self to service, the Christian could draw near to God's will and hope to receive God's grace for a life well lived.[7] In 1630, Puritan leader John Winthrop used Calvin's ideas to found the city of Boston. Winthrop's covenantal theology was that the Puritans had entered into a stewardship arrangement with the Lord to do his work on earth loyally or suffer his wrath. Winthrop wrote, "Thus stands the cause between God and us. We are entered into covenant with Him for this work. We have taken out a commission. The Lord hath given us leave to draw our own articles. . . . He ratified this covenant and sealed our commission, and will expect a strict performance of the articles contained in it."[8] Calvin's theology thus laid the foundation for the Protestant ethic that gave birth to capitalism.[9]

Independent of Judeo-Christian law, Roman law provided for various forms of stewardship responsibilities. One who held property as security—other people's money, so to speak—to protect a creditor was a *fiducia*.[10] The action was a contractual transfer of ownership of a thing to the creditor, who then acted as custodian or trustee of the property so transferred.[11] Roman citizens could pledge themselves to faithful observance of a covenant by saying "*Spondeo*," or "I so assume to do," to make themselves sureties for an obligation.[12] Calvinism and Roman fiduciary legalities merged in English common law and constitutional practice. The principle that public office was a public trust was acknowledged by John Locke in his *Second Treatise on Civil Government*, which shaped the American Declaration of Independence and the U.S. Constitution.

English common law conceptions of stewardship as legal obligation have descended into modern commercial and corporate law in the law of agency, partners, trustees and corporate officers, including members of boards of directors. Fiduciary duties imposed by law to prevent abuse of power by one in a position of trust and responsibility include a duty of loyalty to those dependent on the management of the trust and a duty to those same persons to take due care in the management of their interests. The fiduciary standard in law is to avoid both selfish expropriation of opportunity and malfeasance in decision making.

So the idea that society holds powerful private financial intermediaries responsible for producing public goods and reducing public bads is not new. Standards of fiduciary conduct should not be seen as illogical or objectionable. These principles go back to ancient times and are the pillars upholding both capitalism and Western civilization.

WHAT SOCIETY WANTS FROM
FINANCIAL INTERMEDIARIES

Society grants licenses to financial institutions to intermediate financial transactions. The contract terms pertain to the side effects, or externalities, that flow from such business. Given that capitalism systematically creates wealth, society's motivation is to make capitalism possible.

The good that society desires from financial intermediation is timely support for more prosperity. As Smith said, "All industry is employed, and has and will be to the end of the world, in increasing and multiplying the objects of human desire; that is, goods and money: goods as the end and money as the means."[13] Society's expectation of finance is to create and sustain many different kinds of inducements to industry to make goods and services and thus create jobs. Financial intermediaries stand between the seller, or maker of the good or service, and the buyer. They have a dual role: they assist producers and sellers who bring goods and services to market, and they ensure that buyers have ready money to purchase what they need and desire.

Like any customer seeking satisfaction, society wants good value for money. It will provide a favorable license in exchange for excellent service.

Society looks upon financial intermediation as a government office, a position with independent authority created to achieve certain ends. The holder of any office is not the owner with the benefits and powers that come with the position, but a servant. As a servant, their responsibility is to share power and put the needs of others first, described by author Robert Greenleaf as "servant leadership."[14]

Financial intermediaries broker and arrange the contracts for the exchange of rights to use funds. Society needs them to broker and arrange funds in the appropriate amounts for enterprises to thrive. The social contract with financial intermediaries is a simple one in concept: freedom to arrange financing in return for sustained wealth creation that promotes sufficient social welfare for society's stakeholders.

WHAT SOCIETY WANTS FROM FINANCIAL INTERMEDIARIES
- To attract funds from investors for investing and credit
- To invest those funds on good terms
- To accurately calculate risks and returns
- To invest wisely and profitably
- To maintain consistent prices of funds and avoid pricing volatility
- To prudently estimate the value of financial assets

Society expects financial intermediaries to make available more liquidity than there is cash money in circulation. To permit economic growth, society wants to optimize its ability to pay for investments on the one hand and for purchases on the other. Thus financial intermediaries coordinate arrangements for future sharing of wealth made possible by current investments and transactions. As the economy grows, more funds become available—we say that the money supply expands. Current promises to share in the distribution of such future wealth will entice present owners of funds to part with them now. The basic financial contract, therefore, is the present transfer of funds in exchange for contract rights that provide for future payments.

Financial intermediaries thus find themselves caught between another pair of opposing interests: those who have ready money now, and those who don't but who are willing to hire it for a time. Financial intermediaries stand between those with money seeking to invest it and those seeking funds, and endeavor to connect the two.

Accordingly, the social contract responsibilities of intermediaries are, on the one hand, to place funds on good terms, and, on the other, to attract funds from investors. Society expects that the funds will be placed, first of all, on such terms as will convince the owners of wealth to trust care of their money to others and, second, on such terms as will bring about a net increase in wealth. Fortunately, the second expectation makes the first possible. If funds are not put to work wisely and profitably, there is no likelihood that the private expectations of investors can be met. Thus, financial intermediation—when well managed—simultaneously satisfies both social and private expectations. Society gets its wealth creation, and private investors get their profits.

Intermediaries collect funds and place them well by prudently calculating the risks of success and the probable rewards. The intellectually rigorous calculations of risks and returns are central to the disciplines of bank lending, investment banking, securities analysis, asset management and wealth management advising. When such calculations are sound, financial intermediaries hit their key performance indicators: funds for investment and extensions of credit. A separate term in society's contract with financial intermediaries applies to the quality of such risk/return calculations.

Now, in addition to mere success in raising funds and putting them to work, society has additional expectations as to the scope and quality of such intermediation. Wealth creation benefits from low volatility in the price of funds. When funds are too expensive, investment falls, and conversely, when the price is too low, funds are not forthcoming and investment also falls. Cheaply priced funds, usually the result of an oversupply, risk causing the value of assets to rise in the short term, only to collapse in the future. Thus, the supply of liquidity should be neither too much nor too little. Society prefers that both inflation and deflation be avoided.

Further, society benefits when financial intermediaries prudently estimate the value of financial assets. Misleading or stupid valuations, especially unsustainably high ones, lead to losses for investors and less economic activity. Unreasonably low valuations deter investors from consigning their wealth to other people's management. Unreasonable prospects of high valuation draw forth investment, but only to see the funds poorly used or squandered.

Good stewards are well aware of the dangers inherent in extremes of pricing and valuations. They have internalized standards of prudent foresight. By avoiding the highs and the lows, such stewardship aligns with society's basic expectations of financial services.

SOURCES OF MISALIGNMENT

Financial intermediaries are not always aligned with society's expectations of their contract performance. They have their own private expectations that motivate and guide their decision making. While society expects financial intermediaries to hold "office," the intermediaries themselves may not see their role in such a light. They may much prefer to see themselves as "owners" of opportunities to profit.

In short, society expects the common good to be served, while the financial intermediary is actually acting in self-interest. Instead of Adam Smith's ideal of an "invisible hand" coordinating self-interested actions to create positive results for many, the model is self-aggrandizement at the expense of others, or Social Darwinism.

Experience has shown that there can be serious misalignment between what society expects from financial intermediation and what the financial sector delivers to society. This misalignment results directly from the self-serving negligence that can arise in dealing with other people's money. Whenever norms and circumstances permit excessive deference to self-interest in financial intermediation, this misalignment grows, sometimes even to the point of causing the industry to break its contract with society. The contract can then only be repaired through a process of realignment. The realignment occurs through a return to stewardship norms and practices.

THE 2008 BREACH OF CONTRACT

Three developments led to the financial industry's shift away from good stewardship and breach of contract that caused the 2008 collapse of global credit markets. They were: the emergence of "quants" in decision making; the conversion of investment banking firms into publicly traded corporations; and speculation as a major source of revenue for the industry.

Beware of Quants Bearing Gifts

First, the emergence of quants who predicted price movements in trading markets for financial contracts changed the dynamic of financial intermediation. The mathematical skills of quants created opportunities to profit from short-term speculation while sidelining long-term business realities. This use of statistical algorithms to determine much more accurately than ever before the regression of efficient market prices to an assumed norm was thought to have eliminated much of the risk in trading. With risk conceptually eliminated—but not so in real life, as it turned out—returns were thought to be much more certain. Such certainty drew forth increased systemic allocation of funds to trading, which raised the prices of financial instruments traded.

The use of computers in trading, especially high-frequency trading, permitted millions of trades to be directed by algorithms so that small profits per trade could be aggregated into large profits over time. This technology further encouraged the shift of financial intermediation to speculative trading.

Speculation is at odds with society's contract with finance. Society seeks new wealth creation, while speculation merely moves money from one pocket to another. Economist John Maynard Keynes was serious when he compared stock markets to casinos. And the origin of trading algorithms lies in statisticians who tried to write probability equations that would beat the house in Las Vegas casinos. When investors borrow funds in order to speculate, there will be winners and losers. The losers can suffer heavy losses that often force them into financial distress. From society's point of view, this is a bad outcome. Such investing on margin was a primary cause of the collapse of the New York Stock Exchange in 1929.

Renters, Not Owners

Second, the reorganization of most investment banks from partnerships into publicly traded corporations made a big difference. Now financial intermediaries were no longer protecting their own money, but were working with other people's money. Financial houses borrowed money to trade with and exposed themselves to collapse if the market prices of those assets lost value.

Investor psychology changes when one turns from seeking long-term value appreciation to short-term profit taking. An owner's prudence becomes a renter's more casual mind-set of not worrying about the future. They become trendy consumers rather than real investors. Investors with funds to put into financial markets bought and sold financial contracts largely to profit from market price movements, which added volatility to prices. As Keynes trenchantly noted in his *General Theory* of the economy, trading in financial contracts exposes traders to the myopia of herd behavior.[15] They come to follow the herd and thus fail to look beyond immediate herd concerns in order to place their bets on price movements.

Speculative Trading

When speculative desperation takes over pricing, the prudence demanded by society evaporates, and pricing and valuation fail to protect continued wealth creation. Importantly, the nature of many investment products made and sold by financial intermediaries, and the nature of the clients seeking funds, contributes to destabilization of markets under conditions of speculation.

Starting with the Tulip Mania of 1627 in Holland, financial markets breach the terms of their social contracts by overcharging now for a contractual right to future returns. Financial instruments are legal contracts, not goods or services. They are abstractions—promises to pay in the future, whether in stocks, bonds, warrants, debentures, shares of mutual funds, limited partnerships or shares in packages of loans such as collateralized debt obligations.

As such, the marginal cost of issuing more of them is very low. Only a promise is needed, formalized in a legal contract enforceable in court. Naked promises can be had on the cheap. The marginal cost of new contracts does not reflect the increasing risk that comes with selling into an asset bubble. The new contracts are mispriced because they do not compensate for a rising risk of future loss.

To add insult to injury, when the issuers of contract rights sell off their interest in future payments for an up-front fee, they have little incentive to be prudent in the creation of sound contracts or to keep the probable valuation of the rights stable as promised. Not only do the architects of such contracts fail to put their own money at risk, they are playing exclusively with other people's money and leave the last one who bought the contract holding the bag.

When such negligent issuance of contract rights builds into an asset bubble, as it did with subprime mortgages starting in 2004, financial intermediation turns into a game of musical chairs: when the music stops, someone is destined not to have a chair to sit on. This sudden inability to sit securely leads to economic loss and a breach of society's expectations.

Perhaps the best illustration of the imprudence of financial intermediation leading up to the 2008 collapse of credit markets came from Citigroup CEO Chuck Prince: "As long as the music is playing, you've got to get up and dance."[16]

Trading for speculative purposes wounds stewardship practices in another way as well. Trades, especially when they are executed in nanoseconds by computers, are not relationships where long-term consequences between the parties matter. In a trade, one party leaves with the item purchased and the other with the money. Traders lend themselves to the morality of "take the money and run" and "*caveat emptor.*" They are one-off transactions, mostly with unknown buyers or sellers. In the language of game theory, they are "noniterative" games that maximize zero-sum calculations of self-advantage. They are mechanical and not personal and so cannot draw forth from participants any moral sense of concern for the other party. In the formulation of Martin Buber, they submerge "I/Thou" relationships beneath instrumental "I/It" exploitations and fears.[17]

CONCLUSION: RESTORING THE SOCIAL CONTRACT

Leadership arises from values and principles. The following code of conduct sets forth a template for good leadership by banks and other financial intermediaries.

SUGGESTED CODE OF CONDUCT

1. **Mission:** Our mission is to provide liquidity to empower economic growth and prosperity on reasonable terms that are commensurate with the risk we assumed. We recognize that the social well-being of society depends on the quality of our services.
2. **Standard of Due Care:** As stewards for both those who provide capital and those who use capital, we will be prudent and diligent in our valuations, providing sustainable liquidity support and reasonable returns commensurate with the risk we assumed for our customers. Our duty is to provide effective risk management for the benefit of our stakeholders. As part of this standard of due care we will be knowledgeable about what constitutes best business practice and will instruct our managers to accept nothing less than the most thoughtful and responsible practices.
3. **Compensation:** We seek no more than a level of profit commensurate with the value we create for our customers. We will compensate our employees appropriately in line with common best practices in our society and generously commensurate with their successful implementation of this Code of Conduct.
4. **Duty of Loyalty:** As stewards and trusted intermediaries, we will avoid conflicts of interest with our customers, we will place their interests above our own and we will require our employees to faithfully execute these responsibilities. We will safeguard customer

information, and we will not misuse information for our own advantage.

5. **Criminal and Illicit Activities:** We will not tolerate or facilitate any criminal or illicit activity or knowingly engage in any violation of laws and regulations.

6. **Stakeholders, Communities and the Natural Environment:** We acknowledge our ability to enhance the well-being of all of our stakeholders, the communities in which we do business and the natural environment supporting those communities—both domestic and global. Acting in good faith, we will not knowingly bring harm to any of these. We will act transparently, according to our best judgment, to maintain a balanced and sustainable approach to promoting the well-being of those stakeholders, communities and natural environments.

7. **Governance and the Public Trust:** We will adhere to best practices of governance to ensure maximum material transparency, fairness and honesty in our communications and prudential accountability to our stakeholders.

Financial intermediaries can indeed mend their ways, restore good stewardship practices and realign their industry with society's expectations of service for the common good. All that is required is leadership from the top.

NOTES

1. Suzanne Kapner, Stephanie Armour, and Julie Steinberg, "Bad News Drew Citi CEO to Rush Home," *Wall Street Journal*, March 28, 2014, A1.
2. Ibid.
3. Adam Smith, *An Inquiry into the Origins and Causes of the Wealth of Nations* (New York: Modern Library, 1937), 700. Fifth edition, 1789; first edition published 1776.
4. Adam Smith, *Lectures on Jurisprudence* (Indianapolis: Liberty Fund, 1982), 87, 93; Smith, *Wealth of Nations.*
5. Code of Hammurabi, trans. L. W. King, http://eawc.evansville.edu/anthology /hammurabi.htm.
6. I Samuel 8: 1-22.
7. John Calvin, *Institutes of the Christian Religion*, ed. John T. McNeill (Philadelphia: The Westminster Press).
8. John Winthrop, *A Modell of Christian Charity* (1630), https://history.hanover .edu/texts/winthmod.html.
9. Max Weber, *The Protestant Ethic and the Spirit of Capitalism* (New York: Charles Scribner, 1958); Richard Brookhiser, *The Way of the WASP* (New York: The Free Press, 1991).

10. Fritz Schulz, *Classical Roman Law* (Oxford: Oxford University Press, 1951), 400.
11. Ibid., 406.
12. Rudolph Sohm, *The Institutes of Roman Law* (Oxford: Clarendon Press, 1892), 38.
13. Smith, *Lectures on Jurisprudence*, 380.
14. Robert Greenleaf, *Servant Leadership* (Mahwah, NJ: Paulist Press, 2002).
15. John Maynard Keynes, *The General Theory of Employment, Interest, and Money* (London: Palgrave Macmillan, 1936).
16. Michiyo Nakamoto and David Wighton, "Citigroup Chief Stays Bullish on Buy-outs," *Financial Times*, July 9, 2007, http://www.ft.com/intl/cms/s/0/80e29 87a-2e50-11dc-821c-0000779fd2ac.html#axzz3EvgVtoFi.
17. Martin Buber, *I and Thou* (English trans. 1932) (New York: Scribner, 1958).

CHAPTER 3

FINANCE AND THE GOOD SOCIETY

Robert J. Shiller

Economist, Yale University

What are we to make of the phrase *finance and the good society*? To some readers, this may seem an incongruous coupling of concepts. The word *finance* is commonly thought of as the science and practice of wealth management—of enlarging portfolios, managing their risks and tax liabilities, ensuring that the rich grow richer. The phrase *good society* is a term used by generations of philosophers, historians and economists to describe the kind of society in which we should aspire to live; it is usually understood as an egalitarian society, one in which all people respect and appreciate each other. So at first glance *finance*, at least as commonly understood, seems to be working *against* the achievement of the *good society*.

But it is not so simple. Finance has become ever more associated with capitalism. Since the Industrial Revolution, intellectuals have focused their often-heated debates about the good society on issues related to capitalism, including the system of markets, private property, legal rules and class relations. These institutions and issues have increasingly come to define modern society throughout the world. After democracy, few ideas have been as pervasive and contentious in defining the good society as capitalism.

Debates about capitalism and the good society, from Karl Marx's incendiary criticisms in the nineteenth century through Milton Friedman's spirited defenses of free markets in the twentieth, have tended to center on industrial capitalism: the system of production, banking and trade that shaped modern society up through the end of World War II. But the past several decades have witnessed the rise of financial capitalism: a system in which finance, once the handmaiden of industry, has taken the lead as the engine driving capitalism. Much ink has been spilled over the purely economic aspects of financial capitalism. I too have contributed to this discussion, in my scholarly writings on market volatility and in books such as *Irrational Exuberance*. The recent financial crisis has called forth questions not only about the system's parts but also about financial capitalism as a whole. This crisis, dubbed by Carmen Reinhart and Kenneth Rogoff as the "Second Great Contraction"—a period of weakened economies around the world starting in 2007 but continuing for years after, mirroring the Great Contraction that followed the financial crisis of 1929—has led to angry rejections of the value of financial capitalism.[1]

Given this experience, many wonder: What is the role of finance in the good society? How can finance, as a science, a practice and a source of economic innovation, be used to advance the goals of the good society? How can finance promote freedom, prosperity, equality and economic security? How can we democratize finance so it works better for all of us?

WHAT'S IN A PHRASE?
FINANCIAL CAPITALISM EVOLVING

The term *financial capitalism* developed negative connotations as soon as it first became popular in the 1930s with the publication of George W. Edwards's *The Evolution of Finance Capitalism*.[2] Edwards saw a conspiracy of large financial institutions, with J. P. Morgan at the lead. He called it the *Pax Morgana*. During the Great Depression critics and much of the public at large blamed the financial system for their plight; they viewed the system as almost feudal, with financiers replacing the lords.

The term has recently been revived, and again it is used with hostility. President Nicolas Sarkozy of France has said, "Purely financial capitalism has perverted the logic of capitalism. Financial capitalism is a system of irresponsibility and is . . . amoral. It is a system where the logic of the market excuses everything."[3]

Tony Blair, former British prime minister, speaking of the severe financial crisis that began in 2007, remarked, "What is plain is that the financial system has altered its fundamentals, and can never be the same again. What is needed is radical action to deal with the fallout of the crisis."[4]

Grigory Yavlinsky wrote the 500 Days Program of 1990, which outlined the Russian transition to a free market economy, and was promoted to deputy prime minister to implement it. He began to express similar doubts after the crisis. In his 2011 book *Realeconomik*, in a section entitled "Structural Shift: From Industrial Capitalism to Financial Capitalism," he noted that "the fundamental structural shifts [are] directly related to a gradual slackening of moral constraints in developed countries. Structural shifts like these follow very fast growth of the financial sector and services directly related to it."[5]

While critics are correct in some of their indictments, the changes that must be made, rather than having the effect of constraining the innovative power of financial capitalism, should instead broaden its scope. We will make little progress if we simply condemn financial capitalism as a system of irresponsibility. But we have the potential to support the greater goals of good societies—prosperous and free societies in the industrialized as well as the developing world—if we expand, correct and realign finance.

THE INEXORABLE SPREAD OF FINANCIAL CAPITALISM

At this time, we still well remember the severe financial crisis of 2007–09. We still tend to associate finance with the problems like those revealed by that crisis, such as the mortgage and debt hangovers in the United States and Europe, and with the legal and regulatory errors that preceded these events. But we should not lose sight of the bigger picture. The more important story is the proliferation and transformation of successful financial ideas. Financial innovations emanating from Amsterdam, London and New York are developing further in Buenos Aires, Dubai and Tokyo.

The socialist market economy, with its increasingly advanced financial structures, was introduced to China in 1978 by Deng Xiaoping, who adapted to the Chinese environment the examples of other highly successful Chinese-speaking cities: Hong Kong, Singapore and Taipei. The economic liberalization of India, which allowed freer application of modern finance, was inaugurated in 1991 under Prime Minister P. V. Narasimha Rao by his finance minister (later prime minister) Manmohan Singh, who was educated in economics at Nuffield College, University of Oxford. The voucher privatization system introduced to Russia in 1992–94 under Prime Minister Boris Yeltsin by his minister Anatoly Chubais—which followed a modification of the Yavlinsky plan—was a deliberate and aggressive strategy to transform Russia's economy. The intent was not simply to match the rest of the world in the degree to which finance permeated the daily lives of the Russian people, but to have Russia rank first in the world in public ownership of capital.

Such sudden integrations of sophisticated financial structures, originally designed in more financially advanced countries, were not achieved entirely smoothly in these countries, and there was a degree of anger about the inequality of benefits that accrued to some as opportunists amassed great wealth quickly during the transitions. But China, India and Russia have seen a flourishing of financial sophistication and amazingly high economic growth rates. And it is not just these countries. According to International Monetary Fund data, the entire emerging world—including the Commonwealth of

Independent States, the entire Middle East, sub-Saharan Africa and Latin America—has proved able to generate annual gross domestic product growth of over 6 percent during the past decade, when not compromised by world financial crises.[6]

In addition, a host of international agreements have created institutions that work for the betterment of humankind using sophisticated financial tools. The World Bank, founded in 1944 and today expanded into the massive World Bank Group, has engraved on its headquarters in Washington, D.C., the motto "Working for a World Free of Poverty." The World Bank was only the first of the multilateral development banks: the African Development Bank, the Asian Development Bank, the European Bank for Reconstruction and Development, the Inter-American Development Bank Group and many others.

Modern financial institutions are pervasive throughout the world today. Moreover, it is not just stocks or bonds that represent financial markets. One might not at first consider the price of agricultural commodities as relevant to a discussion of financial instruments, but the prices that they fetch on futures exchanges are entirely analogous to prices in the stock and bond markets. Wheat and rice markets are financial markets too, in the sense that they engage in similar activities and rely on comparable technical apparatus, and they are similar in their fluctuations and their impact on the economy. The fact that the very lives of low-income people around the world depend on food prices in some of these markets only underscores the significance of our financial institutions—and the importance of getting these institutions right.

FINANCIAL CAPITALISM COMES OF AGE

We do indeed live in the age of financial capitalism. We should not regret that. Regulations and restrictions can and should be placed on financial institutions to help them function in the best interests of society, but the underlying logic and power of these institutions remain central to their role. Financial institutions and financial variables are as much a source of direction and an ordering principle in our lives as the rising and setting sun, the seasons and the tides.

Indeed, there appears to be no viable alternative. We never hear talk of *nonfinancial* capitalism as a model—although one could use such a term to refer to a market economy with poorly developed financial institutions, as we still see today in some poorer regions of the world. As much as we might like to criticize finance, no one seems to view these alternatives as suitable models for anyone's future.

Our task, both in the financial sector and in civil society, is to help people find meaning and a larger social purpose in the economic system. This is no small feat, with all the seemingly absurd concentrations of wealth the system brings about, the often-bewildering complexity of its structures and the games—often unsatisfying and unpleasant—it forces people to play.

Definitions matter, and so how we define *financial capitalism* will help us develop a working theory of this most important force. It should set a norm for how finance works and what leaders within business, the public sector and civil society must do to harness emerging developments within the field of finance to support the goals of a robust and prosperous economy, to curb its excesses, to smooth its volatility and to consider how finance can be brought to bear to address the needs of advanced and developing economies alike.

Toward a Working Theory of Financial Capitalism

At its broadest level, finance is the science of goal architecture—of the structuring of the economic arrangements necessary to achieve a set of goals and of the stewardship of the assets needed for that achievement. The goals may be those of households, small businesses, corporations, civic institutions, governments and society itself. Once an objective has been specified—such as payment for a college education, a couple's comfortable retirement, the opening of a restaurant, the addition of a new wing on a hospital, the creation of a social security system or a trip to the moon—the parties involved need the right financial tools, and often expert guidance, to help achieve the goal. In this sense, finance is analogous to engineering.

It is a curious and generally overlooked fact that the very word *finance* actually derives from a classical Latin term for *goal*. The dictionary tells us the word derives from the classical Latin word *finis*, which is usually translated as "end" or "completion." One dictionary notes that *finis* developed into the word *finance* since one aspect of finance is the completion, or repayment, of debts. But it is convenient for our purposes to recall that *finis*, even in ancient times, had two meanings, both "termination" and "goal," as does the modern English word *end*, and we might assume that it is the second of the two meanings that is relevant to the etymology of the word *finance*.

Most people define finance more narrowly. Yet financing an activity really is creating the architecture for reaching a goal—and providing stewardship to protect and preserve the assets needed for the achievement and maintenance of that goal.

The goals served by finance originate within us. They reflect our interests in careers, hopes for our families, ambitions for our businesses, aspirations for our culture and ideals for our society; finance in and of itself does not tell us what the goals should be. Finance does not embody a goal. Finance is not "just about making money" per se. It is a "functional" science in that it exists to support other goals—those of the society. The better aligned a society's financial institutions are with its goals and ideals, the stronger and more successful the society will be. If its mechanisms fail, finance has the power to subvert such goals, as it did in the subprime mortgage market of the past decade. But if it is functioning properly, it has a unique potential to promote great levels of prosperity.

The attainment of significant goals and the stewardship of the assets needed for their achievement almost always require the cooperation of many people. Those people have to pool their information appropriately. They must ensure that everyone's incentives are aligned. Imagine the development of a new laboratory, the funding of a medical research project, the building of a new university or the construction of a new city subway system. Finance provides structure to these and other enterprises and institutions throughout society. If finance succeeds for all of us, it helps to build a good society. The better we understand this point, the better we will grasp the need for ongoing financial innovation.

WHAT FINANCE DOES

Economists and finance professionals tend to define and discuss finance in narrower terms than those we've been employing here. Much research in academic finance is focused on short-term trading strategies and results, and on the related topic of risk management. In its canonical form, academic finance is the science of designing optimal portfolios of investments. Day-to-day activities on Wall Street likewise tend to be concentrated on highly specified activities. But this is only part of what finance really involves.

An essential part of what finance professionals actually do is deal making—the structuring of projects, enterprises and systems, large and small—an activity that brings convergence to individuals' often-divergent goals. Financial arrangements—including the structuring of payments, loans, collateral, shares, incentive options and exit strategies—are just the surface elements of these deals. Deal making means facilitating arrangements that will motivate real actions by real people—and often by very large groups of people. Most of us can achieve little of lasting value without the cooperation of others. Even the archetypal solitary poet requires financing to practice her or his art: an income to live on, publishers, printers, arrangers of public readings, the construction of suitable halls for public readings—there is a hidden financial architecture behind all of this.

All parties to an agreement have to want to embrace the goal, do the work and accept the risks; they also have to believe that others involved in the deal will actually work productively toward the common goal and do all the things that the best information suggests should be done. Finance provides the incentive structure necessary to tailor these activities and secure these goals.

In addition, finance involves discovery of the world and its opportunities, which ties it in to information technology. Whenever there is trading, there is price discovery—that is, the opportunity to learn the market value of whatever is being traded. This in turn involves the revelation of people's feelings and motivations, and of the opportunities that exist among groups of people, which may in turn make even more ambitious goals possible.

Along with being the science that structures the achievement of goals, finance embodies a vital technology. As such, it has demonstrated continuous progress over the centuries, from the beginnings of money lending in the ancient world through the development of modern mortgage markets as well as the legal and regulatory structures necessary to sustain these innovations. And it will continue to progress. Finance, suitably configured for the future, can be the strongest force for promoting the well-being and fulfillment of an expanding global population—for achieving the greater goals of the good society.

FINANCE MEETS THE GOOD SOCIETY

The real cure for the problem that Marx addressed lies not in destroying the capitalist system but in improving and democratizing it, and improving it means serving the greater goals of the good society. That has always been the best response, to the dismay of radicals.

The essential challenge for leaders to contemplate in coming to terms with the future of finance is to understand that it can be used to help broaden prosperity across an increasingly wide range of social classes and that its products can be made easier for people to use and can be better integrated into the economy as a whole.

On the first point, there is nothing in financial theory that specifies that control of capital should be confined to a few "fat cats." Think of the broadly democratic proliferation of insurance, mortgages and pensions—all basic financial innovations—in underwriting the prosperity of millions of people in the past century. Further perfecting financial institutions and instruments through innovations large and small will enable society to enlarge the scope of this prosperity and reverse the growing trend toward social inequality.

Regarding the second point, designing financial institutions around real human quirks will make it easier for people to adapt financial innovations to their lives and for the financial system as a whole to function more smoothly. This means that psychologists have to be on the financial team, and we must also take account of the revolution in behavioral economics and behavioral finance that has occurred in the past few decades.[7] It means that we must smooth the rough edges off our financial system—those aspects that can cause trouble when people make mistakes. It means that people have to be told the truth about the financial contracts into which they enter, and about the ways in which those contracts could be hurtful in the future, so that they can take full account of their emotions and wants before they sign a contract.

If we extrapolate historical trends, it will be possible to further extend the scope and range of financial capitalism and render Marx's criticism—the fundamental basis for his vision of the communist extreme—forever obsolete. Accomplishing this goal will require a degree of government intervention, but not intervention that would frustrate market solutions. Government's task in this endeavor is to provide a clear set of rules for the game, one that protects consumers and promotes the public interest while enabling the players to compete in doing what they do best: delivering better products and services. A real challenge in this regard is that these rules must have an international dimension, as today's financial markets are both global in reach and instantaneous in effect.

FINANCE: AN ESSENTIAL SOCIAL INSTITUTION

I realize that critics think that preparing students for careers in finance merely exacerbates a trend toward greater economic travail for the many. Certainly some who work in finance or related fields often reap great material rewards for their efforts, while others earn far less. Modern society is, indeed, on a trend toward higher levels of economic inequality,[8] and contributing to that trend has been the tendency to reward especially well some of those who go into activities that relate to finance, while those who make their livings primarily in other sectors of the economy, including most of the middle class and the poor, lose ground. The government bailouts of well-to-do bankers have redoubled public concerns about inequality.

But finance should not be viewed as inherently or exclusively elitist or as an engine of economic injustice. Finance, despite its flaws and excesses, is a force that potentially can help us create a better, more prosperous and more equitable society. In fact, finance has been central to the rise of prosperous market economies in the modern age—indeed, this rise would be unimaginable without it. Beyond headlines incriminating bankers and financiers as self-aggrandizing perpetrators of economic dislocation and suffering, finance remains an essential social institution, a necessity for managing the risks that enable society to transform creative impulses into vital products and services, from improved surgical protocols to advanced manufacturing technologies to sophisticated scientific research enterprises to efficient public welfare systems.

The connections between financial institutions and individual people are fundamental for society. Clarifying the terms of these connections and establishing a proper context for implementing and enhancing them is a critical subject.

It seems a paradox that the very financial system that is the facilitator of some of our greatest achievements can also implode and create such a disaster. Yet the best way for society to proceed is not to restrain financial innovation but instead to release it. Such an approach can reduce the impact of such disasters and at the same time democratize finance.

The financial crisis reminds us that innovation has to be accomplished in a way that supports the stewardship of society's assets. And the best way to do this is to build good moral behavior into the culture of Wall Street through the creation and observance of best practices in its various professions—CEOs, traders, accountants, investment bankers, lawyers, philanthropists.

When Adam Smith wrote his classic *The Wealth of Nations* in 1776, a book long acclaimed as marking the beginning of modern economics, the pressing economic issue for thinkers and critics of the day was tariffs.[9] Private interests lobbied governments to put their interests ahead of public interests and push tariffs up so high as to make it impossible for lower-cost foreign producers to compete. But Adam Smith and other economists who followed him were successful in clarifying the importance of trade for the widespread wealth of nations. Since Adam Smith, lobbyists for special interests have found it much harder to push up tariffs, and trade is substantially free today—a vital institution in creating the remarkable growth and widespread prosperity we have seen since the revolutions of the eighteenth century.

Following a time of severe financial crisis, the point of contention among thinkers and critics is not trade but finance itself. Hostility runs high toward societal institutions that are even tangentially associated in people's minds with finance. This hostility is reminiscent of the public state of mind during the last major world financial crisis—the Great Depression after 1929—which led ultimately to a degree of unrest that shut down much of the world economy and contributed to the tensions that led to World War II.

Hostility among the general public generated by the crisis may have the unfortunate effect of inhibiting financial progress. Ironically, better financial instruments, not less activity in finance, are what we need to reduce the probability of financial crises in the future. There is a high level of public anger about the perceived unfairness of the amounts of money people in finance have been earning, and this anger inhibits innovation: anything new is viewed with suspicion. The political climate may well stifle innovation and prevent financial capitalism from progressing in ways that could benefit all citizens.

FINANCIAL INNOVATION OFFERS HOPE

To be sure, financial innovation is still percolating, at a slow and conservative level. Socially productive financial innovations could be moving rapidly, given the information revolution and with so many more countries experimenting with different economic structures and competing in the world marketplace. In coming decades we could see rapid development in the breadth of financial contracts, with extensions in the scope of markets, for the purpose of safeguarding our fundamental economic assets. Innovations could include the implementation of new and better safeguards against economic depression, including the proliferation of new kinds of insurance contracts to allow people to be more adventuresome in their lives without fear of economic catastrophe. We could also see innovative measures developed to curtail the rising plague of economic inequality that threatens to create serious social problems in our society.

What I want most for my students—near and far, young and old—to know is that finance truly has the potential to offer hope for a more fair and just world, and that their energy and intelligence are needed to help serve this goal.

NOTES

1. Carmen Reinhart and Kenneth Rogoff, *This Time Is Different: Eight Centuries of Financial Folly* (Princeton, NJ: Princeton University Press, 2009), 248.
2. George W. Edwards, *The Evolution of Finance Capitalism* (London: Longmans, Green, and Co., 1938).
3. Nicolas Sarkozy, speech at "New World, New Capitalism" symposium, Paris, France, January 8, 2009, http://www.gouvernement.fr/gouvernement /ouverture-du-colloque-nouveau-monde-nouveau-capitalisme.
4. Tony Blair, speech at "New World, New Capitalism" symposium, Paris, France, January 8, 2009, http://www.tonyblairoffice.org/speeches/entry/speech-by-tony -blair-at-the-new-world-new-capitalism-conference.
5. Grigory Yavlinsky, *Realeconomik* (New Haven, CT: Yale University Press, 2011), 48.
6. International Monetary Fund, "Global Outlook," figure 1.6, April, 2011, http:// www.imf.org/external/pubs/ft/weo/2011/01/.
7. A living history of this revolution can be seen on Robert Shiller's behavioral finance website at http://www.econ.yale.edu/~shiller/behfin/index.htm, which shows a list of the seminars that Richard Thaler and he have organized since 1991, and also at the behavioral macroeconomics website, http://econ.yale .edu/~shiller/behmacro/index.htm, which shows a list of seminars that George Akerlof and Robert Shiller have organized since 1994. Books about behavioral economics include *Inefficient Markets* (2000) by Andrei Shleifer; *Beyond Greed and Fear* (2007) by Hersh Shefrin; and *Nudge* (2008) by Richard H. Thaler and Cass R. Sunstein.
8. This trend, visible in many individual countries, has been offset for the world as a whole by the rise of the emerging countries. See Xavier Sala-i-Martin, "The World distribution of Income: Following Poverty and . . . Convergence, Period," *Quarterly Journal of Economics* 121 (May 2006): 351–397.
9. Adam Smith, *The Wealth of Nations* (1776; repr. New York: Random House, 1937).

PART II

COMPLETING FINANCIAL REGULATORY REFORM

INTRODUCTION

John G. Taft

[A]n intense debate is underway internationally about the role of finance.
—Andrew Haldane et al., "What Is the Contribution
of the Financial Sector: Miracle or Mirage?"

Are regulations striking the right balance between safety and profitability?
—*Economist*, May 2012

Years after the financial crisis of 2008–09, the task of rewriting the rules of the road for finance remains at or near the top of the policy agenda for most developed nations. This reform effort is unparalleled in our lifetimes in terms of its scope, complexity, global reach and the sheer number of organizations and people involved. And it is a long way from being completed.

The goal of reform efforts is not to eliminate instability in the financial system. No regulatory regime can eliminate that, and trying to do so can often cause more harm than good. Instead, the appropriate goal is to strike the right balance between social stability, the profitability of financial firms and economic growth.

Just how well we strike this balance between too much and too little regulation will have enormous long-term consequences for society. Yet remarkably, we are flying blind when it comes to really knowing whether current regulations are already choking off economic growth, or if we still need more regulation to prevent future crises.

The contributors to this part, Sheila C. Bair, Ricardo R. Delfin and Karen Shaw Petrou, are three of the most knowledgeable, respected and engaged experts on financial regulatory reform in the world today. After guiding the Federal Deposit Insurance Corporation (FDIC) through the financial crisis, Bair became the inaugural chair of the Systemic Risk Council, an independent joint venture between the CFA Institute and the Pew Charitable Trusts. Delfin served as executive director of the Council.

Karen Shaw Petrou was once described by *American Banker* as "the sharpest mind analyzing banking policy today, maybe ever." She was also praised by *New York Times* columnist Joe Nocera for coining the phrase *complexity risk* to capture the challenge financial institutions face when navigating through the new regulatory landscape, a topic Bair and Delfin address in their essay as well.

Bair and Delfin suggest that major gaps still exist in the regulatory fabric, gaps that need to be addressed if we are to prevent the systemic meltdown we experienced in 2008–09. "Many essential reforms remain incomplete and significant structural weaknesses remain," they write.

Their analysis matters because, notwithstanding the regulatory progress we've made, systemic risk may be greater today than in the past. In a world where financial institutions are more interconnected, more interdependent, where their operations reach into every corner of the world, the ripple effects from problems at any one firm, any one country or any one sector of the economy can spread much more quickly and cause much more damage than ever before. As author Nassim Nicholas Taleb points out in *Antifragile: Things That Gain from Disorder*, the more complex a system, the more likely it is to break.

Petrou focuses on what's going on in the world of nonregulated financial firms. It's a world in which nonbanks such as hedge funds, private equity firms, business development companies and real estate investment trusts are increasingly engaging in practices such as asset-based commercial lending, from which more stringently regulated banks have withdrawn. This so-called shadow banking can be good for the economy, but unless regulatory agencies monitor, track and correct excesses in nonregulated firms, they can in fact become the next source of systemic risk, as the firm Long-Term Capital proved to be in the late 1990s. "It makes no sense to regulate the living daylights out of big banks and leave nonbanks just as they were. Many firms . . . are becoming ever more embedded in the fabric of financial intermediation," she writes.

CHAPTER 4

THE PROGRESS, PITFALLS AND PERSISTENT CHALLENGES OF RECENT FINANCIAL REGULATORY REFORM

Sheila C. Bair

Former Federal Deposit Insurance Corporation Chair

Ricardo R. Delfin

Former Executive Director, Systemic Risk Council

Though the U.S. financial regulatory structure is stronger than it was before the 2008 financial crisis, many essential reforms remain incomplete and significant structural weaknesses remain. Several of these ongoing weaknesses, including the problems of "too big to fail," money market mutual funds and mortgage securitization, played a central role in that crisis. Other potential risks, such as those posed by clearinghouses for derivatives transactions, may now be even larger. Our hope is that regulators will continue their progress and take the steps necessary to address obvious structural weaknesses before the next crisis. A number of these structural weaknesses are identified in this piece, along with some potential solutions.

THE DODD-FRANK ACT

The 2010 Dodd-Frank Act (DFA) was a landmark law designed to dramatically update our financial regulatory framework to address weaknesses identified during the financial crisis, including too big to fail, mortgage securitization and the regulation of over-the-counter derivatives. It also established a new "macroprudential" regulatory regime, designed to identify and address potential systemic risks before they develop into financial crises. Though wide-ranging, the law did not establish many bright-line prohibitions. Instead it provided regulators with substantial new authority and discretion in implementing its goals. Thus far, progress has been steady, but also slow and often unnecessarily complex. Many key reforms remain outstanding.

TOO BIG TO FAIL

The financial crisis—and the need for unprecedented government support and individual company bailouts—highlighted the problems of too big to fail and the moral hazard for markets going forward. Having seen the market disruptions caused by the failure and potential failure of megafinancials and the ensuing government bailouts in 2008, markets may be more willing to lend to these firms, believing that governments cannot allow them to fail. This moral hazard can create funding advantages for these firms, fueling more size and risk. DFA included a number of reforms to address and reduce this problem, including the establishment of an enhanced prudential regime, living wills and fallback resolution authority that provides clear authority for the Federal Deposit Insurance Corporation (FDIC) to resolve potentially systemic large, complex financial institutions without taxpayer bailouts. Though DFA provided important tools for ending too big to fail, it remains to be seen if regulators will implement the strong policies necessary to achieve the statute's goals.

Financial Stability Oversight Council. One macroprudential reform was the establishment of the Financial Stability Oversight Council (FSOC), an interagency body made up of the heads of the federal financial regulatory agencies, state regulatory representatives, an independent insurance representative and the head of the new Office of Financial Research. The FSOC is tasked with identifying potentially systemic risks and nonbank financial institutions whose failure could threaten financial stability, as well as sharing information among regulators and reporting to Congress on risks and potential reforms.

The FSOC is a significant improvement over the ad hoc President's Working Group on Financial Markets that preceded it. That organization met infrequently and, while it lacked regulatory authority, occasionally undermined needed reforms rather than supporting them. The FSOC is a structural improvement. It meets regularly to discuss risks and market events and provides more detailed information to the Congress and the public about the financial sector.

Though an improvement, the FSOC has not yet achieved its full potential. Some weakness is the by-product of statutory constraints. For example, the FSOC is generally limited to making "recommendations" to functional regulators for dealing with risks—it cannot simply raise standards itself. Accordingly, even when the FSOC identifies a systemic risk such as money market funds, it cannot take action and address that risk directly. Instead, it must rely on the relevant functional regulator, in this case the Securities and Exchange Commission (SEC), to take action. If functional regulators are unwilling or unable to take the necessary action, the risk can continue and grow unabated.

Other limitations, however, are self-inflicted. Though the FSOC now has identified a few nonbank financial firms, such as insurance companies, for enhanced prudential supervision by the Federal Reserve Board, the pace of designations has been slow, and the nature of these new requirements remains undefined. In addition, though the FSOC has taken some action to highlight the ongoing risks posed by money market mutual funds, it has been less vocal on other systemic issues, such as too big to fail.

Orderly Liquidation Authority and Bankruptcy. DFA also established a new resolution regime to provide for the orderly liquidation of large, complex financial institutions. Rather than policy makers having to again choose between financial catastrophe or bailouts as they did in 2008, the statute allows the FDIC to put a potentially systemic financial firm into receivership, to manage its failure and sell it off in parts or ultimately recapitalize it with private funds. While the existence of this process is a significant step toward enabling an orderly failure of a large, complex institution, important reforms for effective implementation remain outstanding.

To truly end too big to fail, large, complex financial institutions must be able to fail like all other firms, *in bankruptcy* and without causing systemic risk or requiring government support. (For insured banks, the FDIC has its own bankruptcy-like process that has proven to be highly effective in dealing with traditional banks that it insures.) To its credit, DFA recognizes this and requires that large firms submit living wills that show they can credibly fail, in bankruptcy, and it gives regulators the authority to order breakups or activities restrictions if firms cannot. While large firms have submitted living wills, there is little evidence firms have made the changes needed so they can fail in bankruptcy without causing systemic risk. We have urged regulators to address these risks and provide greater transparency to markets about the credibility of living wills and the feasibility of winding down institutions in bankruptcy.

Given the continued doubts that bankruptcy is a credible option for the largest firms, DFA's orderly liquidation process will likely be the tool used to resolve a failing systemic firm in the near term. However, without additional regulatory measures, companies, investors and counterparties have real incentives to try to game the orderly liquidation process. As currently envisioned, the FDIC would use a "Single-Point of Entry Process"[1] to resolve large firms—in effect—allocating losses to the holding company while permitting the firm's subsidiaries to function normally. This approach could help reduce the difficulties associated with resolving these firms' highly complex corporate structures. But it also provides an incentive for firms (and their counterparties) to fund the firm through its likely "protected" operating company subsidiaries, rather than through the likely "loss-absorbing" holding company. Former Fed chair Ben Bernanke, current Fed chair Janet Yellen, Fed governor Daniel Tarullo and FDIC chair Marty Gruenberg have publicly discussed the need to require potentially systemic firms to have sufficient loss-absorbing capacity at the holding company, but such a rule has not yet been implemented.

Designations and Enhanced Prudential Regulation. To help understand and reduce the potential systemic risks posed by large complex financial institutions *before* their failure, DFA requires that the Federal Reserve Board (FRB) establish an "Enhanced Prudential Regime" for bank holding companies with greater than $50 billion in assets and for nonbank financial firms designated by the FSOC.[2] This regime would help address a key shortcoming that existed before the financial crisis, when a host of nonbank financial firms, like Lehman Brothers and AIG, grew in size and complexity without a mandatory or effective consolidated oversight regime. This new construct could help avoid similar outcomes, but thus far, the FSOC has been slow to designate nonbanks for heightened oversight by the Federal Reserve, and the Federal Reserve has not yet promulgated its enhanced prudential rules for such firms.

Derivatives and Clearinghouses. Another significant structural improvement was DFA's new authority for the Commodity Futures Trading Commission (CFTC) and the SEC to regulate over-the-counter derivatives, or "swaps." Prior to the crisis, swaps were largely outside the regulatory framework and created a web of interconnections and potential for sudden, cascading losses, as epitomized by AIG. By bringing these transactions under the regulatory umbrella, DFA improved transparency, pricing and basic risk management requirements such as capital and margin requirements. Further, by requiring that certain swaps be "cleared" through central clearing parties, DFA could also help reduce interconnections and counterparty risk.

The growth of clearinghouses, however, increases the potential for systemic risk from these institutions. This risk may have been exacerbated by

DFA's creation of a separate, *and weaker,* regulatory regime for clearinghouses when compared to the other designated nonbank financial institutions discussed above. Rather than designating and subjecting these firms to the stronger enhanced prudential standards, DFA creates a separate regime for these firms (called "designated financial market utilities"), and allows them to operate with a weaker FRB backstop oversight. In addition, unlike the nonbank Systemically Important Financial Institution (SIFI) regime, which provides no benefits for being large and systemic, the Designated Financial Market Utility designation *provides* potential for FRB support otherwise not available. This not only creates an incentive for certain types of firms to become large and complex, but the possibility of potential support could embolden these for-profit entities to reduce risk management and increase risk thresholds.

MORTGAGE SECURITIZATION

Problems and perverse incentives in mortgage finance, particularly in the securitization of private-label, mortgage-backed securities, played an outsized role in the crisis. Traditionally, mortgages were made by lenders who held onto and serviced the loan and had a strong incentive to ensure that borrowers had the ability and incentive to repay. This lender risk resulted in strong underwriting processes, high down payments and good loan performance.

The years prior to the crisis, however, saw the rise of securitization, a process whereby mortgages were originated by one entity and quickly sold through a chain that ended in a mortgage-backed security sold to investors. This "originate to distribute" model had a host of different incentives that resulted in more complex products, weaker underwriting standards and higher leverage. In addition to providing minimum loan origination standards and improving consumer protection efforts, DFA sought to align incentives in the mortgage securitization process by requiring "risk retention."

Under the DFA, regulators were tasked with establishing rules requiring mortgage securitizers to retain a portion of risk in the loans they securitize. This "eat your own cooking" requirement would give them "skin in the game" regarding mortgages they sell. While the regulator's initial proposal was strong, industry and consumer group opposition led regulators to repropose a dramatically weaker approach, which would largely gut the risk-retention requirement and leave many of the same perverse incentives that contributed to the crisis.

Initial strong risk retention efforts were also tied to improved securitization disclosures proposed by the SEC. Unfortunately, years later, important parts of those rules remain stalled.

OTHER CHALLENGES AND RISKS

Though DFA provides significant authority to federal agencies to address risks and problems, it established few bright lines. As a result, regulators face a difficult rule-writing dynamic for agencies trying to balance many competing interests with a broad regulatory mandate.

One unintended consequence of this regulatory dynamic is massive, vague and unnecessarily complex rules. Regulators, facing difficult trade-offs and tremendous industry opposition, have issued a number of highly complex rules that are almost unintelligible. This complexity not only raises costs for institutions, but it also undermines effective oversight and accountability by both regulators and bank boards.

Another related outcome is the risk of regulatory micromanagement. Hypercomplex rules empower regulators and a small group of specialists. When the purpose of rules is lost in complexity, a culture of "compliance" and bureaucratic box-checking can take the place of thoughtful oversight and effective management. A better approach would be for financial regulators to establish strong, simple rules that are easy to understand, follow and enforce. Though such rules may be more difficult for regulators to promulgate, politically (as industry, the public and Congress would be better positioned to challenge the particulars) the long-term benefits of clear and understandable rules, for bank governance as well as regulatory accountability, are overwhelming.

GLOBAL CAPITAL REGIME

There is broad consensus that the pervasive use of excessive leverage—that is, the use of borrowed money instead of shareholder equity—by large financial firms to fund their risky loans and investments was a key driver of the crisis. Yet more than five years after the failure of Lehman Brothers, only incremental progress has been made in strengthening the capital position of large financial firms. A study by the Center for Financial Stability indicates that most large banking organizations have improved their capital ratios by 1 to 2 percent, with much of the increase being attributable to acquisition activity, not regulatory action.[3]

Regulators have also made improvements in the global capital regime for large complex financial institutions, but they have not been fully implemented. Moreover, existing capital regimes continue to rely on hypercomplex regulatory capital frameworks with an overreliance on internal modeling. Prior to the crisis, these approaches not only failed to appropriately measure risk, they provided a host of perverse incentives that contributed to the crisis. Though some progress has been made, more substantial reforms are required.

In the United States, banking regulators have taken a variety of steps to improve loss absorbency and resolvability. For example, U.S. regulators are implementing a supplemental leverage ratio for the large U.S. financial institutions. This approach would work in tandem with the existing risk-based framework, providing an important buttress. While this is a very good step, the levels proposed remain relatively low. (They would bring about $90 billion of much-needed additional capital into the banking system. In addition, a 2011 agreement by the Basel Committee to impose capital "surcharges" on the world's largest financial institutions has not yet even been proposed in the United States.)[4]

Since the crisis, it appears that large U.S. financial institutions have incrementally deleveraged—on a risk-based capital basis, but, in terms of pure size and leverage, these institutions remain quite large and levered. Given weaknesses in risk-based capital frameworks generally—and the problems and perverse incentives associated with internal risk-based models in particular—obvious risks remain.

Basel III. International regulators have also made improvements in response to weaknesses identified in the financial crisis, including establishing an international leverage regime to reduce the capital advantages for large institutions and improve liquidity and countercyclical buffers. Challenges remain, however, particularly involving leverage and resolvability. Slow progress in these areas leaves the financial system exposed to destabilizing failures and the moral hazard associated with too-big-to-fail policies. To more effectively address these risks, U.S. and foreign regulators should strengthen and finalize supplemental leverage requirement and capital surcharges on potentially systemic institutions, eliminate reliance on internal models for establishing regulatory capital and address the remaining challenges associated with cross-border resolutions.

MONEY MARKET MUTUAL FUNDS

Money market mutual funds remain a serious threat to financial stability. Because of their unique pricing structure (the "stable NAV," or net asset value), money market funds have a structural weakness that makes them susceptible to destabilizing runs. This threat revealed itself during the financial crisis at a most inopportune time—when the Reserve Primary Fund "broke the buck" and triggered a massive run on money market funds that shut down the short-term lending markets and resulted in an unprecedented taxpayer guarantee. Though the SEC made modest changes in 2010 and some structural changes in 2014, the reforms are not yet effective and do not fully address the structural risks in these instruments. The SEC's primary structural reform (the "floating NAV") only applies to a subset of money funds and its secondary reform (so-called gates and fees) could make run dynamics worse. The SEC should address the stable NAV head-on and require that all money market fund prices "float" like other mutual funds.

RELIANCE ON SHORT-TERM FUNDING

The stable NAV in money market funds contributes to instability in other ways as well. By permitting the stable NAV, the SEC's rules (known as 2a-7) provide an incentive for investors to put their money in assets that are 2a-7 eligible, relative to other types of assets. This increases availability of this type of short-term funding relative to other types of short-term funding or even longer-term funding. Given the better pricing, borrowers, such as banks and broker-dealers, have an incentive to use this funding source over more stable, long-term funding.

Short-term funding is often cheaper for borrowers when markets are stable, but reliance can prove catastrophic during a crisis, when money market funds can pull back en masse to avoid breaking the buck or because of a run. In such cases, this previously plentiful—and subsidized—short-term funding evaporates, and many large institutions can find themselves, all at the same time, needing new sources of funding.

Though regulators have discussed taking steps to reduce this reliance, few reforms have been implemented.

MARKET REGULATORS

While DFA provided substantial new authority to the SEC and the CFTC, it did not provide these institutions with a reliable funding source. Though other financial regulators are "self-funded" by their activities and assessments, the SEC and CFTC must rely on the congressional appropriations process for funding. Too often this uncertain, and highly political, process leaves these two agencies underfunded and unable to make long-term strategic plans that could improve their abilities to police the markets and achieve their missions.

These risks are particularly acute now that the agencies have expanded missions over financial products and activities with significant systemic importance. Through robust market-based regulation and enforcement, these agencies can play an essential role in market functioning and appropriate risk mitigation—reducing the pressure on our macroprudential framework. Unfortunately, however, funding constraints undermine the agencies' ability to perform some of the vital duties required. This raises pressure on the FSOC and the Federal Reserve to try to find ways to monitor and address the risks that cannot be addressed by the functional regulator. The best solution

SHEILA BAIR'S TO-DO LIST

1. **The Financial Stability Oversight Council:** Can identify systemic risks and make recommendations to other agencies, but cannot directly address risks.
2. **Orderly Liquidation Authority and Bankruptcy:** Companies, investors and counterparties have real incentives to game the bankruptcy/orderly liquidation process, and the initial living wills have not yet credibly shown that companies can fail in bankruptcy.
3. **Designations and Enhanced Prudential Regulation:** FSOC has been slow to designate nonbanks, and the Fed has not yet promulgated its enhanced rules for nonbanks.
4. **Derivatives and Clearinghouses:** Designating these financial utilities with only light regulations and potentially giving them support from the Fed may actually be encouraging risk taking.
5. **Mortgage Securitization:** The "originate to distribute" model prevails, and securitizers still don't have to eat their own cooking. Further, securitization market disclosure remains weak.
6. **Complex Rules:** Some rules are almost unintelligible and there are massive numbers of them, raising costs and undermining their effectiveness. Strong, simple rules are essential.
7. **Capital Positions of Large Firms:** Leverage rules are improving, but many institutions still remain just as large and leveraged. Capital requirements continue to rely on hypercomplex regulatory frameworks and internal risk models.
8. **Money Market Mutual Funds:** They remain a serious threat to financial stability, and the SEC's proposed fixes are inadequate. All money market fund prices should float like other mutual funds.
9. **Overreliance on Short-Term Funding:** Can dry up in a crisis, contributing to instability.
10. **SEC, CFTC Are Resource-Strapped:** Despite expansion of their missions under Dodd-Frank, both rely on Congress for funding. Should be self-funding like other federal financial regulators.

would be for Congress to allow these agencies to self-fund, as is the case with the other federal financial regulators, so that the agencies can fulfill their vital missions.

The reforms enacted since the 2008 financial crisis have significantly improved the financial regulatory framework, but substantial work remains with regard to risks that were revealed during the financial crisis. Dodd-Frank empowered regulators with substantial authority to address these issues. Now the challenge remains to deliver.

NOTES

1. Resolution of Systemically Important Financial Institutions, Federal Deposit Insurance Corporation, Notice and Request for Comments, Federal Register, December 18, 2013, https://www.fdic.gov/news/board/2013/2013-12-10_notice _dis-b_fr.pdf.
2. The Dodd-Frank Act, Sec. 113.
3. Diane B. Glossman, Robin L. Lumsdaine and Lawrence Goodman, "Bank Capital Observations," Center for Financial Stability, January 13, 2014, http:// www.centerforfinancialstability.org/research/CFS_Bank_Capital_011314.pdf.
4. "Measures for Global Systemically Important Banks Agreed by the Group of Governors and Heads of Supervision," Bank of International Settlements, Press Release, June 25, 2011, http://www.bis.org/press/p110625.htm.

CHAPTER 5

BIG BANKS AREN'T THE ONLY PROBLEM

Karen Shaw Petrou

Managing Partner, Federal Financial Analytics

While small banks are often seen as bastions of their communities, big banks are loathed. Big banks, many say, have broken an inviolable social contract that once gave them special advantages. In return for their monopoly charters and the protection of Federal Deposit Insurance Corporation (FDIC) insurance for their depositors, big banks were expected to support economic growth and resist the temptation of more profitable activities that might harm society as a whole. Is the contract really broken? If so, are still more punitive rules for big banks needed?

Not only are more rules not needed, piling more and more rules on big banks will only lead to unintended and often-perverse consequences. The most damaging is that encumbering banks actually empowers "shadow" entities. These private equity firms, hedge funds and asset managers become ever more critical to financial intermediation, without even a suggestion of a social contract or tough rules to constrain their short-term profit maximization. Even though nonbanks are in the same business lines as banks, and even though they have far less capital and fewer controls than banks, they are often unregulated. In fact, their customer, market and systemic risk profiles could be the same or even higher than those of a big bank. But since these do not have a bank charter, they fall outside the regulations, including the Dodd-Frank reforms.

To resolve this double standard, a robust regulatory framework should be activity based, not charter based. That is, current and emerging financial activities should be understood for the roles they play in financial intermediation and the risks they pose to general financial stability or vulnerable individuals. Regardless of charter, an institution offering a high-impact/high-risk activity should be highly regulated; one outside this sphere can be less regulated or even unregulated. All institutions dealing with vulnerable customers should be comparably regulated, since customers don't much care if it's a bank or nonbank that costs them their home or livelihood. The Fed already has the regulatory power to make this happen.

Since the 2008 crisis, consensus has been firmly established on the need for tough rules for the biggest banks. Reasonable people can argue over whether the new rulebook is tough enough, or if big banks remain "too big to fail." However, there's little question that the postcrisis rulebook may well convert the largest companies into financial utilities. This poses many risks to the biggest banks—profit first among them—but it also presents a policy challenge few have yet recognized, let alone addressed: although many nonbanks caused the crisis alongside their big-bank brethren, few prudential rules yet govern them. And the pace at which nonbanks enter what was once traditional banking has only increased since 2008.

If bankers are neither more nor less inherently evil than nonbankers—an assumption history strongly supports—then it makes no sense to regulate the living daylights out of big banks and leave nonbanks just as they were. Many firms, including technology pioneers not usually considered financial ventures (such as Google and PayPal), are becoming ever more embedded in the fabric of financial intermediation. Regulation by charter—one set of rules for banks, another or even none at all for nonbanks—must quickly be replaced by regulation by function so that risks to financial stability or vulnerable citizens are averted no matter where they emerge.

HOW BANKING WENT BAD

In the wake of the Great Depression of the 1930s, the U.S. government made a very hard decision about the structure of financial market regulation. It segregated certain activities—most notably gathering deposits from the general public—into monopoly franchises (insured depositories) that received this unique status. In exchange, banks accepted rules that limited where they could be located and the financial risks they could take. The Federal Deposit Insurance Act, along with the Glass-Steagall Act and many other laws, carved finance into distinct activities housed in wholly separate charters subject to very different rules.

This charter-regulatory framework remained almost unchanged until the mid-1980s. It started breaking down when bank holding companies (BHCs) began to offer brokerage services. Meanwhile, nonbanks from Sears Roebuck to Merrill Lynch acquired "nonbank banks"—that is, carefully structured insured depositories that allowed the parent nonbanking companies to engage in banking without all the muss and fuss of most prudential rules and activity restrictions. The Competitive Equality Banking Act of 1987 nominally shut down nonbank banks, but it did so with many exceptions and by grandfathering prior charters.

With those precedents set, barriers tumbled between banking and nonbank financial services, and between banking writ large and commerce. Then the Gramm-Leach-Bliley Act of 1999 created financial holding companies (FHCs) authorized to engage in a wide array of activities. Nominally now a functional-regulatory framework, the act in fact ratified the charter approach because like-kind activities within an FHC were regulated very differently depending on the brass plate on the front door. Nothing in the law, for example, forced any nonbank bank parent companies to become an FHC, while it left untouched many exemptions for bank securities, insurance and similar activities from like-kind regulation. Even the Dodd-Frank Act of 2010 didn't address this fundamental issue. It only put a three-year moratorium—now expired—on permissible nonbank banks like those Wal-Mart has long sought to open.

The barriers between banking and nontraditional activities also became mostly moot over the past 20 years because so many activities were characterized as "the business of banking" by the Office of the Comptroller of the Currency. Even though these activities were virtually identical to insurance, securities or even commercial-investment businesses, they became embedded within national banks and further blurred the barriers, creating numerous opportunities for regulatory arbitrage, albeit this time in the banks' favor.

REFORM RULEBOOK:
RATIFYING REGULATION BY CHARTER

By 2008, the Great Depression functional-regulatory apparatus was in complete tatters, with banks engaged in all sorts of activities and nonbanks challenging them outright in core financial intermediation businesses such as mortgage origination. In each case, the rules varied dramatically—not depending on the function involved, but on the charter of the institution that was engaged in that activity. As noted, Dodd-Frank only slapped the wrists of nonbank banks. It does subject all large retail financial institutions to the not-so-tender mercies of the new Consumer Financial Protection Bureau (CFPB). But Dodd-Frank is focused on banks. Section 165 of the act specifies that all bank holding companies with assets over $50 billion are to be subject to stringent systemic rules. Yet it's unclear if any of these firms but the very largest pose any type of systemic risk. This provision is regulation by charter at the extreme, since dozens of BHCs are governed by rules designed to make them safe and sound in concert with their subsidiary insured depositories.

The 2008 crisis is often blamed on lax banking regulation, and indeed, this was a problem, but there was also a lot of bad behavior at the very biggest banks. But what sparked the subsequent lethal combination of leniency and cupidity? Are bankers just so bad that rules must be so tough on them, and so costly that the largest BHCs are essentially converted into utilities? And must these utilities be forever yoked to low-risk, low-return activities?

Answering this question requires a careful understanding of the economics of risk taking. If financial market risk flees from banks because the rulebook alone makes taking risk uneconomic, then these risks will find a new home in a nonbank if the nonbank can make money at it under whatever regulatory regime—if any—applies. But, if the nonbank takes on critical financial intermediation activities because its rules are more lenient than those governing a bank for a like activity, little has meaningfully been done to protect long-term financial stability or to protect vulnerable borrowers and investors.

ARE NONBANKS A REAL WORRY?

In short, yes, nonbanks are a real worry. The Financial Stability Board (FSB) has in recent years undertaken analyses of "shadow banking" to determine its significance in each member nation. The FSB is a global organization whose members are banking, insurance and securities regulators. Most recently, it found that global shadow finance accounted for $71.2 trillion in the nations it surveyed. In the United States, shadow firms were equivalent to 174 percent of the U.S. banking system. On average, shadow nonbanks were 52 percent of the banking system in 20 jurisdictions and the euro area combined.[1]

Despite these startling numbers, a close look at the FSB data shows that they still underestimate the magnitude of shadow banking. Shadow banking is largely defined by reference to wholesale banking and capital market activities like securities financing, asset securitization and money market funds because each of these activities is deemed a cause of the last crisis. Although finance companies are included in the data, critical financial intermediation activities, such as gathering funds from ordinary citizens and making loans to them, are not counted in the FSB's data.

Further, the FSB data do not capture the transmission of key activities often dubbed "financial market infrastructure" into entities that are not clearly regulated and that do not have mandated resolution regimes. Another cause of the crisis is attributed to undue opacity and illiquidity in over-the-counter (OTC) derivatives and similar clearing markets. As a result, an urgent global priority—one reflected in the Dodd-Frank Act—transfers OTC-derivative clearing from dealer banks to central counterparties (CCPs). These CCPs are coming under prudential rules in the United States, but resolving them in a crisis remains problematic. Further, other types of financial market infrastructure, such as entities that handle large volumes of foreign exchange or commodities trading, have yet to be addressed for safety and soundness, or orderly resolution concerns. As trading-related risk transfers from dealer banks to new financial market infrastructure, it often moves to de facto shadow entities yet to be governed by functional prudential regulation. This vital business is being drained from banks—which are required to follow the capital, liquidity and resolution rules—to unregulated entities.

IS BIG-BANK REGULATION ENOUGH?

To be sure, big banks are huge, with the top ten U.S. BHCs now holding $11.4 trillion in on-balance sheet assets.[2] But size can be deceiving, especially if measured only by on-balance sheet assets. Financial intermediation now can often be executed by securitization—meaning that loans touch a balance sheet only for an instant—or by syndication, secondary market activity of a different name with similar balance sheet impact. Fee-based activities—for example, prime brokerage—leave few balance sheet traces but can have a big systemic footprint, as do CCPs and similar market intermediaries. Conversely, securities financing has a big impact on nominal balance sheets but little direct credit risk since the real hazard in this sector comes from the liquidity side of the book.

Asset managers, private equity firms and hedge funds are quickly entering what were once traditional lending activities. They have been spurred to do so not only by new big-bank capital rules that alter pricing, but also by the Volcker Rule and other bank-only activity barriers that drive structuring and securitization activities out of the banking system. Google, Apple, PayPal and other technology firms yet to even rate FSB notice as shadow banks are also offering deposit, payment and lending services that surveys suggest are more appealing to younger customers. Not only do technology firms usually innovate light-years ahead of traditional banks, but these customers are more than happy to do business with anyone that isn't a bank.

Consider some examples where nonbanks are heading fast into what was once traditional banking:

- taking deposits, which nonbank providers of prepaid cards do by virtue of converting salaries into bank account equivalents;
- servicing loans, which in the case of mortgages is rapidly restructuring a longtime bank business into a nonbank activity due in large part to new capital rules;
- providing wealth management services, which is increasingly being done by nonbanks less fearful of anti–money laundering rules since there's little shareholder capital to seize in sanctions;
- offering new payment systems, which may well work on smartphones and the like until something goes wrong and no one knows where the money went;
- lending to small businesses, which eBay and PayPal are doing outside banks even as crowd-sourced funding supports small and midsized firms;
- engaging in peer-to-peer lending, which could transform finance from an intermediation into a social media function; and
- providing an array of digital currencies such as Bitcoin that pose a raft of financial market and law enforcement challenges as depositors and counterparties try to erect a payment system outside the reach of banks and their regulators.

TWENTY-FIRST-CENTURY FUNCTIONAL REGULATION

In concert with the build-out of new, tough rules for big banks, several leading U.S. policy makers have argued for the reinstatement of still tougher charter regulation, up to and including reinstatement of the Glass-Steagall Act. Senators Elizabeth Warren (D-MA) and John McCain (R-AZ), for example, have proposed effective reinstatement of the Glass-Steagall Act, while Senators Sherrod Brown (D-OH) and David Vitter (R-LA) take a different approach. They try to cut big banks down to a smaller size through punitive capital regulation and other rules. The president of the Federal Reserve Bank of Dallas, Richard Fisher, and FDIC vice-chair Thomas Hoenig have proposed variations on this theme, seeking either to ban banks from nonbanking activities or at the least to circumscribe them as tightly as the "Vickers" rule, new standards that separate traditional banking from other financial services, does in the United Kingdom.

Importantly, the Federal Reserve Board (FRB) as a whole has so far resisted revisiting the past, in large part due to the challenge of crafting a new law that defines "traditional" banking. The FRB's fear is that disentangling charters will prove complex because of integrated functions across the financial services industry. Their concern is that new rules could take a long time to implement and, worse, could serve as a still-greater impetus to shadow banking. As a result, the FRB hopes to craft rules that limit the interaction between big banks and shadow firms. The FRB hopes this will choke off systemic linkages between big banks and shadow firms that now empower these shadow institutions.

However, the already formidable power of shadow firms demonstrates that our chance to shut down the shadows may well have passed. As a result, bank-centric rules will only increase the shadows' growth.

The Dodd-Frank Act gives the Federal Reserve in concert with Treasury and other U.S. policy makers a ready-made statutory vehicle. Instead of trying to inoculate banks from "nontraditional" activities, a better approach would be to define which activities and practices pose risks to vulnerable borrowers and investors and the financial system. This statutory vehicle should be quickly deployed to ensure that firms regardless of charter are functionally regulated to protect themselves, the financial system and their customers, regardless of charter.

This authority is in Section 120 of the Dodd-Frank Act. It gives the Financial Stability Oversight Council (FSOC) power to designate activities or practices that pose risk from either a systemic or retail-customer perspective. When any such activity or practice is identified, FSOC can then propose a rule that lays out how it should be regulated and demand that primary regulators implement these standards. While the primary federal or state regulator is not required to do what FSOC recommends, the law pressures regulators to do so. If all else fails, these actions will alarm the marketplace so that meaningful self-regulation ensues.

So far, FSOC's record of using this functional-regulation power is at best underwhelming. Instead, the Council has haltingly used its Dodd-Frank powers to name "systemic non-bank financial institutions." Four years after the law's enactment, FSOC has done so for just three firms. More are to come, but this is regulation by size—another poor criterion for prudential standards.

A ROADMAP TO EFFECTIVE FUNCTIONAL REGULATION

One obstacle to prior efforts to make functional regulation a reality has been Congress's usual unwillingness to take anything away from powerful constituent interests. As a result, to make effective prudential regulation work before the next crisis, regulators must rely on the tools in current law and their own willingness to act decisively. Otherwise, regulators risk having their hand forced by costly debacles and losses.

First, the FSOC should use its authority to designate systemically important activities and practices. It should go beyond the tentative effort on money market funds and lay out a list of high-risk/high-impact activities from both a market and consumer perspective. Where activities pose risk to retail depositors and borrowers, the CFPB should use its power to pressure primary regulators: if these risks land in the laps of retail consumers or investors, the CFPB or the Securities and Exchange Commission (SEC) should act; if the risks are to retail insurance policy holders, then FSOC should stipulate its concerns and press for rapid action by state insurance regulators.

In areas where retail customers are exposed to risks that are not under the jurisdiction of the CFPB, SEC or insurance regulators—for example through systemic failure by new providers of retail payment products, perhaps like those provided by PayPal, Google and Apple—the FSOC should name its concern, lay out its recommendations and, if industry reform is not swift and sure, work with regulated institutions to curtail access by unregulated entities to critical payment-system and similar resources.

Where risks are found in capital market and other wholesale finance arenas, the FSOC has its firmest and strongest hand. That's because primary regulators for these businesses—at least in the United States—are mostly under its sway. FSOC should name names for products and activities, lay out the best path for meaningful prudential regulation and again block critical access to systemic infrastructure if necessary.

All of these risk determinations and—far more important—regulatory responsibilities are fully within the scope of current law. This means regulators should be held accountable for setting a framework for functional regulation that goes beyond sanctioning institutions just because they are banks or just because they are big.

However, Dodd-Frank gave regulators another critical power with which to prevent too big to fail. They have tools with which to shutter financial institutions regardless of size or systemic risk if financial stability is threatened. If investors, management and counterparties fear that they will absorb the cost of their own risk taking or negligence, caution and due diligence will be encouraged, if not also required. Should neither still result, pain will come to those who deserve it, and the next round of systemic risk may be averted if this resolution framework—still incomplete—is credible. Thus, in tandem with a new focus on risk by function, not by charter, U.S. regulators should move quickly to complete a strong resolution regime.

THE CRISIS NEXT TIME

Many nonbanks are small in comparison with the $11.4 trillion now housed in the top ten banks. Does size correlate with systemic risk? Not if the 2008 crisis is any guide: One money market fund with barely $50 billion in investments had to be rescued by the U.S. Treasury. Does being a big bank dictate systemic risk? Again no, as judged by a crisis precipitated in part by Lehman Brothers and characterized by rescues of Bear Stearns, AIG, Fannie Mae and Freddie Mac. Even if most risk now resides in big BHCs, will it stay there? Not if economic risk analytics and market incentives have anything to do with it.

NOTES

1. Financial Stability Board, *Global Shadow Banking Monitoring Report 2013*, Financial Stability Board, November 14, 2013, http://www.financialstability board.org/publications/r_131114.pdf.
2. Federal Financial Institutions Examination Council, Top 50 holding companies (HCs) as of December 31, 2013, https://www.ffiec.gov/nicpubweb/nicweb /top50form.aspx.

PART III

RESTORING TRUST, INTEGRITY AND CLIENT FOCUS TO THE FINANCIAL SYSTEM

INTRODUCTION

John G. Taft

> *For the system to operate with integrity, penalties for misconduct cannot be seen as a cost of doing business. Rather, banks must recognise that only exemplary behaviour can confer social license to global financial capitalism. . . . More fundamentally, integrity cannot be legislated, and it certainly cannot be bought. Only a perspective that takes into account the wider implications of actions can guide proper behaviour.*
>
> —Mark Carney, governor of the Bank of England, Remarks at World Economic Forum in Davos, January 24, 2014

The financial services industry has a "trust deficit," in the words of PIMCO CEO Douglas M. Hodge in his chapter for this part of the book. That's the bad news. The good news is it knows it has a trust deficit. And encouragingly, green-shoot efforts are sprouting, like the CFA Institute's Future of Finance Initiative, which aspires to address not just the reputational and public relations aspects of this trust deficit, but also the underlying behaviors that caused it in the first place.

But is it even possible to elevate the ethics of an entire sector of the economy, to restore integrity to an industry that encompasses all points along the profession-to-business continuum? And, if so, how?

Charles D. Ellis and John C. Bogle epitomize, for me, our moral exemplars in the world of finance. To see what I mean, meet Charley for coffee in the Great Room at the Yale Club of New York City, or make a pilgrimage to visit Jack in his office at Vanguard, the firm he designed and built on his pioneering vision of the role institutional asset managers should play in society.

Ellis's essay is a cautionary tale of "mission drift"—showing how easy it is, even for firms committed to excellence, to lose touch with that "iconic statement, 'the needs of our clients always come first.'" This is a particular risk for the large, complex financial institutions that dominate financial services today and which also interact with lots of folks who *aren't* clients. Not fully understood or appreciated, but profoundly important, is the fact that the obligations a financial institution has to trading counterparties (fair dealing) differ from those it has to customers (full and accurate disclosure and best execution), which are in turn different from those it has to clients (fiduciary standards of care). Ellis argues that "an important step toward attaining the respect and trust" is to be clear about those differences, and to "give up unrealistic promises and stop asking for unrealistic credence."

Fiduciary obligations, and the importance of fiduciary principles, are topics John C. Bogle has been writing about throughout his career, never more articulately than in his classic essay "The Fiduciary Principle: No Man Can Serve Two Masters." At the risk of oversimplifying, Bogle's recommended cure for what ails finance is to more broadly apply and strictly observe what he calls "the highest duty known to the law"—a fiduciary duty of care.

Donald B. Trone is a lifelong proponent of fiduciary process who heads the Leadership Center for Investment Stewards, known as 3ethos. In his essay, he goes a step beyond Bogle and Ellis to suggest that merely observing fiduciary standards will not be enough to repair the finance sector's trust deficit. He argues that trust is to be found at the intersection of fiduciary principles, governance principles and stewardship. Trone suggests that individual investors are looking not so much for "trusted guides," as wealth management advisors have called themselves for decades, but for principled and empowered "leaders," whose values align with their own.

CHAPTER 6

RESTORING TRUST

Douglas M. Hodge

CEO and Managing Director, Pacific
Investment Management Company

This is a consequential time. Structural realignments are reshaping the global economy and the financial services industry. Financial firms are adapting to post-2008 regulations, even as the Federal Reserve steps back from policy experimentation and hopes remain for economic growth here and abroad.

As to how this all plays out, well, there are many unknowns. In the immortal words of Yogi Berra, "It's tough to make predictions, especially about the future."

It is particularly difficult to make predictions about the future of our industry. What will be our role in 2015, 2016 and beyond? Such uncertainty makes us all anxious. Yet some things are clear. It's clear that our industry will be shaped by macroeconomic and regulatory developments and, of course, by the behavior of capital markets themselves. It's also clear that our deepest challenge is not an external one. It's something more basic and intrinsic: trust.

As stewards of the capital markets, trust is our most valuable asset. It's what gives investors enough confidence to engage with us, to entrust us with their savings with the expectation that we will help them achieve their investment goals, protect their money and provide appropriate liquidity. Yet over a period of several years, both prior to and indeed through the crisis of 2008, our industry as a whole has squandered this trust. We forgot the most basic principle of our profession: that finance is a means to an end. That whether we work for a bank, a broker or an investment manager, our core function is that of an intermediary and service provider.

In short, too many of us forgot the second word: "services." We're in the financial services industry. We exist to serve others.

Restoring trust means once more acting as stewards. Stewardship must be our guiding principle as we restructure our businesses, work with regulators and interact with clients and the public. If we succeed, our reputations will rise, our contributions to society will spread and we can reclaim our pride in what we do.

TARNISHED TRUST

But we face a difficult challenge. Trust in our industry has fallen to new lows. The most recent reading of the Financial Trust Index, which is based on a survey done by the business schools at Northwestern and the University of Chicago, shows that only 38 percent of respondents trust banks.[1] As an industry, we've fallen into the same boat as lawyers and journalists. I suppose we can take some comfort in the fact that Congress still ranks lower. Then again, maybe not.

However, our low standing shouldn't come as a surprise. Now, in the seventh year since the onset of the financial crisis, millions of Americans remain unemployed or underemployed. The human suffering has been immense and the fallout may last for generations. Far from helping, we've been hurting our own cause. There's been a steady stream of dismaying news in recent years. We witnessed the robo-signing debacle amid the housing collapse, billions of dollars in trading losses by the London Whale, the Libor rate-rigging scandal and, more recently, Leonardo DiCaprio portraying a Wall Street wolf and Michael Lewis's scathing book on high-frequency trading.

What these and other scandals show is that, whether through simple incompetence or deliberate action, some within our industry have been guilty of deceptive communication, duplicitous motives and, in the most egregious cases, outright dishonesty. As a representative of the asset management industry, it's tempting to lay the blame on bad bankers. But the Financial Trust Index shows an even lower reading for the mutual fund industry: only 31 percent of people trust asset management companies.[2]

We have a serious trust deficit!

Trust is developed on a personal level. It's achieved by acting consistently and honestly; by demonstrating expertise and competence; by communicating openly and accurately; and by showing concern and compassion toward the clients we serve.

On these counts, we all have plenty of work to do.

THE ROAD AHEAD

Our job of restoring trust will be even more challenging because the ground has shifted in fundamental and distressing ways. The decades leading up to the financial crisis were an era of deregulation, globalization and credit entitlement. These forces produced economic growth and outsized returns for financial assets. Most of us lived in this environment for so long we stopped noticing it; we began to take it for granted.

That is, until it stopped—and suddenly went into reverse. Rather than credit entitlement, the winds shifted to reregulation and delevering. For a time, monetary policy experimentation boosted asset returns, pushing investors out the risk spectrum. Taper Talk likely marked the end of that stage of recovery.

So what are we dealing with? We've got a financially burned consumer who trusts us less than ever. We've got tepid economic growth in the United States, and more volatile markets and uncertainty as global economies adjust to shifts in monetary policies. It's in this context that we've enacted the most sweeping overhaul of financial regulation in our lifetimes, and frankly, so far we haven't done it very well. There's a widespread sense that the regulatory responses have fallen short. Many people on Main Street—and Wall Street too—remain unconvinced that the fundamental sources of systemic instability within the financial system have been resolved.

All this is why we believe informed and responsible reforms are called for. But reforms need to be smart and coordinated, not protective or politically motivated. They must differentiate among the various types of financial intermediaries and how they should be treated. And they need to spur growth by promoting the market's ability to discover prices, provide liquidity and allocate risk capital efficiently.

For instance, it is important that we differentiate between regulation that is designed to ensure the safety and soundness of balance sheets, which is the foundation of our depository institutions and the banking system, and the regulation of capital markets, which is designed around the tenets of transparency and disclosure. We need to remember that the overarching role of capital markets is to provide a forum for exchange that fosters the flow of risk capital from those who have it to those who need it.

American capital markets have served this purpose well for generations. They are the largest and deepest in the world. They serve those who need capital to support and grow their businesses in order to innovate and create jobs. The capital markets also serve those who invest in order to preserve and grow their wealth so they can fund their retirement or a college education, or buy a first home.

Our markets are the envy of the world. We attract and facilitate the flow of international capital like no one else can. But for the markets to function properly, we need to ensure the integrity of balance sheets. Whether you are a capital market participant or a simple depositor with a passbook account and an ATM card, we learned this lesson: in the near-death experience of 2008 when the capital markets froze, it became clear that the balance sheets of some of the largest and most venerable financial institutions had been compromised.

There should be no question about the importance of preserving the integrity of balance sheets. However, regulators, both domestic and foreign, need to consider the impacts on the global capital markets as they institute their reforms. Our challenge is to expand credit, but to do so in a way that is both safe and sustainable. If we are to achieve our long-term growth potential, then we will need well-functioning capital markets.

TOWARD A CULTURE OF TRUST

Of course, regulations can only take us so far. They quickly become outdated. And they cannot guarantee that fraud and other financial misdeeds won't happen. That's why it's imperative that we restore a culture of trust in the financial services industry. It's time we enter a new era, an era of cultural transformation. We need to rediscover our core values.

I wrote a piece in July 2012 about culture in our industry.[3] I said that the culture of the financial services industry should rest on three basic principles:

- Number one, the client must come first. It's an old adage but one that has never been more true. This principle must be more than mere words printed on a page in an employee handbook or memorialized on a plaque in your lobby or cafeteria. All the financial services we provide must meet a legitimate client need. We must live, honor and respect this value above all others.
- The second element is risk management. Risk management must be integral to everything all financial institutions do.
- The third and broadest element is that we embrace a sense of stewardship. It's a simple concept but one that can reliably guide us in the right direction.

MAKING THINGS HAPPEN

I've laid out some cultural principles that I believe most of us would agree with. So the question becomes, How do we make them happen?

The simple answer is that it starts at the top, with the leaders of the financial services industry. Both as firms and individuals, we need to personify trustworthy values. Great organizations are built from the inside out. We should strengthen and reinforce the key elements of our service culture, including a reexamination of management objectives. We should put in place reward systems that incentivize our people to place the interests of the client ahead of the firm and the interests of the firm ahead of the individual employee.

We all make mistakes. But mistakes have consequences, and the individuals and institutions who commit them need to be held accountable. Willful violations of the rules should not be tolerated by any of us. Firms should adopt a culture of compliance. This involves increased training and putting a stronger emphasis on ethics and integrity.

Once lost, financial trust—like any other kind of trust—is hard to restore. But it's not impossible. I have absolutely no doubt that if we commit ourselves to reviving a culture centered on client needs, risk management and stewardship, then we will all be better off.

NOTES

1. "Chicago Booth/Kellogg School Financial Trust Index Reveals Public Concern over Income Inequality, Broken Education System," 2014, The University of Chicago Booth School of Business and Kellogg School of Management, http://www.financialtrustindex.org/resultswave22.htm.
2. Ibid.
3. Douglas M. Hodge, "It's All about Culture," *PIMCO*, July 2012, http://www.pimco.com/EN/Insights/Pages/Its-All-About-Culture.aspx.

CHAPTER 7

WHAT IT TAKES

SUCCESS CHALLENGED

Charles D. Ellis

Author of Winning the Loser's Game

Every organization—and every great firm—will, inevitably, experience trouble. A truly great organization will identify troubles early *and* will overcome them through leadership and strengths in culture, past recruiting and training, and its internal commitment to the firm's mission. And that's how Goldman Sachs proved itself a great firm.

The multiple crises that Goldman Sachs confronted a few years ago were at least several decades in the making. They can be traced to major changes in the firm's mission and culture during five different leadership tenures. The biggest change is that Goldman Sachs has gone from an investment bank whose purpose was to serve its clients to a trading firm whose purpose is to trade with counterparties. While its primary business principle remains ostensibly the same—"Our clients' interests always come first"—too many customers, competitors, regulators and even past partners wonder whether it has become mere lip service.

Before the Great Crash of 1929, all the Goldmans and the Sachses wanted was to have their small firm accepted by the owners of Wall Street and to prosper by serving corporate clients with great care. In the 1970s and '80s, John Whitehead and John Weinberg brought the focus back to investment banking for corporations, building Goldman Sachs into a leading Wall Street—and eventually international—firm. The two men ran the firm together and served as cochairs and co–senior partners. Their mission was to serve clients so well that Goldman Sachs would rise to a leading position at each client organization and win more and better corporate clients.

There was no sudden turning point for the firm's aspirations and standards. But before they left, Whitehead and Weinberg may have quite unintentionally launched the firm into businesses that were by nature destined (if successful) to be incompatible with the service-intensive, risk-averse culture they had previously built. They committed the firm to becoming the global leader in finance, acquired a commodities business, built up the bond dealing business, launched investment management and increased profitability, capital and the firm's prowess in capital-at-risk trading.

Their successors, Bob Rubin and Steve Friedman, differed from the two Johns in significant ways. Rubin and Friedman were also cochairs and co-senior partners and ran the firm together; both saw being senior partner as a job, not as a career or a calling. The firm was a vehicle, not a destination. To increasing numbers of partners, Goldman Sachs itself was important, but not *that* important. As Friedman later said, "There *is* life after Goldman Sachs." Impatient to increase profitability, they accelerated the pace of activity and empowered anyone with the drive and determination to make it happen.

THE RISE OF TRADING

Rubin and Friedman focused increasingly on changing the mix and pace of the firm's many businesses to increase profits and payouts to partners. Serving clients more intensively was still considered important as a means of augmenting profits, but client service was increasingly matched and even superseded by trading skills and capital commitments—deliberately taking market risks in bonds, foreign exchange, oil and commodities—and increasingly gathering and applying proprietary information. Numerous accomplished people were hired in from other firms and never learned to treasure the iconic values of the Whitehead-Weinberg era. Rubin was primarily a *strategic* leader and Friedman primarily a *transactional* leader. Friedman's abrupt departure—during a loss-making bond market and without a plan in place for leadership succession—set a new benchmark for putting personal interests ahead of the firm's. Trading and transactional leadership—and increasingly visible and forceful power politics—were becoming dominant at Goldman Sachs.

For Jon Corzine, the firm's first chair and CEO, the initial goal was stark: save the firm by terminating enough people to cut out a billion dollars in bloated costs—and trading out of money-losing bond positions. Later, he came to see the investment banking agency business—doing transactions for others—as slow-growth, low-margin and passé, and he resolved to expand proprietary trading for the firm's own account, make acquisitions and go public. As Corzine twisted arms to get votes for the initial public offering, politics flourished, and the prospect of huge individual payoffs tempted even the most company-minded among them. Even for those who had been almost romantic about the mission of serving clients, the real purpose had become clear: it was all about the money. Very little attention was given to the "soft" values and protecting the primacy of the firm's culture.

Hank Paulson, a former relationship banker and a forceful, pragmatic CEO, further increased the independent strength of the firm as an aggressive, profit-maximizing global capitalist. He build up private equity investing, joined in hostile takeovers (a major change) and expanded asset management, technology and trading while making more than 70 trips to establish the firm in China. Paulson's ability to play hardball showed in his leading the putsch that removed Corzine and later dismissing his own promise to pass the baton of leadership to others.

Finally, the current CEO, Lloyd Blankfein—skilled in sales, trading and politics—thrived in this era of transformation and was a creature of the new kind of firm that Goldman Sachs—and all its major competitors—was fast becoming: a profit-focused trading powerhouse that also did banking. Blankfein's mission began with further increasing the firm's profitability and power á la the great J. P. Morgan—until the global financial crisis required refocusing his attention on defending the firm politically, legally and in the court of public opinion.

It might seem that Goldman Sachs's mission, in Blankfein's era, had come full circle, but that would miss a fundamental difference. Weinberg had wanted to serve prestigious corporate clients and develop a strong business with profit as the *means* of building a great firm. In his era, payouts to partners came later, and were modest. Well before Blankfein's era, those two objectives were reversed: build a powerful firm in order to maximize profits paid out to the partners. What insiders saw as a spectacular success—as measured by competitive rankings, profits and payouts to partners—would increasingly be seen by customers, regulators and government leaders—and by the press and the public—as excessive and suspicious.

By stages, committing capital and taking risks in trading transactions had eclipsed long-term, service-based client relationships at Goldman Sachs and among its competitors. Common denominators increasingly became not qualitative and "all about people," but quantitative and "all about numbers": capital, risk and profit—particularly profit. The focus on profit kept increasing.

Taken together, the firm's complex, fast-moving businesses form an extraordinary network of activities that enable Goldman Sachs to gather and deliver to the point of decision a plethora of proprietary information that the firm can and does act on to make profits. The time horizon for conducting business moved from years—even decades to develop a primary relationship with a major corporation—down to hours, even minutes to do a trade. The language of Goldman Sachs changed: In the past, it was all about clients; now it was about accounts and counterparties, and the terminology turned toward locker-room crudeness.

Power within the firm had always gravitated toward those divisions that made the most profit, so it soon moved away from banking to trading. Partnerships and compensation shifted from the bankers to the traders. The identification of profits with particular trades made it easier for specific individuals to insist on being paid for the reported profit of specific transactions, which inevitably shifted the focus even further from firm to individual—from *we* to *me*. Twenty-five years ago, 85 percent of the partners were bankers and 75 percent of the profits came from banking. Today, banking is less than 10 percent of the profits, and a large majority of the partners—and both the CEO and the COO—are from trading.

Trading businesses are naturally friendless. Success depends primarily on the individual traders. So moneymaking traders are free agents, while individual investment bankers or research analysts or securities salespeople are almost captives of the complex organizations they depend on and represent. They cannot easily leave and take the firm's clients with them. But traders can move overnight to new firms. So the competition for traders has become a "spot" market, and compensation for top traders has soared.

Trading, taking risks and committing capital to make more profit became the driving forces within Goldman Sachs. Observers began to define the firm as an aggressive, highly leveraged hedge fund with an appendage in investment banking. Major transformational changes gained momentum: geographically, the firm went from a New York–Chicago–London concentration to a dispersed global organization of several hundred different "market-facing" entrepreneurial business units connected by a powerful, centralized, level-by-level risk management and reporting system—so formidable it was dubbed "The Federation." The securities business was changing rapidly, and Goldman Sachs was changing even more rapidly so its skillful, driven people could stay ahead of the curve of change and excel at making money.

Compared with the Goldman Sachs of 20 or 30 years ago, Blankfein's Goldman Sachs is huge, with 33,000 people and a trillion-dollar balance sheet. As the firm has grown in scale and complexity, the time horizon for management decisions has gotten shorter and shorter. As Goldman Sachs got much more aggressive and hard-dealing in its pursuit of maximum profit, it often appeared too aggressive and too profitable.

During the global financial crisis, Blankfein—one of the most capable transactional leaders the firm has ever had—had the toughest job any

Goldman Sachs CEO had ever faced as a strategic leader. The firm made that job much tougher by not recognizing that when you're the world's leading financial organization with a reputation for exceptional talent, skill and expertise, much more is expected—not on the hard, quantitative metrics on which the firm focused, but on the softer, qualitative dimensions on which clients, customers, regulators, the media and the public focused. No matter how skilled and powerful it is, no firm can expect to continue being the leading firm in its field unless it is the firm that earns the most well-deserved client and customer trust, as well as public goodwill and respect.

As Goldman Sachs repeatedly demonstrated its ability to make money for itself, clients could react in two ways: one negative and one positive. The *negative* reaction could be: Goldman Sachs is good at making money for itself because that's its whole focus—but that's not always good for us, so we should try to avoid them. The *positive* reaction would be: Goldman Sachs is a superb moneymaker, so we should align ourselves with them and make money too. Senior people at Goldman Sachs were confident that the positive view would prevail because that's how they themselves would have reasoned. But those with regular business dealings with the firm, still widely recognized as the most capable of all its competitors, judge Goldman Sachs not by what it says, but by what it does and what they see day after day. All too often, they experience tough "firm first" behavior. As Wall Street cynics say, "If Goldman Sachs wants to buy, you don't want to sell, and if Goldman Sachs wants to sell, you don't want to buy."

THE BUSINESS STANDARDS COMMITTEE

After nearly two punishing years of being behind the curve and not appearing to recognize the validity of the public furor, Goldman Sachs accepted that the world saw things differently. The Security and Exchange Commission's (SEC's) fraud charges and the record-setting settlement paid by the firm gave substance to the aggressive articles in the press and the hostile questions posed in the Washington hearings. At the May 2010 annual meeting, undertaking an initiative larger and more public than any corporation had ever taken before, Lloyd Blankfein announced the creation of a major self-examination by a committee cochaired by vice-chair Mike Evans, head of Goldman Sachs Asia, and partner Gerald Corrigan, for many years chair of the powerful firm-wide risk committee. This Business Standards Committee included 17 of the firm's most senior leaders, plus a distinguished Wall Street attorney and securities industry wise man, Rodgin Cohen of Sullivan & Cromwell, and former SEC chair Arthur Levitt—but no clients. As part of the committee's extensive exploration effort, more than 100 partners led small study groups in examining every facet of every business for six intense months. In

January 2011, the committee presented 39 specific recommendations. All were promptly approved by the board of directors and by senior management.

The committee's 63-page report[1] was made public, an extraordinary, highly visible commitment to action. Its first page was devoted to the iconic Goldman Sachs Business Principles; it began, "Our clients' interests always come first," and concluded, "Integrity and honesty are at the heart of our business. We expect our people to maintain high ethical standards in everything they do."

For a skeptical audience familiar with spin, the obvious question was whether the report would lead to vigorous corrective actions. Corrigan was determined to see it done. He had come to Goldman Sachs after 25 years in the Federal Reserve System, culminating in nine years as president and CEO of the powerful New York Fed. A genial Irishman with a ready smile, he is a tough career public servant who earned a reputation as a man of integrity who gave no quarter even in past negotiations with the U.S. Treasury. Fifteen years before, he and John Thain had designed and installed Goldman Sachs's sophisticated risk management system, and ever since he had cochaired the powerful, firm-wide risk committee. This position had given him great credibility with the firm's many traders; they knew they depended on that system for every major decision every day.

Corrigan summarized his view of reality: "There is only one word to describe our business today—complex. Risk metrics and the information we need to manage risks are evolving quite rapidly. Over the past five years there has been a major change in our business due to quantification and computers." Then he turned from the industry to focus on Goldman Sachs: "There *had* been culture slippage. The industry *and* the firm are more short-term focused. The orientation is less about clients and more about the firm and current profits." Then he reflected, "All great firms go through difficult periods. The key question is whether a calamity is seen for what it really is and taken as an opportunity to self-evaluate and rebuild."

Phrases throughout the Business Standards Committee's report signaled determination to get things right: "fundamental recommitment," "not just can we, but should we," "making the firm a better institution," "transparency," "strengthen our culture," "focus on serving clients," "we must be clear to ourselves and to our clients about the capacity in which we are acting." The committee's primary organizational recommendation was to change the firm's structure to move mortgage-backed securities product distribution over into investment banking, where due-diligence disciplines were traditionally strong. For reporting purposes, the firm's three major business segments would be made into four, with principal investing and lending clearly segregated. Securities services would move from investment management to institutional client services where it belonged. Mike Evans, a Canadian Olympic oarsman who still looks the part, chaired the committee, tracking the implementation of each of the 39 recommendations. "We get weekly reports on progress and meet every month for four hours to hear the progress on each recommendation and discuss ways to keep advancing and keep the pressure on. Some are already done, but some—like the new software required for pricing and pre-and post-trading—had to take longer. We intend to complete all 39 actions this year."

Regular reports on progress were made to the Federal Reserve, the firm's regulator that has several of its people full time at Goldman Sachs (as it does with all major banks), as well as to the board of directors and to employees. No reports on results were made public, but the internal view is that desired changes have been made successfully and that external observers will, in time, accept that reality too.

In publicly endorsing the committee report, Blankfein said, "We believe the recommendation in this report represent a fundamental recommitment of Goldman Sachs to our clients and to reputational excellence in everything the firm does." Setting aside the no-longer-credible idea that each business of the firm was separate, Blankfein declared, "Goldman Sachs has one reputation. It can be affected by any number of decisions and activities across the firm," and added, "It is important to articulate clearly both to our people and to clients the specific roles we assume in each case."[2] In private conversation, as he was leaving for yet another trip to China—to conduct a few more of the three dozen Chairman's Forum meetings he has been holding around the world to articulate the firm's commitments, answer questions and give clients access to the CEO—Blankfein was clear: "This will be my legacy." Given the firm's bad press in those days, he usually opened those sessions with a few self-deprecating jokes to acknowledge that there were problems and to encourage people to ask their real questions.

Goldman Sachs continues to perform more skillfully in more areas than any competitor and is clearly rebuilding its reputation as the industry's leading firm. Doing so requires that no more examples be found of Goldman Sachs breaking the rules or laws. Implementation of the final report of the Business Standards Committee also had to be convincing—inside the firm *and* with external observers, particularly any skeptics. Surely, a difficult challenge for the firm has been to recognize that the iconic statement, "The needs of our clients always come first," cannot be promised or delivered to its trading customers and counterparties, but only to its traditional relationship-based clients in such major businesses as investment banking and asset management.

CLIENTS OR COUNTERPARTIES?

Most of the organizations Goldman Sachs works with are *not* clients. Some are customers—even important customers—but not clients. And still others are not customers, but counterparties. They should all know from experience which they are and what the securities business has become, and the firm should be clear with them—and with itself too—about the limits of its responsibilities and promises. It should concentrate on demonstrating comparative excellence again and again. Over and over, Goldman Sachs has, with unrelenting persistence, out-performed its competitors in major markets around the world. No longer attacked automatically in the media, the firm's next most important step will be to implement the day-to-day behavior that would bring the 39 important change recommendations of the Business Standards Committee to life in the real world of transactions with clients, customers, and counterparties.

Goldman Sachs has continued to show the largest aggregation of talented, skillful, committed men and women ever combined in a single securities firm. It consistently recruits the most capable and highly motivated young people; is the best place to learn the business; has the strongest internal culture and collective commitment; is the market leader in a vast array of specific markets and products; works on transactions with the largest number of major corporations, investing institutions, central banks and governments; has the most effective internal communications; has the best financial management, operating management and risk management at all levels—particularly at the top; and can get more complex deals done faster. And, of course, it makes the most money.

Qualitatively, Goldman Sachs may not always be considered by clients, customers and competitors to be as fine a firm to work with as it was 20 years ago, but that's because the securities business has changed and so the firm itself has had to change too. Surely, the firm has the resources and the determination at the top, so now time will tell whether it will, as is now widely expected, continue to earn the mantle of unquestioned industry leadership.

NOTES

Unless noted otherwise, quotes from individuals in the text come from interviews with the author during the past decade.

1. Goldman Sachs, "Report of the Business Standards Committee," January 2011, http://www.goldmansachs.com/who-we-are/business-standards/committee-report/business-standards-committee-report-pdf.pdf.
2. Goldman Sachs, "Business Principles and Standards Committee Report," Executive Summary, http://www.goldmansachs.com/who-we-are/business-standards/committee-report/business-standards-committee-report.html.

CHAPTER 8

THE FIDUCIARY PRINCIPLE

NO MAN CAN SERVE TWO MASTERS

John C. Bogle

Founder, The Vanguard Group

I write at a time of financial and economic crisis in our nation and around the globe. I venture to assert that when the history of the financial era which has just drawn to a close comes to be written, most of its mistakes and its major faults will be ascribed to the failure to observe the fiduciary principle, the precept as old as holy writ, that "a man cannot serve two masters." No thinking man can believe that an economy built upon a business foundation can permanently endure without some loyalty to that principle. The separation of ownership from management, the development of the corporate structure so as to vest in small groups control over the resources of great numbers of small and uninformed investors, make imperative a fresh and active devotion to that principle if the modern world of business is to perform its proper function.[1]

Alas, the words in the preceding paragraph are not mine. Rather, they are the words of Harlan Fiske Stone, excerpted from his 1934—yes, 1934—address at the University of Michigan Law School, reprinted in the *Harvard Law Review* later that year.[2] But his words are equally relevant—perhaps even more relevant—at this moment in history. They could hardly present a more appropriate analysis of the causes of the recent collapse of our financial markets.

One could easily react to Justice Stone's words by falling back on the ancient aphorism "the more things change, the more they remain the same," and move on to a new subject. But I hope financial professionals will react differently and share my feeling, that in the aftermath of the Great Depression and the stock market crash that accompanied it, we failed to take advantage of the opportunity to demand that those who lead our giant business and financial organizations—the stewards of so much of our nation's wealth—measure up to the stern and unyielding principles of fiduciary duty described by Justice Stone. So, for heaven's sake, let's not make the same mistake again.

Justice Stone's stern words force us to focus on the ethical dilemmas faced by today's business leaders. Included among these leaders are the chiefs who manage our nation's publicly held corporations—today valued in the stock market at some $27 trillion—and the professional managers of "other people's money" who oversee equity investments valued at some $18 trillion of that total, owning 70 percent of all shares and therefore holding absolute voting control over those corporations.[3] Like their counterparts in business, those powerful managers have not only an ethical responsibility, but a fiduciary duty, to those whose capital has been entrusted to their care.

FIDUCIARY STORY

The concept of fiduciary duty has a long history, going back more or less eight centuries under English common law. Fiduciary duty is essentially a legal relationship of confidence or trust between two or more parties, most commonly a fiduciary or trustee and a principal or beneficiary, who justifiably reposes confidence, good faith and reliance on his trustee. The fiduciary is expected to act at all times for the sole benefit and interests of the principal, with loyalty to those interests. A fiduciary must not put personal interests before that duty and, importantly, must not be placed in a situation where his fiduciary duty to clients conflicts with a fiduciary duty to any other entity.

It has been said, I think accurately, that fiduciary duty is the highest duty known to the law. It is less ironic than tragic that the concept of fiduciary duty seems far less imbedded in our society today than it was when Stone expressed his profound convictions. As ought to be obvious to all educated citizens, over the past few decades the balance between ethics and law on one hand and the markets on the other have heavily shifted in favor of the markets. As I have often put it: we have moved from a society in which there are some things that one simply does not do, to one in which "if everyone else is doing it, I can do it too." I've described this change as a shift from moral absolutism to moral relativism. Business ethics, it seems to me, has been a major casualty of that shift in our traditional societal values. You will hardly be surprised to learn that I do not regard that change as progress.

We forgot the fundamental principle expressed by the apostles Matthew and Luke, and repeated by Justice Stone: "No man can serve two masters."[4]

My principal objection to moral relativism is that it obfuscates and mitigates the obligations that we owe to society and shifts the focus to the benefits accruing to the individual. Self-interest, unchecked, is a powerful force, but a force that, if it is to protect the interests of the community of all of our citizens, must ultimately be checked by society. The financial crisis of 2008–09—which I have described as "a crisis of ethic proportions"—makes it clear how serious that damage can become.

CAUSES OF THE RECENT CRISIS

The causes of the recent crisis are manifold. Metaphorically speaking, the collapse in our financial system has 1,000 fathers. But one major cause is the radical increase in the power and position of the leaders of corporate America and the leaders of investment America. These leaders have failed to exercise their power. The agents of investment in America have failed to honor the responsibilities that they owe to their principals—the last-line individuals who commit much of their capital wealth to stock ownership, including mutual fund shareowners and pension beneficiaries. The record is clear that, despite their controlling position, most institutional investors have failed to play an active role in board structure and governance, director elections, executive compensation, stock options, proxy proposals, dividend policy and so on.

Given their forbearance as corporate citizens, these managers arguably played a major role in allowing the managers of our public corporations to exploit the advantages of their own agency, not only in executive compensation, perquisites and mergers and acquisitions, but even in accepting the "financial engineering" that has come to permeate corporate financial statements, endorsed—at least tacitly—by their public accountants.

The failures of our institutional investors go beyond governance issues to the very practice of their trade. When they fail to honor their traditional fiduciary responsibilities, these agents do not meet the high standards that our citizen/investors have every reason to expect of the investment professionals to whom they have entrusted their money.

THE ROLE OF INSTITUTIONAL MANAGERS

The failure of our newly empowered agents to exercise their responsibilities to ownership is but a part of the problem we face. The field of institutional investment management also played a major, if often overlooked, role. As a group, we veered off course almost 180 degrees, from stewardship to salesmanship, in which our focus turned away from prudent management and toward product marketing. We moved from a focus on long-term investment to a focus on short-term speculation. The driving dream of our advisor/agents was to gather ever-increasing assets under management, the better to build their advisory fees and profits, even as these policies came at the direct expense of the investor/principals whom, under traditional standards of trusteeship and fiduciary duty, they were duty-bound to serve.

As control over corporate America moved from owners to agents, our institutional money managers seemed to forget their duty to act solely in the interest of their own principals, those whose savings were entrusted to mutual funds and whose retirement security was entrusted to pension plans. These new investor/agents not only forgot the interests of their principals, but also seemed to forget their own investment principles. The predominant focus of institutional investment strategy turned from the wisdom of long-term investing, based on the enduring creation of intrinsic corporate values, to the folly of short-term speculation, focused on the ephemeral prices of corporate stocks. The own-a-stock strategy of yore became the rent-a-stock strategy of today.

Here, again, we can't say that we hadn't been warned well in advance. Way back in 1936, John Maynard Keynes warned us, "when enterprise becomes a mere bubble on a whirlpool of speculation, the job of capitalism will be ill-done."[5] Today, the job of capitalism is being ill-done, and the consequences have not been pretty. In 1958, speaking before the convention of the National Federation of Financial Analysts Societies, Benjamin Graham, legendary investor and author of the classic *The Intelligent Investor*, described "some contrasting relationships between the present and the past in our underlying attitudes toward investment and speculation in common stocks."[6] He further commented:

> In the past, the speculative elements of a common stock resided almost exclusively in the company itself; they were due to uncertainties, or fluctuating elements, or downright weaknesses in the industry, or the corporation's individual setup. . . . But in recent years a new and major element of speculation has been introduced into the common-stock arena from outside the companies. It comes from the attitude and viewpoint of the stock-buying public and their advisers—chiefly us security analysts. This attitude may be described in a phrase: primary emphasis upon future expectations. . . .
>
> The concept of future prospects, and particularly of continued growth in the future, invites the application of formulas out of higher mathematics to establish the present value of the favored issues. But the combination of precise formulas with highly imprecise assumptions can be used to establish, or rather to justify, practically any value one wished, however high. . . .

Have not investors and security analysts eaten of the tree of knowledge of good and evil prospects? By so doing have they not permanently expelled themselves from that Eden where promising common stocks at reasonable prices could be plucked off the bushes.[7]

This obvious reference to original sin reflected Graham's deep concern about quantifying the unquantifiable (and doing so with false precision). The implications of that bite into the apple of quantitative investing were barely visible when Graham spoke in 1958. But by the late 1990s, this new form of investment behavior had become a dominant force, and continues to be a major driver of the speculation that has overwhelmed our financial markets.

It is little short of amazing how long ago these prescient warnings were issued. Justice Stone warned us in 1934. John Maynard Keynes warned us in 1936. Benjamin Graham warned us in 1958. Isn't it high time we stand on the shoulders of these intellectual giants and shape national policy away from the moral relativism of peer conduct and greed and short-term speculation—gambling on expectations about stock prices? Isn't it high time to return to the moral absolutism of fiduciary duty, to return to our traditional ethic of long-term investment focused on building the intrinsic value of our corporations—prudence, due diligence and active participation in corporate governance?

Yes, now *is* the time for reform. Today's agency society has ill-served the public interest. The failure of our money manager/agents represents not only a failure of modern-day capitalism, but a failure of modern-day capitalists. In all, our now-dominant money management sector has turned its focus away from the enduring nature of the intrinsic value of the goods and services created, produced and distributed by our corporate businesses and toward the ephemeral price of the corporation's stock—the triumph of perception over reality. We live in a world in which it is far easier to hype the price of a company's stock than it is to build the intrinsic value of the corporation itself. And we seem to have forgotten Benjamin Graham's implicit caution about the transience of short-term perception, compared to the durability of long-term reality: "In the short run, the stock market is a voting machine; in the long run it is a weighing machine."[8]

TO BUILD THE FINANCIAL WORLD ANEW

We must now restructure the nature and values of the entire money management business—to build the financial world anew. I am well aware of how difficult it will be to accomplish that sweeping task.

And yet we dare not stand still.

For the fact is that there has been a radical change in our investment system. The ownership society of a half century ago is gone, never to return. It has been replaced by the agency society of today, in which our agents have failed to serve their principals—mutual fund shareholders, pension beneficiaries and long-term investors. Rather, the new system has served the agents themselves—our institutional managers.

Further, by their forbearance on governance issues, our money managers have also served the managers of corporate America. To make matters even worse, by turning to short-term speculation at the expense of long-term investment, the industry has also damaged the interests of the greater society, just as Lord Keynes warned.

Of course American society is in a constant state of flux. It always has been, and it always will be. I've often pointed out that our nation began as an agricultural economy, became largely a manufacturing economy, then largely a service economy, and most recently an economy in which the financial services sector had become the dominant element. Such secular changes are not new, but they are always different, so enlightened responses are never easy to come by. To deal with the new and complex economic forces that our failed agency society has created, of course we need a new paradigm: a fiduciary society in which the interest of investors comes first, and ethical behavior by our business and financial leaders represents the highest value.

BUILDING A FIDUCIARY SOCIETY

While the challenges of today are inevitably different from those of the past, the principles are age-old. Consider this warning from Adam Smith way back in the eighteenth century: "Managers of other people's money [rarely] watch over it with the same anxious vigilance with which . . . they watch over their own. . . . They very easily give themselves a dispensation. Negligence and profusion must always prevail."[9] And so in the recent era, negligence and profusion have prevailed among our money manager/agents, even to the point of an almost complete disregard of their duty and responsibility to their principals. Too few managers seem to display the "anxious vigilance" over other people's money that once defined the conduct of investment professionals. So what we must do is develop a new fiduciary society to guarantee that our last-line owners—those mutual fund shareholders and pension fund beneficiaries whose savings are at stake—have their rights as investment principals protected. These rights must include:

1. The right to have money manager/agents act solely on their principals' behalf. The client, in short, must be king.

2. The right to rely on due diligence and high professional standards on the part of money managers and securities analysts who appraise securities for their institutions' portfolios.[10]
3. The assurance that agents will act as responsible corporate citizens, restoring to their principals the neglected rights of ownership of stocks and demanding that corporate directors and managers meet their fiduciary duty to their own shareholders.
4. The right to demand some sort of discipline and integrity in the mutual funds and financial products that our manager/agents offer.
5. The establishment of advisory fee structures that meet a "reasonableness" standard based not only on rates but on dollar amounts, and the assurance of fairness with regard to the fees and structures available to all clients of the manager, regardless of portfolio size.
6. The elimination of any conflicts of interest that could preclude the achievement of these goals.

It will take federal government action to foster the creation of this new fiduciary society that I envision. Above all else, it must be unmistakable that government intends, and is capable of enforcing, standards of trusteeship and fiduciary duty under which money managers operate with the sole purpose and in the *exclusive* benefit of the interests of their beneficiaries—largely the owners of mutual fund shares and the beneficiaries of our pension plans. As corporate reformer Robert Monks accurately points out, "capitalism without owners will fail."[11]

While government action is essential, the new system should be developed in concert with the private investment sector, an Alexander Hamilton–like sharing of the responsibilities in which the Congress establishes the fiduciary principle and private enterprise establishes the practices that are required to observe it. This task of returning capitalism to its ultimate owners will take time, true enough. But the new reality—increasingly visible with each passing day—is that the concept of fiduciary duty is no longer merely an ideal to be debated. It is a vital necessity to be practiced.

A lot is at stake in reforming the very nature of our financial system itself, which in turn is designed to force reform in our failed system of governance of our business corporations. The change in the rules that I advocate—applying to institutional money managers a federal standard of fiduciary duty to their clients—would be designed, in turn, to force money managers to use their own ownership position to demand that the managers and directors of the business corporations in whose shares they invest also honor their own fiduciary duty to the holders of their shares. It is these two groups that share the responsibility for the prudent stewardship over both corporate assets and

investment securities that have been entrusted to their care, not only reforming today's flawed and conflict-ridden model, but also developing a new
model that, at best, will restore traditional ethical mores.

And so I await—with no great patience!—the return of the standard so
beautifully described by Justice Benjamin Cardozo years ago: "Those bound
by fiduciary ties . . . [are] held to something stricter than the morals of the
marketplace . . . a tradition unbending and inveterate . . . not honesty alone
but the punctilio of an honor the most sensitive . . . a level of conduct . . .
higher than that trodden by the crowd."[12]

In his profound 1934 speech that has been the inspiration for this essay,
Justice Harlan Fiske Stone made one further prescient point on serving the
common good:

> In seeking solutions for our social and economic maladjustments, we are
> too ready to place our reliance on what [the policeman's nightstick of] the
> state may command, rather than on what may be given to it as the free
> offering of good citizenship. . . . Yet we know that unless the urge to indi-
> vidual advantage has other curbs, and unless the more influential elements
> in society conduct themselves with a disposition to promote the common
> good, society cannot function . . . especially a society which has largely
> measured its rewards in terms of material gains. . . . We must [square] our
> own ethical conceptions with the traditional ethics and ideals of the com-
> munity at large. [There is] nothing more vital to our own day than that
> those who act as fiduciaries in the strategic positions of our business civili-
> zation, should be held to those standards of scrupulous fidelity which [our]
> society has the right to demand.[13]

Justice Stone's landmark speech reminds all of us engaged in the profession of investment management how far we have departed from those
standards of scrupulous fidelity, and gives us yet one more opportunity to
strengthen our resolve to meet that test and build a better financial world.

NOTES

1. Harlan Fiske Stone, "Address to the University of Michigan School of Law,"
   June 15, 1934, reprinted in the *Harvard Law Review* 48, no. 1 (November 1934):
   8–9.
2. Harlan Fiske Stone (1872–1946) received his law degree at Columbia in 1898
   and served as dean of Columbia Law School from 1910 to 1923. In 1925, President Calvin Coolidge appointed Stone associate justice of the United States
   Supreme Court. In 1941, President Franklin Roosevelt appointed him chief

justice of the United States, and he served in that position until his death in 1946. A curious coincidence is that Justice Stone appeared on the cover of *Time* magazine on May 6, 1929, just two days before my own birth on May 8. In its profile story, *Time* accurately speculated that one day Stone would become the chief justice, in part because (in those backward sentences that distinguished the early style of the magazine), "Well he has always tackled the public interest."

3. Federal Reserve Board Release Z.1, "Financial Accounts of the United States: Flow of Funds, Balance Sheets, and Integrated Macroeconomic Accounts," First Quarter, 2014.

4. Luke 16:13, and Matthew 6:34, AV.

5. John Maynard Keynes, *The General Theory of Employment, Interest, and Money* (1936; repr., New York: First Harvest/Harcourt, 1964), 159.

6. Benjamin Graham, "The New Speculation in Common Stocks," reprinted in *Benjamin Graham: Building a Profession*, ed. Jason Zweig and Rodney N. Sullivan (New York: McGraw-Hill, 2010), 79–80, 90.

7. Ibid.

8. Warren Buffett, "Letter to Berkshire Hathaway Shareholders, 1993," March 1, 1994.

9. Adam Smith, *An Inquiry into the Nature and Causes of the Wealth of Nations* (1776; repr., New York: Bantam Books, 2003), 941. In those days, *profusion* was defined as a "lavish or wasteful expenditure or excess bestowal of money, substance, etc., squandering, waste." *Oxford English Dictionary*, 2nd ed., vol. 12, s.v. "profusion."

10. Alan Murray, "Future of Finance (A Special Report)—Principles for Change: Peter Fisher on How to Avoid Financial Crises in the Future," *Wall Street Journal*, March 30, 2009. Peter Fisher, widely respected BlackRock executive and former Treasury Department official, believes we should force institutional investors to do a better job of analysis and establish demanding minimum standards of competence.

11. Robert Monks and Allen Sykes, *Capitalism Without Owners Will Fail* (London: Centre for the Study of Financial Innovation, 2002).

12. Benjamin N. Cardozo, *Meinhard v. Salmon*, 164 N.E. 545 (N.Y. 1928).

13. Stone, "Address to Michigan School of Law," 4, 13.

CHAPTER 9

TRUST DEPENDS ON AUTHENTIC LEADERSHIP, STEWARDSHIP AND GOVERNANCE

WHY WE MUST GO BEYOND COMPLIANCE

Donald B. Trone

Chief Ethos Officer, 3ethos

We need to hold critical decision makers in the wealth management industry to an authentic leadership, stewardship and governance standard.

Individual investors have grown cynical about Wall Street firms and major banks that claim to put the interests of clients first, then demonstrate otherwise. As an industry sector, financial services ranks lower than any other. However, the vast majority of wealth management advisors are honest and are committed to serving their clients. It is the dishonesty and, in some cases, criminal conduct of a relatively few bad actors that has destroyed the public's confidence.

The question that consumes both Washington and Wall Street is *How do we restore trust?* Washington's response has been fairly predictable: write more rules and regulations, particularly in the form of fiduciary standards. *Fiduciary* is defined as having the legal responsibility for managing the assets of another. There is a three-part test to determine whether a fiduciary standard has been met. The fiduciary must be able to demonstrate (1) the details of its decision-making process; (2) that the decision-making process was prudent; and (3) that decisions were made in the best interests of the client.

On the surface, a uniform fiduciary standard for all advisors appears to be the prescriptive solution. And, in fact, President Obama in 2010 signed the Dodd-Frank Act, which included language (Section 913) charging the Securities and Exchange Commission (SEC) with determining whether a uniform fiduciary standard of care would be in the public's best interests. (As of spring 2014—when this chapter was written—the SEC has yet to make such a determination. Likewise, the Department of Labor has made several unsuccessful attempts to subject more retirement service providers to a fiduciary standard.)

Such efforts by regulators to promulgate more rules and regulations—even if they are in the form of fiduciary standards—are not likely to have a material impact on the moral and ethical conduct of the industry. Time and time again, we have seen that morality cannot be legislated. Any teenager can testify to the fact that there is no correlation between more rules and better behavior. Voluminous regulations only make it easier for bad actors to hide within the system, and complicated financial disclosures make it more difficult for clients to make informed decisions. The fact that Bernie Madoff was "registered" with the SEC (and subject to a fiduciary standard) no doubt lulled certain of his investors into thinking that the SEC had conducted appropriate due diligence, and there was no need to replicate the effort. And despite a bevy of existing rules and regulations, Madoff found a way around them all.

Equally important, it is not the role of regulators to define the gold standard for the wealth management industry. The role of regulators is to define the minimum standard of care that must be met in order for an organization to conduct business. If a uniform fiduciary standard of care is promulgated, it will likely be a *de minimus* standard—a bronze, rather than a gold, standard.

What is needed is a more fundamental approach to evaluate whether a wealth management organization, or person, is worthy of trust. Is that firm or advisor authentic? We need an answer that doesn't depend on understanding arcane securities rules and regulations. We need a framework anyone can use to evaluate the effectiveness of a firm that is being considered for a critical leadership and stewardship role in advising and taking care of their clients' assets.

Distinguishing great wealth management firms from the rest is actually not that difficult; we do it every day with other industry sectors. If given a choice, what airline would you prefer to fly? Do you favor a particular hotel chain or rental car company? Have you ever paid more for a product because it was backed by spectacular customer service? And when you're in a strange town, have you ever gone out of your way to find a particular coffee chain?

In all these situations we have made decisions to be loyal to companies that demonstrate authentic leadership, stewardship and governance.

ETHOS—THE CONTINUUM OF BEHAVIORS, CORE VALUES AND DECISION MAKING

Fear, greed and envy are part of our human condition. Since the beginning of time, they have been the root causes for more bloodletting, pain and suffering than any other malady. The ancient Greek philosophers were passionate about understanding these conditions and developed guiding principles (not rules, but principles—I will discuss the differences between the two later in the chapter) to raise the social consciousness of society. Socrates wrote, "The more men value money-making, the less they value virtue."[1] It was Socrates's protégés, Plato and Aristotle, who wrote that you can learn a lot about an organization by studying its *ethos*, which they defined as the distinguishing leadership behaviors, core values and decision-making process of a person, group or institution.

My research on ethos dates back to 2007, when I was offered the opportunity to head the newly established Institute for Leadership at the U.S. Coast Guard Academy. One of my pet projects was to try to find a concise answer to this question: Why was the Coast Guard so successful in its response to Hurricane Katrina, which hit New Orleans on August 29, 2005, when nearly every other government agency failed? The other agencies all had hurricane preparedness plans, staffs and budgets, yet the Coast Guard was the only one able to execute an extraordinary response to the crisis.

I was about nine months into my research when I came across the word *ethos*—immediately I recognized ethos as the concise answer to the Coast Guard question. It's because it has a well-defined ethos. No matter where you take a slice out of the organization, the most senior officers to the most junior enlisted men and women understand the Coast Guard's lifesaving role and mission. During Katrina, Coast Guard personnel didn't have to wait for orders or fill procurement forms out in triplicate—they knew what was expected of them, and they executed with confidence, knowing that their superiors would back them up. They were inspiring, and they demonstrated their capacity for principles-based service.

It doesn't take a hurricane for an organization to demonstrate that it has a well-defined ethos—that within the organization there is a consistent relationship between behaviors, core values and decision making. We see it every day with outstanding organizations such as Starbucks, Nordstrom, the Ritz-Carlton, Southwest and JetBlue. In the wealth management industry we also have a number of firms and organizations that have a well-defined ethos, and we must do more to reward and to promote these organizations.

ETHOS AND TRUST: THE CONTINUUM BETWEEN LEADERSHIP, STEWARDSHIP AND GOVERNANCE

For the wealth management industry, I would define *trust* as the point of intersection between leadership, stewardship and governance. The essence of trust is the modern-day expression of ethos. If you want to know whether an organization can be trusted, look at how it demonstrates its capacity for leadership, stewardship and governance. (See figure 9.1.)

Governance

Simply defined, governance is how we manage a prudent decision-making process. The financial services industry is highly regulated; it would seem that nearly every decision that needs to be managed has been fenced off by rules and regulations. Yet, being merely compliant with regulations is not the same as good governance.

You can tell some things about an organization by reading its disclosure documents and services agreements. Does the organization imply a certain relationship in the large print, then define a different one in the small? Are agreements written in plain English, or incomprehensible legalese? You can't learn to trust an organization if you're uncomfortable with its governance.

FIGURE 9.1   TRUST: THE CONTINUUM BETWEEN LEADERSHIP, STEWARDSHIP AND GOVERNANCE

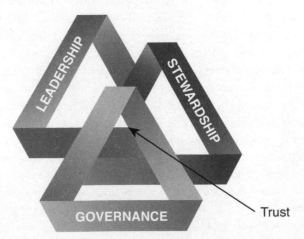

Source: Donald Trone, 3ethos

But it also is important whether an industry or organization is governed by rules or principles—does it have a code of conduct or a code of ethics? Most people use the terms interchangeably, but there are significant differences, especially when you want to establish trust. A code of conduct is based on rules, and a code of ethics is based on principles.

To illustrate the important differences between rules and principles, how do you react to the following statement? Thou shall not kill. If you are like most people, your mind is probably thinking of a number of exceptions: What about in the time of war, or in self-defense? What if, on the other hand, I said, Love one another. Now where does your mind go? You're caught, aren't you? There is no exception to be found.

Thou shall not kill is a rule; Love one another is a principle. A rule merely requires compliance, whereas a principle requires discernment, the ability to judge wisely and objectively. If you want to define a higher standard of care based on trust, you must do so with principles, not rules.

Stewardship

Stewardship is the passion and discipline to protect the long-term interests of others. Discernment is a prerequisite to stewardship: a good steward must be able to judge wisely and objectively. Obviously, when looking for a financial advisor, you want an advisor who is a great steward.

Imagine if we could build a Trust Thermometer. It might look something like figure 9.2:

FIGURE 9.2   THE TRUST THERMOMETER

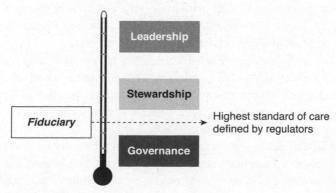

Source: Donald Trone, 3ethos

We could then put a thermometer under the financial advisor's tongue to see how high trust is registered. We could do away with rules and regulations and rely upon the advisor's temperature. If the advisor's temperature fell below Stewardship, you would know it was time to replace the advisor.

Note also where the legal definition of *fiduciary* would register on the thermometer—midway between Governance and Stewardship. Consistent with the theme of this chapter, higher standards of care are defined by leadership, stewardship and governance, not by being merely compliant with rules and regulations.

Leadership

In a world of complexity, individual investors are looking for advisors who are more than the trusted guides we've heard about for decades: they're looking for leaders. Authentic leadership can only occur when governance is aligned with principles and there is a high capacity for genuine stewardship. Leadership differs from being merely compliant in that it evokes a higher calling and requires a significantly higher level of trust.

Every worthwhile endeavor has a leadership component; this is especially true in wealth management. The simplest definition of leadership that can be applied in any situation is that a leader has the ability to inspire and the capacity to serve. Two questions arise from this definition:

Does your financial advisor inspire you?

Does your financial advisor have the capacity to serve your best interests?

If the answer is no to one or both these questions, then you're working with the wrong advisor, and probably the wrong financial services firm.

Each of the two leadership principles—the ability to inspire and the capacity to serve—can be further broken down into discrete elements to facilitate an assessment of a financial advisor's trust potential.

Integrity is the essence of a leader's ability to inspire—only a person of integrity can effectively serve as a leader. In turn, integrity is composed of three elements: character, competence and courage. Similar to ethos, one must demonstrate a continuum and a balance between the three elements to be known as a person of integrity.

In the wealth management industry, we can access public documents to get a good sense of a financial advisor's competence: their academic achievement; the regulatory licenses they possess; professional designations they may have earned; and special honors and awards that may have been bestowed by the industry. What is more difficult to assess is an advisor's character and courage, which are situational. We can get a sense of these two elements by observing the advisor's behavior, but no test has ever been devised to help determine when, and under what circumstances, an advisor may be tempted to subvert the best interests of his or her clients. However, we do know there is a high correlation between the conduct of a financial advisor and that of the advisor's firm. What is the tone at the top? Does the firm place a greater emphasis on growing revenue and profits than developing genuine leaders and stewards?

Engagement is the essence of the capacity to serve— only a financial advisor who is fully engaged can protect the best interests of clients. The three elements that must be kept in balance are purpose, process and passion. The absence or shortfall of any one of these three elements will result in disengagement.

Unlike the ability to inspire, which is largely subjective, the capacity to serve is much more objective. Of particular importance is the advisor's stated purpose and process—the details of the advisor's decision-making process, which brings us back full circle to an understanding of the advisor's governance and sense of stewardship.

The remaining element to engagement is passion. Does the financial advisor love:

- the work?
- the people the advisor works with?
- the firm to which the advisor belongs?

An answer of no to any of the above three questions should also raise a red flag. Love and passion are essential elements to effective leadership. A deficiency of either impacts a leader's ability to inspire others. In the absence of love and passion, an advisor may be more tempted to rationalize inappropriate behavior.

IN SUMMARY

In a free enterprise economy, the public has the capacity to reward good behavior and punish bad. However, the public has been reluctant to use the full force of that power to rid Wall Street of its bad actors. If your financial advisor does not inspire you, or is not authentic or aligned with your best interests, then you have the wrong advisor. If your wealth management firm does not have the capacity to serve your best interests—is not engaging with you—then you are working with the wrong firm.

Fear, greed and envy will not be kept in check by more rules and regulations. Legally defined standards of care, such as a fiduciary standard, will

merely define compliance requirements that must be met in order for a firm
or an advisor to conduct business. Such rules and regulations will never restore trust in the financial services industry.

The vast majority of wealth management firms and advisors are committed to serving their clients and to using their resources to "become a force for
good in the world," as John Taft writes in his preface to this book. The most
effective way to identify these great organizations is to look at how they demonstrate their capacity for authentic leadership, stewardship and governance.

NOTE

1. Plato, *Republic*, c. 360 BC, 4, Stephanus 550E. Quoted in Jerry Z. Muller, *The
   Mind and the Market: Capitalism in Modern European Thought* (New York: An-
   chor Books, 2002), 4.

PART IV

RESTORING CONFIDENCE IN EQUITY MARKETS

INTRODUCTION

John G. Taft

We need investors to trust in the markets again.
—Richard Ketchum, President and CEO,
the Financial Industry Regulatory Authority, May 2014

One of the facts of life in today's altered world is that the Federal Reserve and other central banks continue to engage in financial repression. This is the suppression of interest rates, at the expense of savers, for the benefit of borrowers. With short-term interest rates hovering close to zero percent, the stealth penalties for individuals who park savings in cash are significant. Savers see their purchasing power for the goods and services they consume eroded at the rate of inflation. That is a loss of 2 percent a year in today's environment, and more than 40 percent over the course of a typical retirement.

Intermediate- and longer-term bonds offer investors the prospect of earning a real rate of return, but at the risk of losing principal if and when interest rates rise again.

Only equities offer the potential of preserving purchasing power over long periods of time.

Yet ever since the financial crisis, individual investors have lost confidence in financial markets. Consequently, they have maintained outsized allocations in what they consider safe investments—cash and fixed-income securities. This has a number of bad social outcomes. For one thing, it will exacerbate the retirement savings crisis discussed in part 6. It also robs the economy of the patient long-term equity capital necessary to foster more robust economic growth.

Yet despite the fact investors are being forced by the Fed to own stocks to preserve their nest eggs, investors have never been more nervous and skeptical of equity markets. Michael Lewis's depiction of the world of high-speed trading in *Flash Boys* and his now-infamous assertion that the market is rigged is just the latest proof, as far as the public is concerned, that the stock and bond markets are financial shark tanks, perilous places to invest hard-earned savings.

But this is a classic case of throwing the baby out with the bathwater. Let's take a moment to remember the purpose of financial markets. Former U.S. Securities and Exchange Commission chair Mary Schapiro makes the case in chapter 10 for the importance of equity capital markets, which fund the "innovation and risk taking" that drives productivity and job growth and, ultimately, improves society.

"In simple terms, equity markets support our economic growth by turning the savings of investors into long-term capital for business, enabling a flow of funds from investors to inventors, entrepreneurs and established companies, and then back again to investors through dividends and capital gains," Schapiro writes.

The proper functioning of equity capital markets depends, more than anything else, on investor confidence. In turn, that requires transparent markets that provide investors with full, timely and accurate information. It also requires honest, competent financial intermediaries and market structures that work (not just some of the time, but all of the time). Ditto effective regulation and, perhaps most important, stewardship of the interests of shareholders through high standards of corporate governance.

Former Rotman School of Management Dean Roger L. Martin takes on what he believes is one of the culprits eroding investor confidence: equity-based compensation. Stock grants and grants of equity options were designed to better align the interests of professional executive managers (agents) with those of principals (the company's shareholders). For Martin, however, equity awards have had the unintended effect of focusing the attention of executives on the performance of their company's stock in the "expectations market" (the stock market) rather than on the performance of their company's physical products and services in the "real market."

The problem is so significant, Martin believes, that stock-based compensation actually *contributes* to stock market crashes and scandals, further undermining public trust in markets. Why? "The answer lies in the fact that executives become so concerned with how to maximize shareholder value for their own gain that they sacrifice long-term, sustainable growth to achieve it," he writes.

CHAPTER 10

EQUITY MARKET DEVELOPMENT AND CORPORATE GOVERNANCE IN EMERGING MARKETS

Mary Schapiro

U.S. Securities and Exchange Commission
Chair, 2009–2012

During this time of crisis and its aftermath, the attention of regulators has been rightly focused on strengthening the banking system and fortifying the regulatory structure that supports it. It is also important, however, that we not lose sight of the criticality of equity financing and capital markets to the economic success of nations, and that we create the necessary conditions for those markets to prosper and fuel growth.

Clearly, a healthy and resilient banking system is central to any nation's economic success. A recent Organisation for Economic Co-operation and Development (OECD) paper makes the point that banks play an "important and pivotal role in the financial system," and when a banking system becomes dysfunctional—as we saw in the United States during the financial crisis—the repercussions are broad and reverberate throughout the national and even the global economy.[1]

While the recent financial crisis and its regulatory response has focused all regulators—including the Securities and Exchange Commission (SEC)—on the banking system and issues of prudential supervision, bank capital standards, large bank resolution and use of derivatives, as a capital markets regulator, we at the SEC also tried to keep our attention squarely on the health and resiliency of the capital formation markets that have contributed so enormously to the success of the U.S. economy over many generations. So, as you can imagine, as a capital markets regulator for nearly 30 years, I am always anxious to talk about the role of equity markets in the success of businesses, economies and nations.

EQUITY FINANCING

While bank financing will always have a critical role to play, I would suggest that equity financing in an environment of transparency, including high-quality accounting, investor protection and resilient market infrastructure, is at least as—or perhaps more—important to economic growth in the long run.

Significant economic research supports the thesis that well-developed capital markets foster greater productivity and job growth. A November 2004 study by William Dudley, then chief economist at Goldman Sachs and now head of the Federal Reserve Bank of New York, and Glenn Hubbard, dean of Columbia University School of Business, found that in the United States and the United Kingdom, capital markets delivered three important benefits. First, they helped improve the allocation of capital and risk throughout the U.S. economy, thereby raising the average return on capital, attracting large inflows from abroad and providing a mechanism by which new businesses could raise capital. Second, higher productivity growth is evident and has resulted in higher real-wage growth. And third, despite higher productivity and wages, employment growth in countries with robust capital markets had been higher than elsewhere.[2]

Empirical evidence from the International Monetary Fund (IMF) suggests that although an efficient banking sector is necessary for the development of an equity market, there can be many constraints that prevent banks from providing long-term investments, including the rising cost of capital. Equity markets directly benefit countries by avoiding reliance on debt during times of rising interest rates, as equity markets serve as channels for savings.[3]

Moreover, equity investments provide managerial discipline to provide a more efficient allocation of capital and ensure that managerial resources are utilized effectively. For instance, according to IMF research, in developing countries, where a majority of the equity ownership is concentrated in the portfolios of large shareholders, these owners find it beneficial to monitor and ensure there is financial discipline within the business entity.[4]

In this same regard, New York University researchers in 1993 sampled 40 industrial and developing countries and found that the higher the ratio of stock market trades to GDP, the higher the growth of per capita income, suggesting a significant relationship between the development of stock markets and overall economic growth.[5]

Despite the clear benefits of equity financing—which I will talk about in a moment—it is no secret that, despite some resurgence in 2013 and 2014, the past decade has seen a dramatic decline in initial public offerings (IPOs) and exchange listings of securities, as well as in the amount of capital raised, particularly in OECD countries. In the United States, critics often point to these declining numbers to suggest that we are witnessing the demise of the public corporation and, hence, equity financing rather than attributing this decline to cyclical or temporary phenomenon. I would suggest that the.dot-com bust; a prolonged, near-zero interest rate environment; a weakening of investor confidence in the integrity of market structure abetted by excessive complexity and volatility; the narrowing of analyst coverage of smaller companies; and the coming of age of foreign exchanges have more to do with the decline in U.S. listings than the demise of the corporation itself.

At the same time, the overall picture for equity markets is actually somewhat more mixed. OECD research shows us that public offerings (initial and secondary) between 2006 and 2011 by emerging market companies increased by more than five times the amount of equity raised between 2001 and 2005, and exceeded total funds raised by OECD companies. And the numbers for secondary public offerings show that, for every year of the last decade, secondary public offerings by OECD-based nonfinancial companies exceeded the proceeds from IPOs.[6]

Despite the disappointing IPO numbers, there is little doubt that equity financing is and will remain the most effective and efficient vehicle for financing long-term ventures. As OECD's Mats Isaksson's recent paper describes, equity "can be used to finance projects with uncertain and long-term returns, such as research, product development, innovation or the opening of new markets. These characteristics make equity unique and the only standardized financial instrument dedicated to finance genuine innovation and value creation."[7]

In simple terms, equity markets support our economic growth by turning the savings of investors into long-term capital for business, enabling a flow of funds from investors to inventors, entrepreneurs and established companies, and then back again to investors through dividends and capital gains. It is funding this innovation and risk taking that equity is so well suited to do, in part because, as the OECD and other commenters have pointed out, equity has only a residual claim on corporate earnings—there is no right to a dividend—and the ability to transfer shares in the secondary market permits a shareholder to have a different time horizon for investment than the corporation has, and to easily exit or increase his ownership interest if his view of the company changes.[8]

In the United States in particular, the regulatory burdens of being a public company—brought about by the Sarbanes-Oxley Act, SEC rules and stock exchange requirements, and most recently the Dodd-Frank Act—are often cited as the primary reasons for the decline in listings. But while equity financing in the public markets brings with it many obligations—disclosure, financial audits, corporate governance requirements and more—it is still a critical path to sustainable growth for many companies. For example, up until the point of its IPO announcement, Twitter had difficulty generating a profit, claiming its investments had limited its margins.[9] CEO Dick Costolo claimed that taking his company public allowed him to ensure Twitter is ready for the "visibility to the future." Further, the IPO filing enabled him to invest in "product innovation and cadence of product innovation" to improve Twitter's capabilities beyond its partnerships, and grow its core business.[10]

Similarly, when the Nasdaq Stock Market chair talked of bringing Nasdaq public, he said, "Offering shares to the public is a natural next step in the evolution of Nasdaq. When the time is right, we will do it. The result will be a Nasdaq with more resources, better able to compete and improve its market for investors and companies around the globe."[11] He added that Nasdaq looked forward to the offering as a chance to increase the market's competitive stance and allow for greater investments in technology. Expenditures for technology development and to open new markets and develop new products, given their magnitude—and riskiness—have spurred Nasdaq and other exchanges to themselves tap the public equity markets.

Before equity markets can flourish, there must exist the basic infrastructure of a banking system and a regime of private property and contract law that allows transfer of ownership with certainty and judicial enforcement, provisions for competition and bankruptcy, sensible macroeconomic policies and capable regulation.[12] And there is just one additional requirement: investor confidence. But it has several critical components:

1. Markets must be transparent. Investors must be provided complete, timely and honest quantitative and qualitative information about the companies they seek to invest in. They require accounting that is rigorous and transparent and not subject to political pressures. Markets need, and investors will demand, well-developed standards of corporate governance. Shareholders—those who own the corporation—must be able to exercise their governance rights, and those rights should be protected by law.

2. Financial intermediaries must be competent, financially capable and honest.

3. The market structure—the systems for trading, clearing and settlement of securities transactions and payments—must be fair, resilient and reliable.
4. And finally, investor confidence demands vigilant, informed and adequately funded regulators who promote investor protection and a level playing field, including rigorous enforcement of the law and rules.

Transparency and Disclosure

Because investing is a risk-taking exercise, it is essential that investors have access to the information necessary to make informed decisions. In the United States, this has meant an ever-broadening scope of information made public at the time of a securities offering and thereafter annually, quarterly and even nearly immediately, in connection with specific events.

This disclosure-based system is the foundation of the public equity markets in the United States, since the SEC does not approve or endorse investments. Rather, the role of the agency is to ensure that investors have been told all the relevant information from which they can make their own decisions about how to allocate capital.[13] In this regard, the agency's staff selectively reviews company filings to monitor information quality and completeness and ensure adherence to accounting and disclosure requirements. The agency's staff routinely requires companies to enhance and clarify their disclosure. The scope of required disclosure is continually updated to encompass emerging risks, such as cyber threats, new accounting standards, and legislative and corporate developments.[14]

Of course, all of the requirements and even the vigilance of the regulators do not alone ensure that every company's disclosure will be complete and forthright; certainly the history books are replete with examples of restatements and accounting and disclosure frauds. In this regard, the ability to rely on the critical gatekeepers—auditors, lawyers, research analysts and investment bankers—is an important part of the fabric of truthful disclosure. And when any or all of these fail, rigorous criminal and civil enforcement is vital.

The role of gatekeepers in promoting the fundamental honesty of corporate disclosure has grown dramatically. The gatekeeper's role has transformed from that of an auditor to a protector of public and stakeholder interests.[15] For instance, more than a decade ago, the International Organization of Securities Commissions (IOSCO) adopted a comprehensive set of Objectives and Principles of Securities Regulation (known as IOSCO Principles), which emphasize the importance of the role of a gatekeeper in any institution. One of the ideals states, "Independent auditors play a critical role in enhancing the reliability of financial information by attesting as to whether the financial statements prepared by management fairly present the financial position and past performance of the public enterprise in compliance with accepted accounting standards," ultimately improving investor confidence.[16]

These ideals have grown since the financial crisis to include appropriate mechanisms for continuous improvement in auditing methodology, enforced objectivity within auditing standards and practices, as well as provisions for continuing professional education.[17] The stated goals of the IOSCO Principles are to protect investors through information disclosure, ensure markets are fair and transparent, and reduce systematic risk through efficiency, all of which rely on the soundness and enforcement of our gatekeepers.[18]

Intermediaries

The vast majority of investors interact with the equity markets through intermediaries—either through brokers, who assist them with advice or the execution of securities transactions and custody of their assets, or through collective investment vehicles such as mutual funds, hedge funds or pension funds.

According to OECD and IOSCO data, in 2010, mutual funds, pension funds and insurance companies held roughly half of the listed equities in the world. Thus, a critical component of investor confidence is confidence in the integrity and capability of the intermediaries. Here again, disclosure is the foundation of confidence—disclosure about the risks of particular investments or strategies, costs and fees, and conflicts of interest of the money manager or broker. In addition, safekeeping of investor assets; best execution and fair pricing of securities transactions; competency of advisors; adequacy of supervision; and access to remedies when an investor has been treated unfairly are necessary components for investor trust.

Market Structure

Investor confidence can be deeply shaken by failures of the mechanics of trading markets. When equity market structure breaks down—if it fails to provide the necessary and expected fairness, stability and efficiency—investors and companies pull back, raising costs and reducing growth.

Investors understand that they will make or lose money on an investment depending on the performance of the company in which they have invested. What they do not understand—and should not have to worry about—is whether the trading mechanisms themselves will fail to function and cause them losses or whether the strategies of other traders put them at a serious disadvantage. Whether the failure is caused by technological glitches or human error—events like the Flash Crash in May 2010 or the botched Facebook IPO or the massive trading error in the summer of 2013 by Everbright Securities in China, or any of a number of other exchange or participant failures—serious and potentially long-lasting damage is done to investor confidence. And because the markets are, first and foremost, price-discovery mechanisms, real harm is caused when investors flee and participation declines.

Regulators

Fair rules of the road and effective oversight and enforcement support a system that protects providers and consumers of capital alike, brings stability to a complex marketplace and undergirds robust economic growth. Of course, regulators must always appreciate that regulation has costs. But, as we have seen time and time again, inadequate and ineffective regulation and enforcement have costs as well—oftentimes costs that are far greater than any rule could ever impose.

If we think about issues such as insider trading—an area of particular regulatory enforcement focus in the United States—it would be hard to conclude that rampant insider trading does not severely damage investor confidence in the integrity and fairness of the markets. The willingness and capacity of regulators to prevent and punish such activity is important to maintaining investor confidence and, hence, investor willingness to entrust their capital to the markets.

CORPORATE GOVERNANCE

Last, but in no sense least, corporate governance is critical to the success of equity markets. As Mats Isaksson's paper illuminates, partly to compensate for the lack of a fixed claim on corporate earnings, equity comes with a set of rights that not only protect the equity holder from abuse, but also provide the opportunity to shape the direction of the corporation in a way that aligns the interest of the shareholder and the company in long-term prosperity.[19]

Of the many variations of the definition of *corporate governance*, I think the best has been articulated by the OECD:

> Corporate governance involves a set of relationships between a company's management, its board, its shareholders and other stakeholders. Corporate governance also provides the structure through which the objectives of the company are set, and the means of attaining those objectives and monitoring performance, are determined. . . . The presence of an effective corporate governance system, within an individual company and across an

economy as a whole, helps to provide a degree of confidence that is necessary for the proper functioning of a market economy. As a result, the cost of capital is lower and firms are encouraged to use resources more efficiently, thereby underpinning growth.[20]

Governance exists at both the country level and the level of individual companies. National-level standards are developed in the context of political, cultural, historical and legal infrastructure and characteristics. As a result, there is great variability around the world when comparing governance requirements from country to country. These national standards in turn set the broader context for company-level governance structures.[21] And where those national standards are less developed, or where there is flexibility for a company to define its governance, there is great variability across companies within a country. Research has shown that good governance is significantly related to valuation, and is even more important in countries with weak overall legal systems or weak investor protection from the courts.[22]

In the United States, our debates around corporate governance tend toward the narrow and specific: How granular should the disclosure of executive compensation be? Should the board have both an audit committee and a risk committee? Should the role of CEO and chair of the board be separated? Many other countries are grappling with more fundamental questions of governance, namely, the basic rights of investors, such as the right to access a wide array of audited financial and risk information about the company and management; to vote on important corporate matters such as extraordinary transactions or the election of independent and competent board members; fair treatment and protection of minority shareholders; the exercise of ownership rights; and the effective oversight and monitoring of management.

Extensive academic and industry research tells us that the quality of governance matters to investors, and there is good reason for this. Research by the World Bank shows that better corporate governance is highly correlated with better operating performance and market valuation.[23] And as the OECD notes,

> The degree to which corporations observe basic principles of good corporate governance is an increasingly important factor for investment decisions. Of particular relevance is the relationship between corporate governance practices and the increasingly international character of investment. International flows of capital enable companies to access financing from a much larger pool of investors. If countries are to reap the full benefits of the global capital market, and if they are to attract long-term "patient" capital, corporate governance arrangements must be credible, well understood across borders and adhere to internationally accepted principles.[24]

I believe the OECD has this exactly right. And as it further notes, "Even if corporations do not rely primarily on foreign sources of capital, adherence to good corporate governance practices will help improve the confidence of domestic investors, reduce the cost of capital, underpin the good functioning of financial markets, and ultimately induce more stable sources of financing."[25]

At the end of the day, shareholders are owners. They may take a more or less active role in the governance of the companies they own. But it is important to them, when making investment decisions, to know that they can appropriately influence the direction and conduct of the corporation and that they have options other than selling their stock if they are dissatisfied. As we continue the complex work of rebuilding and strengthening the institutions of our banking system and fortifying supervision and regulation, it is critically important that we also focus our energies on ensuring that the foundations for strong equity markets—disclosure, transparency, competent and honest intermediaries, vigilant gatekeepers and regulators, a robust market infrastructure and well-developed corporate governance—also remain firmly in our sights.

NOTES

1. Organisation for Economic Co-operation and Development, "The Role of Banks, Equity Markets and Institutional Investors in Long-Term Financing for Growth and Development," February 2013, http://www.oecd.org/finance/private-pensions/G20reportLTFinancingForGrowthRussianPresidency2013.pdf.

2. William C. Dudley and R. Glenn Hubbard, "How Capital Markets Enhance Economic Performance and Facilitate Job Creation," Goldman Sachs Global Markets Institute, November 2004, https://www0.gsb.columbia.edu/faculty/ghubbard/Articles%20for%20Web%20Site/How%20Capital%20Markets%20Enhance%20Economic%20Performance%20and%20Facilit.pdf.

3. Manmohan S. Kumar, *Growth, Acquisition, and Investment: An Analysis of the Growth of Industrial Firms and Their Overseas Activities* (Cambridge, UK: Cambridge University Press, 1985).

4. Robert Feldman and Manmohan Kumar, "Emerging Equity Markets: Growth, Benefits and Policy Concerns," *The World Bank Research Observer* 10, no. 2 (August 1995): 181–220, http://www-wds.worldbank.org/external/default/WDSContentServer/IW3P/IB/1995/08/01/000009265_3980420172604/Rendered/PDF/multi_page.pdf.

5. Ibid.

6. Expert Group on Equity Markets and Corporate Governance in Emerging Markets, "Equity Market Development and Corporate Governance: Background Report and Issues for Discussion," Organisation for Economic Co-operation and Development, January 2014.

7. Mats Isaksson and Serdar Celik, "Who Cares? Corporate Governance in Today's Equity Markets," OECD Corporate Governance Working Papers no. 8 (Paris: OECD Publishing), 2013, http://dx.doi.org/10.1787/5k47zw5kdnmp-en.

8. Ibid.

9. Yoree Koh, "Watch Twitter's IPO 'Roadshow' Pitch," *Wall Street Journal*, October 25, 2013, http://blogs.wsj.com/digits/2013/10/25/watch-twitters-ipo-road show-pitch/.

10. "Transcript: Twitter CEO Dick Costolo Speaks One-On-One with CNBC's Julia Boorstin Today," CNBC, November 7, 2013, http://www.cnbc.com/id/10 1179100.

11. "NASDAQ to Go Public in 2002," CNN Money, April 26, 2001, http://cnnfn .cnn.com/2001/04/26/deals/nasdaq/.

12. Dudley and Hubbard, "How Capital Markets Enhance Economic Performance and Facilitate Job Creation," 23.

13. US Securities and Exchange Commission, www.sec.gov.

14. Ibid.

15. Robin R. Radtke, "Auditors as Gatekeepers for Public Interest," The University of Texas at San Antonio, Department of Accounting, June 2004, accessed on the American Accounting Association website, http://aaahq.org/AM2004/cpe /Ethics/Session5A_03.pdf.

16. International Organization of Securities Commissions, "Principles for Auditor Insight: A Statement of the Technical Committee of the International Organization of Securities Commissions," October 2002, http://www.iosco.org /library/pubdocs/pdf/IOSCOPD134.pdf.

17. Ibid.

18. Antonio Marcacci, "IOSCO: The World Standard Setter for Globalized Financial Markets," *Richmond Journal of Global Law & Business* 12, no. 1 (March 27, 2013): 23–43, http://rjglb.richmond.edu/wp-content/uploads/2013/04/RGL102 .pdf.

19. Isaksson and Celik, "Who Cares? Corporate Governance in Today's Equity Markets."

20. Organisation for Economic Co-operation and Development, "OECD Principles of Corporate Governance," 2004, http://www.oecd.org/corporate/ca/cor porategovernanceprinciples/31557724.pdf.

21. Leora F. Klapper and Inessa Love, "Corporate Governance, Investor Protection and Performance in Emerging Markets," World Bank, Policy Research Working Paper 2818, April 2002, http://elibrary.worldbank.org/doi/pdf/10.1596 /1813-9450-2818.

22. Ibid., 19.

23. Ibid.; see also Paul Gompers, Joy L. Ishi, and Andrew Metrick, "Corporate Governance and Equity Prices," National Bureau of Economic Research, Working Paper 8449, 2001, http://www.nber.org/papers/w8449.pdf; Rafael La Porta, Florencio Lopez-de-Silanes, Andrei Shleifer, and Robert W. Vishny, "Legal Determinants of External Finance," *Journal of Finance* 52 (1997): 1131–1150, http://scholar.harvard.edu/shleifer/files/legaldeterminants.pdf; Davide Lombardo and Marco Pagamo, "Legal Determinant of the Return on Equity," Mimeo, 2000, http://ssrn.com/abstract=209310.

24. OECD, "OECD Principles of Corporate Governance."

25. Ibid.

CHAPTER 11

GET REAL

HOW TO RECOVER AUTHENTICITY
IN OUR FINANCIAL SYSTEM

Roger L. Martin

Dean, Rotman School of Management,
University of Toronto, 1998–2013

"*Can we ever trust bankers again?*" The BBC let the question hang over all its reporting on the increasingly sordid details of the London interbank offered rate (Libor) fixing scandal.[1] Barclays, the financial institution at the center of it all, admitted that its actions had likely "decimated" the public trust in banks.[2] Multinational investigations revealed emails between traders and rate setters at banks in the United Kingdom, Europe, North America and Japan that offered bribes for their counterparts' help in fixing the key lending rate. Considering that over $300 trillion in financial contracts are written on the basis of Libor, the scandal had massive global implications.[3]

The ubiquitous interest rate is set by a group of leading banks, which submit their rates for 10 currencies and 15 loan durations. The top and bottom quartiles of these rates are discarded, and an average is calculated.[4] The banks have a choice of what rate to submit—the final decision always rests with an individual within each bank—and so the door was left open for manipulation and abuse. The offending banks took advantage of the opportunity, throughout the 2000s, to artificially inflate or deflate their rates depending on which scenario would most benefit each bank at the time. The rate manipulations were real, illegal and widespread, and touched banks in several developed economies. When they were discovered, the banks faced fines in the billions of dollars.

Still reeling from the 2008 global financial crisis, the banks hardly needed another negative story. Their reputations were already eroded, as demonstrated in the latest survey from the Edelman Group—a public relations firm that publishes an annual "Trust Barometer." Of the industries surveyed, banks and financial services rank as the least trustworthy, trailing even the perennial basement-dwellers, energy and media.[5]

What did people believe were the causes of financial scandals such as Libor? The results Edelman got from this question were telling. Twenty-three percent thought the cause was "a corporate culture driven by compensation/bonuses," namely, that the traders manipulated Libor because the traders earned a higher bonus as a result. Twenty-five percent figured corporate corruption was the culprit, and 11 percent indicated that conflicts of interest were the root of the scandals.[6] All told, a significant majority of people believed the scandals were caused by factors fully under the control of financial services firms, rather than external factors such as a lack of regulation or changes in the economy.

Bankers aren't alone in this type of compensation-driven behavior. In fact, it's endemic to the larger business ecosystem. Our systems of rewards and compensation are misaligned in a way that breeds inauthenticity in our executives. This inauthenticity is at the root of society's current distrust of business writ large, not just the financial sector, although finance is the current poster child.

It wasn't always thus. Forty years ago, if you were a gambler betting that corruption, conflicts of interest and a culture driven by compensation and/or bonuses would be common today, you would have been a contrarian. Yet in hindsight we can see the seeds of scandal, sown almost 40 years ago in the wake of an influential article by two academics, Michael Jensen and William Meckling. Both at the University of Rochester's Simon Business School in 1976, Jensen and Meckling published a paper in the *Journal of Financial Economics* entitled "Theory of the Firm: Managerial Behavior, Agency Costs and Ownership Structure."[7] At the time, they couldn't have known what an impact the article would have on compensation practices across industries. The article introduced the world to *agency theory*, including, as a central concept, the *principal-agent problem*. In Jensen and Meckling's model, shareholders are the *principals* of a firm—that is to say, they own the firm and benefit from its growth and success. Executives and other employees are deemed *agents*—hired on behalf of the principals to manage and run the business in their stead. The principal-agent problem occurs because the agents have an inherent incentive to organize their activities in a way that benefits themselves rather than the principals. For example, an executive may declare commercial air travel to be too inconvenient and tiring, wasting valuable time that could be better spent focusing on the business. In response, the company might purchase a private corporate jet for the executive. Productivity may increase, but the jet likely costs the owners of the company more than that increase in productivity. The purchase of that corporate jet at the expense of earnings for the principals creates an *agency cost*.

Jensen and Meckling argued that it is both bad for shareholders and wasteful for the economy when executives use the firm's resources for cushy perks. Rather, they said, the firm should be laser-focused on one objective—to maximize returns to shareholders. And to achieve that goal, the logic followed, executives must be incented in a way that aligned their interests with those of the principals: agency costs would be eliminated and shareholder profits would be maximized. They suggested stock-based compensation for executives, in essence aligning their interests directly with those of shareholders. Under such a scheme, executives would be intensely interested in increasing shareholder value because their own compensation would increase concurrently.

Despite its logical elegance, the practice has not proved to be without limitation and side effects. Most notably, stock-based compensation had the unfortunate effect of joining together two hitherto distinct markets: the real market and the expectations market.

The real market is the world in which companies build factories and design and produce products (or services) that are bought and sold. Revenue is earned, genuine expenses are paid and actual dollars of profit are shown on the bottom line. Largely, this is the world that is under the control of companies and their executives, and the reason why companies were founded in the first place.

The expectations market, however, differs a great deal, particularly where substance is concerned. Whereas the real market trades in physical goods and services, the expectations market trades company shares between investors. This should sound familiar—the expectations market is more popularly known as the stock market. In this market, investors do their best to estimate the future value of the current real activities of a company. Using that estimate of the future as guidance, investors then decide whether the market price for the stock is likely to go up or down, and they buy or sell on that basis. Since there exists a multitude of investors participating in the expectations market at any one time, the consensus view of these investors for future company performance then determines the share price.

The mechanics of the stock market make intuitive sense. Provided a fair and transparent flow of information (a lofty assumption, in some instances), investors buy and sell shares at fair prices. And if the stock market were left only to investors, the system would work just fine. But because of the popularity of stock-based compensation, we now have sitting executives who also hold large blocks of company stock and future options for additional stock. This is a problem because it produces executives who worry more about how their company behaves in the stock (expectations) market than about how it performs in the real market.

The practice of linking executive compensation to the expectations market was once quite rare. Before the 1970s, executives were evaluated on whether or not the company earned real profits. They were compensated with a base salary and a bonus for meeting real market performance targets. In 1970, for example, stock-based incentives accounted for less than 1 percent of CEO remuneration.[8] Jensen and Meckling turned this practice on its head. The new theory was that the best way to spur executives to perform in the real market was to make their personal compensation significantly dependent on company performance in the expectations market. After 1976, executive compensation became increasingly stock-based, with dramatic upside when executives produced stock price increases.

The list of the ten highest-paid American CEOs of 2012 shows, for the first time, all ten earning over $100 million in total compensation, the vast majority from realized gains on stock options. Facebook CEO Mark Zuckerberg earned a base salary of just over $500,000, but the company's initial public offering netted him nearly $2.3 billion in profits. Second-place finisher Richard Kinder, of energy company Kinder Morgan, earned a salary of just $1 but added more than $1.1 billion in restricted stock profits.[9] The pattern repeats itself down the line. The pervasiveness of granting executives stock options as part of their compensation packages is considered good governance as it properly aligns executive incentives with those of shareholders. The financial crashes of the dot-com bubble from 2000 to 2002 and the broader market in 2008–09 clearly did nothing to diminish the prevailing theory; in fact, they strengthened it.

So why does stock-based compensation lead to stock market crashes and scandals? The answer lies in the fact that executives become so concerned with how to maximize shareholder value for their own gain that they sacrifice long-term, sustainable growth to achieve it. Executives focus on playing in the expectations market (under the guise of maximizing shareholder value) rather than on building sustainable value in the real market (by building real goods, selling real services and earning real profits).

The problem with the expectations market is that it demands continually rising stock prices, *ad infinitum*. And so a CEO must work endlessly to raise the expectations for his company among investors. In reality, of course, they can't rise forever. When it becomes clear that the expectations for the future performance of a company are too far out of line, they come crashing back down. If this crash happens across a sector, it tends to spark a crisis. All too often, investors lose out while the CEO does just fine, having cashed in millions of dollars of options ahead of time.

In theory, the connection between real market performance and expectations market performance should be quite close. As ' ng as profits are made in the real market, the expectations market should reward real success. In actual practice, this link is tenuous at best. Consider the example of Microsoft. For the better part of the last 15 years, Microsoft stock has traded (adjusted for splits) between $20 and $30, trending slightly higher in 2013 and 2014. Despite being criticized in the business press for its poor stock price performance, Microsoft has enjoyed spectacular real market success in the same time frame: the company nearly tripled its revenue between 2000 and 2010. But the expectations for Microsoft were already so high when it traded above $50 in the dot-com heyday that despite phenomenal success in real terms, the expectations market offers no reward to the company. It merely meets, rather than exceeds, its lofty expectations.

So we see that activity in the real market has little bearing on company performance in the expectations market over substantial periods of time. And we know that stock-based executive compensation incents executives to behave in ways that improve the value of their stock options. Therefore, executives must focus on managing the expectations market if they want to maximize their personal compensation.

Despite this powerful drawback, the practice of stock-based compensation could perhaps be excused if, in fact, it produced better returns for shareholders. The numbers, however, show that the results are a wash at best. More likely, investors are worse off when executives receive stock-based compensation. Let's examine why.

To begin, we must travel back in time to 1976 (our stake in the ground as far as aligning executive compensation with shareholder returns). Several decades earlier, American companies were run by CEO-owners with names like Rockefeller, Mellon, Carnegie and Morgan. During the middle of the last century, American business saw the rise of a new class of hired help—the professional manager—who began running companies on behalf of their owners. It was this shift to professional managers (with owners at an arm's length) that Jensen and Meckling found so troubling and sought to fix. They worried that professional managers were enriching themselves at the expense of their owners, behaving in such a way that an owner-manager would not have done. Shareholders therefore earned suboptimal returns as managers squandered firm resources on themselves.

The data do not necessarily bear out this argument. One way of looking at CEO compensation and its effect on shareholder returns is to determine the total compensation earned by the CEO per dollar of net income earned by the company. The higher the resulting amount, the greater the "take" of management, in this case the CEO, versus the shareholders. Between 1960 and 1980, CEO compensation per dollar of net income earned by the 365 largest publicly traded American companies fell by 33 percent.[10] In this time period, CEOs earned more for their shareholders for less and less relative compensation. While these CEOs may have been squandering firm resources in other ways, they were not extracting resources out of the firm to the benefit of their own compensation.

As the Jenson and Meckling theory gained steam in the late 1970s, we see a distinct shift in CEO compensation. After falling steadily for the previous 20 years, from 1980 to 1990, CEO compensation per dollar of net earnings doubled. Between 1990 and 2000, the figure quadrupled—an eightfold increase in CEO compensation after their interests supposedly became aligned with those of shareholders.[11] The story for better incentives for ownership does not appear to hold water.

Yes, these numbers paint a dark picture, but perhaps all would be forgotten if during the same period from 1980 to 2000 shareholders did better as well. As the saying goes, a rising tide lifts all boats, and executives were on one wild, upward ride.

Unfortunately, the numbers once again do not support the argument that stock-based compensation serves shareholders well. The beginning of the shift to professional managers from CEO-owners can be marked from the publication of a seminal 1933 book on management by Adolf A. Berle and Gardiner C. Means called *The Modern Corporation and Private Property*. From 1933 to Jensen and Meckling's article in 1976, total real compound annual return on the S&P 500 was 7.5 percent.[12] Since 1976, the same calculation on the S&P 500 yields a return of only 6.5 percent.[13]

It is difficult to argue that the age of shareholder value maximization has worked out well for shareholders. At the same time, it is also difficult to make the case that shareholders have done definitively worse. While the difference between 7.5 percent and 6.5 percent is meaningful, especially when measured over 30 years, relative parity can be achieved by manipulating the period dates sufficiently. Either way, there is little credibility to the theory that shareholders have done better since 1976 than they had before.

Stock-based compensation is bad for society in other ways too, leading to more sinister outcomes. With executive incentives ever more closely tied to the expectations market, the personal financial rewards for gaming that market grow stronger. And with the promise of those rewards comes inauthentic behavior.

A study in the *Journal of Accounting and Economics* showed that, regardless of the level of performance, a company's stock performs better if the company meets or beats analyst earnings expectations.[14] For instance, a company's share price is likely to perform better if it earned $1.10 a share when the consensus estimate was $1.08 a share than if it earned $1.12 a share when the estimate was $1.15. Superior performance in the expectations market trumps better absolute performance in the real market.

The peer-reviewed evidence left little room for interpretation: the motivation to meet or gently exceed analyst expectations in order to earn better returns in the expectations market is clear. So pervasive is this desire, in fact, that a whole informal field was created in its service—earnings management. In this context, earnings management means tailoring returns to meet market expectations rather than to reflect actual performance. Earnings management manifests itself primarily in two ways: accounting manipulations and expectations management.

The nature of financial accounting is that many of the decisions on how to represent the financial statements are subjective. When executives seek to manipulate their statements, however, they push the boundaries of what would normally be considered acceptable practice. They may account for sales in the current quarter that really should go in the next, shift expenses in the opposite direction or even hide the expenses entirely. All of these manipulations are risky, and sometimes firms get caught. Dell, for example, was accused of manipulating the accounting for certain payments from Intel to buy Intel chips rather than those from competitor Advanced Micro Devices. The ethics of that arrangement aside, Dell was accused of accounting for those payments in such a way to produce the "right" quarterly earnings results for analysts between 2002 and 2006. Despite denying any wrongdoing, Dell nonetheless paid a $100 million fine, with the most senior executives during the manipulations also paying personal multimillion-dollar fines as part of the settlement.[15] This is certainly not the only example of companies flouting accounting standards for their own benefit, yet despite the risk, firms continue the practice because the rewards for doing so are so clear.

For those with less stomach for accounting fraud, there exists another way to manage earnings: attempt to directly influence analyst expectations. In this practice, smooth-talking executives will "talk the analysts down." Rather than report truthfully on the state of the company's real market operations, executives slyly convince analysts that the company will not be as successful as the analysts currently believe it to be (but they stop short of declaring that the company will not meet the targets—that is a huge earnings management faux pas). This practice is not illegal, provided that everybody gets the information at the same time. But it does not do much to engender trust in big business and the financial sector. And it certainly does little to improve firm competitiveness over time.

As executives became more aware of stock price dynamics and the resulting boost to their personal compensation, their proficiency at managing earnings improved at the same time. From 1983 to 1993, companies met or beat earnings expectations roughly 50 percent of the time—a perfectly acceptable output from what ought to be a random system. From 1994 to 1997, however, companies were able to meet or exceed expectations almost 70 percent of time—a dramatic improvement.[16]

The most proficient companies at managing their earnings, however, performed at even higher percentages. As Michael Jensen noted, General Electric, during the heart of the Jack Welch era, met or beat analyst forecasts in 46 of 48 quarters from 1989 to 2001—a 96 percent hit rate. Perhaps even more impressive, GE hit the forecasts to the penny 89 percent of the time. For those rogue quarters where GE missed the exact number, only twice did it miss on the low side (by 1 and 2 cents, respectively).[17] Nobody would argue that GE is incapable of performing well in the real market, but the extreme precision of its earnings suggests that the influence of the expectations market among the executives was as important, if not more so, than performance in the real market.

Regulators periodically try to close loopholes that allow executives to manage their earnings, especially those that involve accounting manipulations. In the wake of the accounting scandals at Enron, WorldCom, Adelphia and others, the U.S. government enacted Sarbanes-Oxley, which regulators figured would make it more difficult for executives to manipulate the books in their favor. John Graham, Campbell Harvey and Shiva Rajgopal set out to investigate that regulatory theory. The good news was that, in looking at 400 executives from major American public companies, they found that in the wake of the Sarbanes-Oxley regulations, executives were loath to use accounting measures to smooth earnings. But the bad news was a worrisome discovery: "The majority of managers would avoid initiating a positive net present value project if it meant falling short of the current quarter's consensus earnings. Similarly, more than three-fourths of the surveyed executives would give up economic value in exchange for smooth earnings."[18]

The upshot is clear: not only are executives willing to talk down analysts to manage earnings, but they are even willing to sacrifice the long-term financial performance of their companies in the real market in order to satisfy the short-term demands of the expectations market. Given these findings, what is surprising about the Edelman Trust Barometer results is not that society doesn't have much trust for the financial sector, but that it has any trust at all!

So what do we do?

There are some quick fixes we can enact to bring authenticity back into the roles of our executives and the financial system. Looking at earnings management, governments have clamped down significantly on accounting manipulations, but they have not taken action on the executive-analyst relationship. Given that executives work to manage analyst expectations to buoy stock prices and sacrifice the long-term real success of their corporations in favor of smooth earnings to appease the analyst community, this relationship needs to be addressed.

Doing away with guidance—quarterly or otherwise—would be a huge step in restoring executive authenticity. In current practice, guidance provides little in the way of societal value. Executives hold conference calls in which they try to predict what will happen in a market over which they exercise little control. Eliminating guidance calls would turn executives away from an obsession for these arbitrary numbers and back toward the real business goal of delighting customers and creating real value.

A first step in achieving this outcome of a guidance-free world would be to repeal the safe harbor provision of the Private Securities Litigation Reform Act. Instituted in 1995, this provision protects company executives offering earnings guidance; executives can therefore make predictions using "forward-looking" statements and avoid lawsuits when their predictions are wrong. The safe harbor provision is too powerful a tool for managing expectations and earnings, because executives exploit its leniency by feeding misinformation to the analyst community. Without it, guidance would prove less meaningful because executives would be unwilling to say anything at all and would therefore diminish the level of importance placed on playing in the expectations market.

Paring back the means by which executives can manipulate the expectations market is one step toward generating greater authenticity. Taking the influence of the expectations market away from those executives is an important complementary step. The irresistible allure of stock-based compensation means that executives will always work tirelessly to game the expectations market in their own favor. Further, this approach has been shown to be of no net benefit to shareholders. So why have stock-based compensation at all?

On the whole, companies that employ significant stock-based compensation packages do not outperform those without. Which is not to say that monetary incentives are across-the-board harmful. Rather, in order to have an authentic executive compensation system and financial system, those incentives must be based in the real market—ideally in measures that include delighting one's customer.

Grounding the executive role back into the real market adds the benefit of delivering authentic rewards—the feeling of pride in contributing to a company's goal, in offering the best product or service to customers and in winning against one's competition. Only by having goals set in this real market can authenticity in our executives and financial systems be restored. The chief financial officer of one of America's largest and most successful companies that has moved closer to real market measures says companies should "let results speak for themselves, and let them speak over time."[19]

NOTES

1. "Libor Scandal: Can We Ever Trust Bankers Again?" *BBC News*, May 8, 2013. accessed March 12, 2014, http://www.bbc.com/news/business-22382932.
2. Jamie Dunkley, "Barclays Admits Libor Scandal 'Decimated' Trust in Banks," *Telegraph*, July 25, 2012.
3. "Libor Scandal."
4. "BBA Libor™—The Basics," British Bankers' Association, accessed March 12, 2014, http://www.bbalibor.com/explained/the-basics.
5. "2013 Edelman Trust Barometer: 2013 Annual Global Study," *Edelman Insights*, http://www.edelman.com/trust-downloads/global-results-2/.
6. Ibid.
7. Michael Jensen and William Meckling, "Theory of the Firm: Managerial Behavior, Agency Costs and Ownership Structure," *Journal of Financial Economics* 3, no. 4 (October 1976): 305–360.
8. Michael C. Jensen, Kevin J. Murphy, and Eric G. Wruck, "Remuneration: Where We've Been, How We Got to Here, What Are the Problems, and How to Fix Them," Working Paper, Social Sciences Research Network, July 12, 2004, http:ssrn.com/abstract=561305.
9. Dominic Rushe, "The 10 Best-Paid CEOs in America," *Guardian*, October 22, 2013.
10. Roger Martin and Mihnea Moldoveanu, "Capital versus Talent: The Battle That's Reshaping Business," *Harvard Business Review* 81, no. 7 (July 2003): 36–41.
11. Ibid.
12. Adolf A. Berle and Gardiner C. Means, *The Modern Corporation and Private Property* (New York: Macmillan, 1933).
13. Compound annual growth rate calculated on S&P returns adjusted for inflation and dividends, using Bloomberg LP terminal data in January 2010.
14. Eli Bartov, Dan Givoly, and Carla Hayn, "The Rewards to Meeting or Beating Analysts' Earnings Forecasts," *Journal of Accounting and Economics* 33, no. 2 (2002): 173–204.
15. Matt Krantz and Jon Swartz, "Dell Settles SEC Charges of Playing Accounting Rules," *USA Today*, July 23, 2000.
16. Bartov, Givoly, and Hayn, "Rewards to Meeting or Beating."
17. Michael C. Jensen, "The Agency Costs of Overvalued Equity and the Current State of Corporate Finance," *European Financial Management* 10, no. 4 (2004): 549–565.
18. John R. Graham, Campbell R. Harvey, and Shiva Rajgopal, "The Economic Implications of Corporate Financial Reporting," *Journal of Accounting and Economics* 40, nos. 1–3 (2005): 3–73.
19. Roger Martin, *Fixing the Game: Bubbles, Crashes and What Capitalism Can Learn from the NFL* (Boston: Harvard Business Review Press, 2011).

PART V

ACHIEVING FISCAL AND MONETARY POLICY EQUILIBRIUM

INTRODUCTION

John G. Taft

We're going to face the most predictable economic crisis in history. It will make what we went through look like a tea party.

—Remarks by Erskine Bowles, May 2014

At the heart of the Great Deformation is a rogue central bank that has abandoned every vestige of sound money. In doing so, it has enabled politicians to enjoy "deficit without tears" by monetizing massive amounts of debt.

—David Stockman, *The Great Deformation:*
The Corruption of Capitalism in America

In the course of researching topics most relevant to the future of finance, the single largest file I compiled was that on fiscal and monetary policy. Why? Because although not directly related to financial markets, the deficit spending practices of developed nations and the ballooning of central bank balance sheets are the most critical precedents to the "normal" functioning of the financial system.

Most commentators agree on the following facts:

- To prevent a global economic meltdown, the United States and other developed nations acted—appropriately—to "nationalize" excessive private sector leverage that led to the financial crisis of 2008–09.
- The governments of these developed nations are engaged in a historic binge of deficit spending—over $1 trillion in the United States alone in each year between 2008 and 2012—adding to already historically high levels of public debt, at a rate that is unsustainable.
- At this pace, public sector debt to gross domestic product (GDP) levels in the United States will exceed 150 percent by 2035—greater than that of Greece at the time of its fiscal restructuring and bailout by the European Union.
- In previous examples of debt overhang resulting from financial crises, whenever debt to GDP ratios exceed 90 percent, economic growth remained depressed for decades following the crisis.
- To address this problem of anemic economic growth caused by overhanging debt, central banks like the U.S. Federal Reserve have deployed monetary policy strategies designed to keep interest rates low and monetary conditions "looser" than would otherwise be the case.
- Through these tactics, specifically "quantitative easing," the Fed has built up a balance sheet that is over $3.5 trillion larger than it was before the financial crisis . . . $3.5 trillion more than what is "normal."[1]

Where we might disagree is whether it will be possible to unwind this unsustainable state of affairs in an orderly way, and even if we can, what the consequences will be. Is the United States on a glide path to fiscal disaster? Or can we manage to pull off what one commentator termed "the miracle of the immaculate monetary exit"?[2] Are we in or about to enter what economist Gary Shilling calls "the age of deleveraging"?[3] If so, will policy makers be able to effect what Bridgewater hedge fund manager Ray Dalio calls a "beautiful deleveraging," or will it be ugly?[4] How long will governments engage in what economists Carmen Reinhart and Kenneth Rogoff have termed "financial repression"—keeping interest rates artificially low as they are now to hold down the costs of financing debt, to the benefit of borrowers, like the U.S. government, over savers, the general population? Will governments eventually try to inflate their way out of their debt burdens, as Janus's Bill Gross predicts? "The primary magic potion that policymakers have always applied in such a predicament is to inflate their way out of the corner," says

Gross. "Expect an attempted inflationary solution in almost all developed economies over the next few years and even decades."[5]

Economists John Mauldin and Jonathan Tepper, authors of *Code Red: How to Protect Your Savings from the Current Crisis*, feel the same way but are far more alarmist, predicting that before long, "inflation will eat away at savings, government bonds will be destroyed as a supposedly safe asset class, and assets that benefit from inflation and money printing will do well."[6]

The most benign solution, of course, is to grow our way out of our problems. But with all this debt hanging over the economy, growth is likely to be even slower in the future, making deflation as potentially great a threat as inflation.

Writing about fiscal policy on the pages that follow is former U.S. Senator Judd Gregg (R-NH), a member of the Simpson-Bowles National Commission on Fiscal Responsibility and Reform and also cochair of the Campaign to Fix the Debt. Writing about monetary policy is Brian Walsh, founder of Saguenay Strathmore Capital. The chief takeaways from their essays are that: (1) fiscal and monetary policies in the United States are seriously out of whack, and (2) until we return to more sustainable conditions, all the work being done to retool the financial system is the equivalent of picking up coins in front of a steam roller. As Erskine Bowles points out, a future public sector deficit and/or debt-driven crisis has the potential to make the last financial crisis look like child's play.

NOTES

1. Board of Governors of the Federal Reserve System, "Credit and Liquidity Programs and the Balance Sheet: Total Assets of the Federal Reserve," accessed September 29, 2014, http://www.federalreserve.gov/monetarypolicy/bst_recent trends.htm.
2. "Buttonwood: Rate Expectations," *The Economist*, August 2, 2014, http://www .economist.com/news/finance-and-economics/21610268-when-interest-rates -start-rising-how-high-will-they-go-rate-expectations.
3. A. Gary Shilling, *The Age of Deleveraging, Updated Edition: Investment Strategies for a Decade of Slow Growth and Deflation* (Hoboken, NJ: John Wiley & Sons, 2012).
4. Ray Dalio, "An In-Depth Look at Deleveragings," February 2012, http://www .bwater.com/Uploads/FileManager/research/deleveraging/an-in-depth-look -at-deleveragings--ray-dalio-bridgewater.pdf.
5. William H. Gross, "Investment Outlook: Cult Figures," *PIMCO*, August 2012, http://latam.pimco.com/EN/Insights/Pages/cult-figures.aspx.
6. John Mauldin and Jonathan Tepper, *Code Red: How to Protect Your Savings from the Coming Crisis* (Hoboken, NJ: John Wiley & Sons, 2014), 10.

CHAPTER 12

THE ISSUE IS DEBT

Judd Gregg

Former U.S. Senator and Former CEO, the Securities Industry and Financial Markets Association

Adam Smith, who essentially defined and created the concept of market economies over 200 years ago, said many things that still resonate today. One of his observations that holds true is that "great nations are never impoverished by private, though they sometimes are by public, prodigality and misconduct."[1] This point was driven home in a slightly more entertaining way by the finest economist of the twentieth century, Milton Friedman, when he wryly observed, "If you put the federal government in charge of the Sahara Desert, in five years there'd be a shortage of sand."[2]

The point, of course, is that government can make a mess of things. Unfortunately, if the federal government continues on its present course of accumulating debt, that is exactly what will happen.

We do not need to look too far to find examples of governments that have gotten themselves into positions of unsustainable debt. Greece, Iceland, Ireland, Italy and soon enough France have all been close to bankruptcy as a result of their profligate policies. The results are not pretty: their economies have stalled out, work is hard to find, productivity has collapsed and the standard of living of their people has dropped dramatically.

Politicians and liberal pundits say this could not happen here in the United States, but of course it could, and will, if we do not get our fiscal house in order.

As the chart in figure 12.1 shows, we are as a nation right up among the top ten countries whose debt to GDP ratio is highest. We do of course have

FIGURE 12.1   SOVEREIGN DEBT AS A PERCENTAGE OF GDP

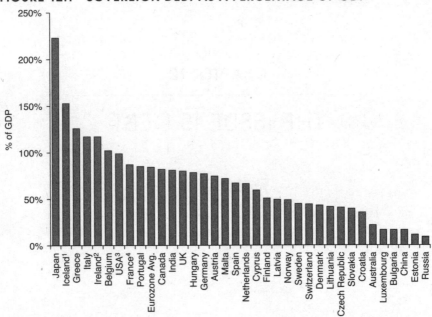

1. Iceland post–IMF bailout; 2. Includes NAMA; 3. Includes TARP & debt held by government accounts; 4. Includes SFEF.

Source: Moody's Investor Service, *Country Credit Statistical Handbook*.

more running room than most of the other unfortunate members of this club because we are America.

The world sees us as a nation of huge resources and hardworking people. A country that addresses issues and solves problems and thus has faith in our currency and our future. But the numbers do not look good; our accumulation of debt due to deficits is heading us over a cliff. As former Clinton administration chief of staff Erskine Bowles has pointed out, "We're the best-looking horse in the glue factory."[3]

Up until 2008, our national debt to GDP ratio since the end of World War II had averaged 35 percent. This was a very strong position. But since 2008, our debt has doubled due to deficit spending that has consistently exceeded $1 trillion; by 2022, it will have tripled. The ratio of debt to GDP is now over 70 percent and headed toward 100 percent. This is a burden that we are placing on our children and that will dramatically reduce their ability to live as well as we have lived.

If we continue on this course, one of the most sacred rules of American governance will be violated, which is that every generation in the history of our nation has passed on to the next generation a stronger and more prosperous country. We are on the verge of reversing this history.

What is the cause and what is the solution? Interestingly, the answer to both questions is rather simple, although the solution is rather complicated.

It does seem like we have waited forever for a coherent policy from Washington on this issue of the debt. This side blames that side, that side then blames this side, and at times people on the same side—usually the Senate and Democrats and the president—blame each other. It gets a little confusing to know who is to blame. But there is something called Sutton's Law, which is named after the famous bank robber of the 1930s. Taught to medical students when learning how to diagnose patients, the rule is that one should first consider the obvious.

If we are honest and look at the obvious, we must return to the sage advice of the old cartoon character Pogo. He famously proclaimed, at least among the small group who read his thoughts, "We have met the enemy and he is us!"[4] No matter how you cut it, the American people are at the core of this failure to have a federal government that is capable of getting out of its own way and governing for the good of the nation.

At the heart of this is the baby boom generation. This is the generation that brought the nation unsurpassed wealth and prosperity during its most productive years, the decades of the 1970s, 1980s, 1990s and into the start of this century. It is also the generation that, in the 1960s, initiated an end to the legacy of discrimination that weighed down our culture by pushing forward the causes of civil rights and women's rights, while raising to unusual intensity the debate over the correctness of the war in Vietnam. It is a generation that has a track record of catalyzing change, mostly positive, in our country and the world. It may not be the "greatest generation," but it is demographically the largest and definitely one of the most impactful in our nation's history.

Now it finds itself at the center of the question of how to get the federal government and its leaders to govern in a manner that continues our great legacy of always passing on more opportunity to our children. The baby boomers represent the largest demographic shift in our culture's experience. As it heads into its retirement years, the consequence is a doubling of the number of people who are leaving the workplace and expecting to be supported by those who are still in the workplace.

The cost implications of going from 35 million retirees to 75 million retirees is staggering, especially as it relates to our retirement-based entitlement programs.[5] We presently have a $60 trillion unfunded liability in just three major accounts: Medicare, Medicaid and Social Security.[6] To try to put this amount in context, all the taxes paid into the federal government since it started collecting taxes in 1789 are approximately $44 trillion. The entire net worth of all Americans, including the value of their houses, stocks, et cetera, minus debts and other liabilities, is approximately $81.5 trillion.[7] This means we have a financial obligation, which we have no idea how we are going to pay, to all these retiring baby boomers that approaches our net worth as a nation. This obligation is growing to a point where in the not-too-distant future Medicare, Medicaid and Social Security will actually cost more to fund annually than the amount the federal government spends today on all its activities, including defense and paying interest on the national debt.

These entitlement programs were built on the assumption that there would always be many more people working and paying into them than retired and taking out of them. With the demographic shift caused by the retirement of the baby boomers, these types of systems cannot maintain themselves. (See figure 12.2.) The issue is primarily one of unsustainable spending, not a lack of revenues.

Almost the entire baby boomer generation now qualifies for Medicare. Even more dramatic in its cost implications is the fact that this generation will live well into its eighties on average, with many people living well beyond

FIGURE 12.2   NUMBER OF WORKERS PAYING PAYROLL TAXES PER SOCIAL SECURITY BENEFICIARY

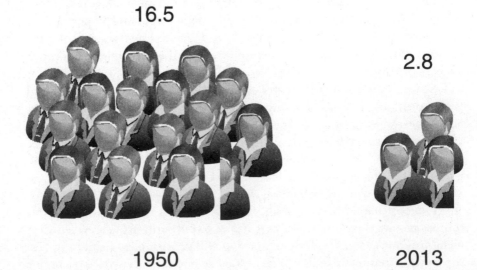

16.5

2.8

1950

2013

Source: 2012 SSA Trustee Report.

that point. In fact, the fastest-growing group will be people living past 100. This will generate an explosion in the most expensive form of health care: long-term care, especially as paid for by Medicaid.

There is not the slightest doubt of any of this.

Of all the issues the baby boom generation has affected, the cost and supply of health care to its members will have the deepest and most dramatic effect on our nation. Because there are so many boomers, and because they tend to vote and because they are affected in a very personal way by federal retirement policy, the folks in Washington are scared to address these issues and programs and to act. This is simple politics. If you do not admit there is a problem, or if you intentionally understate the scale of the problem, you should be able to get through the next election—which, after all, is the primary goal of most people who hold elective office.

There is an opportunity to change this now. Not with another debt-ceiling fight, or a government shutdown, or a false debate over tax burden or even with a straw dog contest over ending Obamacare. But we can change it with a few difficult, but long-lasting, acts of leadership on key issues. First, to accomplish this, the actions and leadership must be bipartisan. On major programs that affect the vast majority of Americans, like Social Security, Medicare and tax reform, people must feel that the decisions are fair or they will not be accepted. They will only be deemed fair in our political system if they are bipartisan.

The goal should be to reduce and stabilize the debt at no more than 70 percent of GDP, and hopefully closer to 60 percent, within ten years. This was the target set by the bipartisan National Commission on Fiscal Responsibility and Reform cochaired by Senator Alan Simpson (R-WY) and former Clinton chief of staff Erskine Bowles, known simply as the Simpson-Bowles Commission, which I supported. It is doable and makes sense. Simpson-Bowles also suggested a broad outline in which approximately three-fourths of this adjustment in deficits comes from changing spending accounts and one-fourth comes from tax reform.

Here are some broad outlines of how these types of policies could be carried out.

The largest costs driving spending by far are the Medicare and Medicaid accounts, which are integrally related with how health care is delivered and paid for in our country. We need to begin the reform of these two entitlement accounts by beginning the reform of how we reimburse for health care costs. Instead of having a system that rewards utilization and cost-plus activity and has virtually no market forces disciplining its costs, we need to move to systems that reward outcomes, promote value and encourage market forces.

This is easy to say but difficult to execute; however, progress is being made in this area. A consortium of medical centers, working under the general framework of ideas and statistics that have been developed at Dartmouth College, are attempting to rationalize the cost of procedures with the outcomes.[8] In addition, a great deal of experimentation is evolving that ties reimbursement to the individual through what is known as capitation.

In the Medicaid area, state governors and state leaders need to be given much more freedom from federal, top-down management so that they can use their creativity, tailored to their states' unique situations, to cover more people for less. This type of approach will allow states for the most part to get a great deal more for the dollars spent with a great deal less bureaucracy.

These types of approaches, along with many others, should lead to a system that maintains quality while limiting cost. There are no easy answers here, but there needs to be an effort to bring about a better, more efficient medical delivery system that is affordable.

Tax reform also needs to be aggressively pursued. Our present tax code is, as everyone knows, massively complex and counterproductive. Instead of encouraging people to invest and work in the most efficient manner, it encourages people to act with the purpose of avoiding taxes. It undermines the productivity of the nation and actually reduces the revenues flowing to the federal government. We have a tax code that encourages investment for the purpose of avoiding taxes instead of supporting investment for the purposes of economic gain that results in jobs and revenue growth.

Again, Simpson-Bowles set out a template for such reform. It proposed reducing or eliminating numerous tax deductions and exemptions in exchange for significantly reducing tax rates and using a small percentage of the revenue to pay for deficit and debt reduction. If passed, such an approach would unleash exceptional economic activity, which would also generate greater revenues and help pay for the cost of government and the reduction of the debt.

Social Security also needs reform before it goes bankrupt. With this program there are only a few moving parts that need to be changed and improved. We need a more accurate cost-of-living adjustment (COLA) calculation, as proposed by President Obama. We need to raise the age of retirement, but in a manner that does not affect anyone over the age of 30. We need to have high-income individuals pay a larger share of the cost of their benefits; this is also true in the Medicare part D drug benefit. There is no reason that a person working in a restaurant should be subsidizing Warren Buffett's prescription drugs.

These are all ideas that can be implemented legislatively. To accomplish them, we simply need leadership in Washington that is willing to stand up to the various interest groups and lobby groups, to step on a few toes and do what everyone who is objective knows is right.

Our nation for all sorts of reasons is on the cusp of a great economic expansion. This expansion will be driven by our special advantages, which include the new availability of domestic energy; the fact that most new, great ideas such as Facebook or Twitter or Tesla still arise here; the fact that we have massive amounts of capital ready to invest and risk on entrepreneurs; and most important, the fact that we are America and our people are problem solvers and doers.

The only thing that might slow or retard this march to greater prosperity is our federal fiscal house and its disorder. This can be corrected. It is not complicated. It just takes leadership.

NOTES

1. Adam Smith, *An Inquiry into the Nature and Causes of the Wealth of Nations*, ed. Edwin Cannan (London: Methuen, 1904). Library of Economics and Liberty [Online], available from http://www.econlib.org/library/Smith/smWN8.html; accessed September 23, 2014.

2. "Milton Friedman in His Own Words," Becker Friedman Institute for Research in Economics, The University of Chicago, November 9, 2012, https://bfi.uchicago.edu/post/milton-friedman-his-own-words.

3. Frank James, "U.S. Is 'Best Looking Horse in Glue Factory': Bowles," NPR, December 1, 2010, http://www.npr.org/blogs/itsallpolitics/2010/12/01/131729414/u-s-the-best-looking-horse-in-glue-factory-bowles.

4. Walt Kelly, Pogo comic strip, August 1970. Derived from Commodore Oliver Hazard Perry on the War of 1812.

5. "The Next Four Decades, The Older Population in the US 2010 to 2050," U.S. Census Bureau, http://www.census.gov/prod/2010pubs/p25-1138.pdf.

6. Rachel Greszler and Romina Boccia, "Social Security Trustees Report: Unfunded Liability Increased $1.1 Trillion and Projected Insolvency in 2033," The Heritage Foundation, http://www.heritage.org/research/reports/2014/08/social-security-trustees-report-unfunded-liability-increased-11-trillion-and-projected-insolvency-in-2033; Robert E. Moffit and Alyene Senger, "The 2014 Medicare Trustees Report: A Dire Future for Seniors and Taxpayers Without Reform," The Heritage Foundation, http://www.heritage.org/research/reports/2014/08/the-2014-medicare-trustees-report-a-dire-future-for-seniors-and-taxpayers-without-reform#_ftn3; The White House, Office of Management and Budget, Summary of Receipts, Outlays and Surpluses or Deficits: 1789–2019, http://www.whitehouse.gov/omb/budget/historicals.

7. Neil Shah, "U.S. Household Wealth Hits Fresh Record" *Wall Street Journal*, September 18, 2014, http://online.wsj.com/articles/u-s-household-wealth-hits-fresh-record-1411056031.

8. The Dartmouth Atlas of Health Care Project, The Dartmouth Institute for Health Policy & Clinical Practice at the Geisel School of Medicine at Dartmouth, http://tdi.dartmouth.edu/, http://www.dartmouthatlas.org/.

CHAPTER 13

REAL-TIME EXPERIMENTS IN MONETARY POLICY

Brian Walsh

Chair and Chief Investment Officer,
Saguenay Strathmore Capital

We are living through a real-time experiment in central bank policy. The Federal Reserve and other major central banks have spent the last six years trying out various forms of monetary stimulation. How expertly this is conducted, and how these unconventional policies unwind, will have profound consequences on financial markets, the economy and the inflation/deflation outlook. These easy-money policies helped prevent a financial Armageddon in the fall of 2008 and have aided the economic recovery of the past five years. However, they also have invisible, unintended consequences, and are partially responsible for the crisis in the first place. The year 2008 marked the end of the massive U.S. private sector debt binge that began in the early 1950s and continued unabated for over 50 years. The Fed's attempts to revive the economy with essentially zero percent interest rates ran straight into this historic unwinding and deleveraging.

While the Fed saved the day in 2008, the unintended consequences were considerable. Low rates have enriched the wealthy thanks to the recovery in housing and the soaring stock and bond markets while destroying safe havens and impoverishing savers, and in the process exacerbating income inequality. Meanwhile, Fed policy has seemingly lost its ability to spur growth and employment, and capital has been misallocated throughout the economy. Trying to understand these and other harmful consequences, or at least provide a framework to think about them, is the major aim of this chapter. "I fear that we are feeding imbalances similar to those that played a role in the run-up to the financial crisis," said Fed governor Richard Fisher, alluding to the unnaturally low rates caused by the Fed policy, and "with its massive asset purchase, the Fed is distorting financial markets and creating incentives for managers and market players to take increasing risk, some of which will result in tears."[1]

First, we'll review how we arrived at the financial crisis of 2008 and consider the Fed's possible role in the creation of the conditions leading to the crisis. Then we'll discuss the need for the unconventional policy tools, review the successes and seeming limitations of these policies, and look at the possible consequences of the inevitable unwinding of these policies and suggestions on what the Fed might do next.

HOW WE GOT HERE

The term *debt supercycle* was coined by the Bank Credit Analyst (BCA) over 25 years ago, when it observed the ever-expanding private sector debt in the United States and many other major countries. The term describes a 50-year cycle during which time private (corporate and individual) debt levels boomed, reached a climax and then burst. Private sector debt in the United States began rising rapidly in the mid-1980s and continued largely unabated until 2008. The reasons for this growth are beyond the scope of this chapter, but during this period of sustained debt growth, there have been a number of financial events cum crises, beginning with the severe equity market correction in 1987 that included Black Monday, the largest one-day decline (25 percent) in the history of the S&P 500. In the last 15 years alone, the Fed has faced four serious threats to the U.S. financial system: first, the collapse of Long-Term Capital Management in 1998, which came on the heels of Russia defaulting; then the tech bubble collapse in early 2000; followed by 9/11 and finally the financial crisis of 2008.

Following the Long-Term Capital implosion, the Fed lowered rates and flooded the banking system with liquidity. The possible contagion to the banking system from the Long-Term Capital collapse was quickly contained, and within a month the equity markets had resumed rallying, with the technology-heavy Nasdaq index moving into a parabolic ascent. In early 2000, the tech equity bubble burst, and the Fed again used easy money to offset the deflationary impacts. Eighteen months later, 9/11 happened, and the Fed aggressively eased once more. By lowering rates and easing monetary conditions, the Fed helped reflate the economy and prevented major recessions.

Generally, the Fed was lauded as a savior following these crises. It had a formula for solving financial crises and it appeared to work, making Alan Greenspan a hero, as exemplified by Bob Woodward's 2000 biography of Greenspan called *Maestro*. However, was the Fed aiding the expansion of this debt burden and inviting subsequent financial accidents? In fact, a central feature of BCA's debt supercycle thesis is "the role that policy has played in promoting increased financial imbalances and indebtedness."[2] The Fed has, in effect, been compliant in the buildup of this debt supercycle. Implicit in the Fed's reflationary policies were easier borrowing conditions, and the private sector acted accordingly, continuing to borrow at a significant rate. As BCA noted, "Policymakers have encouraged an ever-greater accumulation of financial excesses rather than accept the economic pain that would occur if imbalances were allowed to self-correct."[3]

While "it is virtually impossible to identify a normal or ideal level of private sector debt, private debt in the Unites States rose from 53 percent in 1951 to a peak of 179 percent by 2007."[4] Moreover, in the latter stages of this debt binge, it was clear that more and more of the debt was used to finance consumption rather than investment. The law of diminishing returns was settling in, and by 2007, it took $3 of debt to generate a $1 rise in GDP. Hyman Minsky's theory of finance largely anticipated these events. Minsky said there were three stages of finance, the last of which is the Ponzi phase, when borrowing was used or needed to pay interest as well as to refinance existing debt. The theory described perfectly the subprime debacle of no-down-payment, no-documentation loans that, by early 2007, were defaulting just one to three months after issuance! Minsky also explained how stability bred instability: the longer the period of economic prosperity and financial market gain, the more investors let down their guard.[5] On the surface all looked fine. Even as home prices nationally peaked in late 2006, Bernanke et al. believed nothing was wrong with the economy. And was not the Fed, through its easy money policies, adding to the sense of stability? Most important, is the same thing happening again? (More on that later.)

A reasonable observer might have expected the "popping" of the equity bubble in early 2000, and subsequently the events of 9/11, to slow down or even reverse the growth in debt. But from the end of 2000 to the end of 2007, private sector debt in the United States grew by 82 percent (in the United Kingdom it grew by 88 percent, in Ireland by 177 percent, in Spain by 194 percent and in Greece by 215 percent). The rebooting of the economy through lower rates and easy money was what the nineteenth-century French economist Frédéric Bastiat referred to as the first and seen effect of an economic act; the financial excesses, such as the ballooning leverage of the banking system, the financial markets' increasing dependency on Fed bailouts (the "Greenspan/Bernanke/Yellen put") and the growing debt levels were the less overt, or unseen, second effects. The second effect, Bastiat wrote, usually had negative consequences if the first effect was positive.[6]

By the end of 2007, the private sector was reaching the limit of the debt supercycle; unfortunately, no bell was rung in warning. The collapse of Lehman Brothers and subsequent chaos in financial markets was the defining event heralding the end of the debt supercycle. As BCA argued, "The bursting of the credit-fueled housing boom represented a major turning point in the U.S. debt supercycle." Finally, "we reached a peak in the consumer sector's willingness and ability to take on more leverage."[7] The collapse of Lehman threatened the entire banking system, not only in the Unites States but throughout much of the other countries in the Organisation of Economic Co-operation and Development.

After the threat of financial catastrophe passed, the United States found itself in the throes of its first "balance sheet recession" since the Great Depression. A balance sheet recession is one caused by too much debt, in contrast to a more conventional demand-led recession, which is triggered by rising interest rates. It was the inevitable consequence of the debt supercycle. By the beginning of 2009, it was evident that we had stared into the abyss of financial Armageddon and survived. Wall Street was severely scarred, and Main Street's confidence was badly shaken. The economy was already in a recession, business confidence was battered, unemployment was rising quickly, state governments were forced to cut back services and workers to meet mandated balanced budgets, and individuals who hadn't lost their jobs saw their 401(k) values decimated, while home prices, which had peaked in early 2007, declined significantly. The great deleveraging was in full swing, starting with defaulted home mortgages. The Fed was dealing with circumstances not seen since the 1930s; it quickly became clear that the usual monetary formula was essentially impotent. Interest rates were plumbing the "0" bound, and still the economy and markets continued to tank.

The Fed had no choice but to embrace a series of unconventional policy tools. In 2002, when Ben Bernanke was a Fed governor, he speculated in a speech about unconventional tools the Fed could use if interest rates ever reached the "0" bound. He noted that "a money financed tax-cut is essentially equivalent to Milton Friedman's famous helicopter drop of money," which led to the unfortunate moniker "Helicopter Ben."[8] The soon-to-be-unveiled programs of quantitative easing, or QE, and Operation Twist were not quite the equivalent of throwing cash from helicopters, but the desired result was to be the same.

Quantitative easing involved the Fed purchasing significant amounts of U.S. government Treasuries and mortgage-backed paper. The first QE program was unveiled in November 2008 and was instrumental in helping to quell the panic in financial markets. QE II commenced in November 2010 and QE III on September 13, 2012. Prior to the first QE program, the Fed's balance sheet was approximately $870 billion; as of September 24, 2014, it has surpassed $4.4 trillion.[9] Operation Twist was a program to effectively lower long-term interest rates whereby the Fed purchased longer-dated maturities in exchange for shorter (less than five years) government bonds. And today, the Fed owns 45 percent of all of the outstanding Treasuries with 10-to 30-year maturities.[10] This is, plain and simple, monetization of national debt, especially given the Fed's intention regarding these bonds.

MORE INCOME INEQUALITY

The impact of these unconventional monetary policy tools is more pronounced and obvious in financial markets than in real economies. The transmission mechanism to the markets is more direct; the Fed, through its various QE programs, buys trillions of dollars' worth of mortgage paper and Treasuries, thereby lowering overall interest rates and general discount rates. In essence, this is an attempt to increase investors' risk appetites, leading to the purchase of riskier assets such as equities, high-yield bonds and real estate. The subsequent transmission to the real economy theoretically comes through the "wealth effect"—that is, the increase in wealth from rising asset prices, especially housing and equities, is supposed to induce greater consumption. The increase in consumption would then help jump-start the virtuous cycles that drive growth in capitalist economies. Bernanke explicitly argued as much in a *Washington Post* article:

> This approach eased financial conditions in the past and, so far, looks to be effective again. Stock prices rose and long-term interest rates fell when investors began to anticipate the most recent action. *Easier financial conditions will promote economic growth* [emphasis mine]. For example, lower mortgage rates will make housing more affordable and allow more homeowners to refinance. Lower corporate bond rates will encourage investment. And higher stock prices will boost consumer wealth and help increase confidence, which can also spur spending. Increased spending will lead to higher incomes and profits that, in a virtuous circle, will further support economic expansion.[11]

The policies were clearly helpful in increasing wealth, but they also increased income inequality. Since early 2009, overall wealth in the United States has increased from $55.8 trillion to $80.7 trillion—an all-time high.[12] However, much of this increase in wealth has gone to the top 5 percent of the population, thus furthering income inequality. This is not surprising, since the majority of the increase in wealth has come from rising stock prices. A recent study by economists at Ohio State estimates that as of mid-2013, the average U.S. household net worth was still 14 percent below the peak of 2007.[13] So the vast majority of people have not experienced a significant boost in their net worth. As importantly, median household income in 2013 of $51,939 was 8 percent lower than in 2007.[14]

AN ANEMIC ECONOMIC RECOVERY

The Fed's policies were clearly helping Wall Street, as equity and bond prices soared. However, Main Street was left behind. In addition, most households have been focused on reducing debt burdens; at the beginning of 2008, overall household debt was equal to 139 percent of GDP; by the end of 2013, it had dropped to 109 percent of GDP. While this deleveraging is good for the long-term health of the economy, it clearly impaired the short-term recovery. To anyone familiar with the works of Rogoff and Reinhart ("This Time Is Different: Eight Centuries of Financial Folly") and other economists who wrote about balance sheet recessions, the impact of deleveraging on the economy's growth rate was not a surprise. Yet it seems to have been somewhat of a surprise for the Fed because its models consistently overestimated the impact (i.e., the wealth effect) on the economy of various QE and other unconventional policy tools.

Brian Portnoy, in his recent book *The Investor's Paradox*, noted that

> our deleveraging cycle will undercut our growth prospects in coming years. There is no fine-grained algorithm to predict how long it takes for a deleveraging cycle to run its course, nor its precise impact on growth. However, credible analysts suggest that it can take upwards of two decades. The unwinding of excessive debt burdens can lead to extended periods of low interest rates such as we're experiencing now. Yet the availability of cheap financing does not necessarily translate into growth prospects by way of balance sheet expansion. For instance, right now, despite low rates globally, large corporations continue to hold record levels of cash, meaning that the demand for free money is less than one might expect.[15]

Probably the definitive proof of the difficulties for monetary policy in a deleveraging economy is the broken money multiplier, which today is at all-time lows. The Fed's massive purchases of Treasuries and mortgage paper create reserves in the banking system; normally these reserves would lead to lending by banks, thereby increasing the broad money supply. However, since 2009 these reserves have largely remained at the Fed as unborrowed reserves. So while the Fed's balance sheet has more than quadrupled since the beginning of 2008, M2 (the main money supply aggregate focused on by the Fed) has increased by only 33 percent. As importantly, the velocity of money has trended lower during this era of unconventional policy tools. Some commentators attribute the decline to low interest rates, which lowers the opportunity cost of idle money; however, it is probably also related to the generally sluggish recovery of the private sector, as both corporations and consumers continue to behave cautiously.

As a result of private sector deleveraging and the related declines in the money multiplier and velocity of money, the post-2008 recovery has been more anemic than other post–World War II recoveries. The great recession of 2008–09 was the deepest recession since the Great Depression. The only recession in the post–World War II era that came close to it was the 1981–82 recession, which followed the significant interest rate hikes initiated by Fed chair Paul Volcker. The recovery following that recession included a greater than 6.5 percent rise in GDP in 1984; thus far the GDP growth since the end of the most recent recession has averaged less than 3 percent. But a balance sheet recession is more difficult to recover from, and the Fed has been, to a significant degree, the main player in reviving the economy, excluding the economy's own natural healing process. The magnitude of the task is explained by BCA's Martin Barnes, who recently wrote,

> Credit booms and busts have been a feature of economic life for hundreds of years. Periods of cheap and widely-available credit, combined with people's vulnerability to excessive greed and euphoria, represents a powerful and toxic mix that invariably ends badly. And if the bust is bad enough, it can have a lasting impact on borrowers' psychology. The most obvious example was the Great Depression which led an entire generation to embrace financial restraint for the rest of their lives.
>
> The recent economic and financial downturn probably was severe enough to crush the long-running love affair with debt in the Unites States and elsewhere. It is significant that extraordinary monetary stimulus and several years of record-low interest rates have failed to rekindle much of a credit revival throughout the developed world.[16]
>
> Consequently, the terrible mix of private sector deleveraging, the zero interest rate boundary, broken money multiplier and largely unhelpful fiscal policies left the Fed in a difficult situation. It managed to stabilize the economy with these experimental tools, but the recovery was shallow and occasionally stumbling.

But are there other consequences of all the unconventional policy tools used by the Fed? For example, what happens to the massive Fed balance sheet and its effect on all the unborrowed reserves? What are second-order impacts of low interest rates?

PROBLEM OF UNINTENDED CONSEQUENCES

Frédéric Bastiat wrote a pamphlet in 1848 entitled "What Is Seen and What Is Not Seen." The basic premise of the pamphlet was that every economic act has two effects, one that is immediate and seen, and one that is unseen and transpires later. He defined a bad economist as one who *only* focused on the first and seen effect; primarily because if the first effect was positive, usually the second and unseen effect was harmful . . . thus bad policy prescriptions would emanate from focusing solely on the first, seen effects. Bastiat was referring to the law of unintended consequences. With today's unprecedented monetary policy, the first effect is relatively easy to spot, but the second-order effects are much harder to discern and some have probably not yet occurred. The first effects, as defined, should be obvious:

- $4.4 trillion Fed balance sheet, up from $870 billion in 2008;
- Very low interest rates due to a policy of financial repression, or keeping real interest rates low or even negative, with the unstated intention of creating cheap funding for governments;
- A near tripling of the stock market since the bottom in March 2009;
- An end to the housing collapse, as home prices bottomed in 2011 and nationally have risen 16 percent since then;[17]
- A stumbling economic recovery with growth rarely reaching 3 percent, mixed recovery in employment and headline inflation remaining very low; and
- Probably the end of the debt supercycle.

The second-order effects are harder to see and naturally subject to much debate. Some of these second-order effects include:

- **Financial repression** effectively diminishes the value of safe havens; what value is there in a safe short-term government bond if the real return is negative? Consequently, financial repression is bad for conservative fixed-income savers, as the Fed implicitly wants to encourage investing in risky assets.
- **The wrong cost of capital.** As investment researcher Charles Gave has consistently pointed out over the last two to three years, the "wrong" cost of capital can lead to capital misallocation, leading to what he refers to as high cost of free money: "Unnaturally low funding costs undermine the structural growth rate of the U.S. economy, because of capital misallocation. The losers in this deal are usually ordinary folk. Pensioners get no interest on their savings, while rich investors use cheap capital to chase up the cost of property, oil, etc."[18] If the "price" of anything is wrong, common sense dictates it will lead to a misallocation; so if the price of capital is distorted by Fed's actions, is it being misallocated? For example, corporate profits and cash flows are at record levels both in absolute terms and as a percentage of GDP, and corporations are buying back record levels of equity, but capital spending is restrained. The impact on stock prices is great, but are we as a nation underinvesting in productive capacity? Since the beginning of the recovery, capital spending has been MIA, and its widely predicted rebound has yet to happen.
- **Is the Fed an enabler?** Economist and investment advisor John Hussman and others have argued that since the 9/11 attack, the

Fed has actually aided or abetted the housing and other financial disasters. Hussman writes, "There is little demonstrated cause-and-effect relationship between the Fed's actions and the outcomes it seeks, other than provoking speculation in risk-assets by depriving investors of safe yield. That's essentially the same M.O. that got us into the housing crisis: yield-starved investors plowing money into mortgage-backed securities, and Wall Street scrambling to create 'product' by lending to anyone with a pulse. To suggest that fresh economic weakness might justify further efforts at quantitative easing is to assume a cause-and-effect link that is unreliable, if evident at all, and to overlook the already elevated risks."[19] In simple terms, have we reached the limit of usefulness of QE et al., and might the Fed be sowing seeds for the next financial crisis?

- **Six years of free money.** A corollary to the Fed as an enabler is this question: What are the consequences of the Fed overstaying its welcome? The most obvious consequence is inflation, which has usually followed extended periods of negative real interest rates. Until very recently there has been little evidence of inflation; indeed, the economy seems to be having a hard time achieving the Fed's 2 percent target inflation rate. The only evidence of obvious inflation has been confined to risky assets and collectibles such as art, fine wine and luxury real estate. As such, in market parlance, a return of inflation is not being discounted by the financial markets, and such an occurrence would shock markets. The general expectation of little to no inflation worries me, and five years into the recovery, having a central bank so focused on creating inflation does feel odd, especially to someone who entered the financial business in the late 1970s, a time when inflation was rampant. As economist and market strategist David Rosenberg recently wrote, "This is a Fed that seems to desperately want more inflation. It is a Fed that is bent on maintaining their reckless policy of financial repression . . . there is no such thing as a free lunch and heading into six years of free money—negative interest rates—for major industrialized power, is not likely to end very well."[20]

- **Financial risk.** Are our stock and bond markets now addicted to easy money? Thankfully, at this stage it does seem the health of the real economy is much stronger than at any time since 2007, but ironically it can be argued that the markets are currently detached from reality, fueled by a hyperstimulative monetary policy. Most risks assets today appear overvalued. The stock market has almost tripled since the low in March 2009 and has done this without a 20 percent correction; a rally of this magnitude has never occurred without at least one 20 percent correction. In addition, corporate credit spreads are near all-time lows while yields are at all-time lows, and loan covenant patterns are weakening; in 2013 over 50 percent of all leveraged loans issued were covenant-lite. It cannot be healthy long term for financial markets to be hooked on easy money.

- **How will the Fed's balance sheet normalize?** The Fed's June 2011 minutes discussed exit principles to guide its efforts of returning its balance sheet to normal, which today would entail an eventual reduction of $3 trillion of Treasury bonds and mortgage paper.[21] More recently the Fed indicated it is considering a new exit strategy that would not involve normalizing its balance sheet. The Fed over the past year has increasingly demonstrated concerns with QE. Bernanke first began the "taper talk" in May 2013, as the Fed seemingly was losing confidence in QE's ability to effectively stimulate the economy. The market reaction was immediately negative, with ten-year yields increasing from 1.6 percent to 3 percent. The stock market experienced a 7 percent correction. Bernanke was soon trying to soothe markets by arguing that any taper would be based on economic performance and that, no matter what, rates would stay low for the foreseeable future. At the same time, comments from members of the Fed indicated that the majority of the Fed were losing faith (or had lost faith) in QE. In 2014, the Fed did gradually end QE, reducing the size of its purchases in a well-defined schedule. However, it appeared that appeasing the markets continued to be a real concern for the Fed, as it made it clear that notes would remain at current levels for the foreseeable future.

Five years into a recovery, it's worrisome that the Fed winds down unconventional policies like QE but remains hostage, to a degree, to market reaction. What does that imply for the eventual exit and return to normal monetary policy? While it is very difficult to answer this question in any definitive way, it is worth pondering, as is evident in the following remark by Fed governor Charles Plosser. "We have aided the creation of massive excess bank reserves without a clear plan for how to drain them when the time comes."[22] Fed governor Richard Fisher commented in more detail that: "A lot of the shocks that we've faced, certainly in the United States have had lasting effects on the economy. We're not going to close that gap, and to keep thinking we're going to do that means we overplay our hand in terms of policy. I am very worried about the potential for unintended consequences of all this action. Expectations of what central banks can do and should do have risen to unhealthy highs."[23]

Some Fed governors sound very much like market commentators who believe the Fed has overstayed its welcome!

CONCLUSION: TIME TO REMOVE THE PUNCH BOWL

The Fed was the main actor in preventing financial Armageddon in 2008 and in helping get the economy back on its feet. At the same time, the unintended consequences of the Fed's unconventional monetary policies of the last six years increasingly appear to be negative for the economy. That the Fed apparently remains a hostage to market reactions five years into a recovery is problematic; it is akin to a parent indulging a volatile teenager, which rarely ends well. Certain members of the Fed are clearly haunted by Japan's 20-plus years of deflation following the bursting of Japan's stock and real estate bubbles, but are they fighting the last war? And in fighting the last war, are they helping create conditions for the next bust, as argued by David Rosenberg, Charles Gave, Jonathan Hussman, et al., along with Fed governors Fisher and Plosser?

This story could and should have a happy ending. The fundamentals of the U.S. economy look stronger than they have been in some time. The private sector has deleveraged significantly; the Unites States remains at the forefront of technological development; its population is growing, unlike most OECD countries; and its university education system is the strongest in the world. The Fed can help the economy grow, but it needs to be more in touch with Main Street and less concerned with Wall Street; more worried about inflation and less worried about stock prices; more worried about capital misallocation due to the wrong cost of capital than the forward guidance of interest rates. The taper decision and the end of QE is positive. A return to a more normal interest rate environment would be a good next step; the economy probably can stand a 1 percent federal fund rate today, let alone in late 2015 as current Fed guidance suggests. A continuation of current, overly easy monetary policies and the Fed overstaying its welcome will most likely lead to inflation shock and larger economic setbacks. A prudent Fed would be removing the proverbial punch bowl!

NOTES

1. John P. Hussman, "Fed-Induced Speculation Does Not Create Wealth," *Hussman Funds Weekly Market Comment*, March 24, 2014, http://www.hussman funds.com/wmc/wmc140324.htm.
2. Martin H. Barnes, "Deleveraging and the Debt Supercycle," *BCA Research Special Report*, March 4, 2014.
3. Ibid., 1.
4. Martin H. Barnes, "An Update on the US Debt Supercycle: Where Are We Now?" *BCA Research Special Report*, September 6, 2012, http://www.bcaresearch .com/pdf/BCASRsep62012.pdf.

5. Hyman P. Minsky, the Jerome Levy Economics Institute of Bard College, Working Paper No. 74, *The Financial Instability Hypothesis*, May 1992, http://www.levyinstitute.org/pubs/wp74.pdf.
6. Frédéric Bastiat, *Selected Essays on Political Economy*, trans. Seymour Cain (n.p.: Library of Economics and Liberty, 1995), accessed October 1, 2014, http://www.econlib.org/library/Bastiat/basEssNotes.html.
7. Barnes, "Deleveraging and the Debt Supercycle."
8. Ben S. Bernake, "Deflation: Making Sure It Doesn't Happen Here," speech presented at the National Economists Club, Washington, DC, November 21, 2002, http://www.federalreserve.gov/boarddocs/Speeches/2002/20021121/default.htm.
9. Federal Reserve Statistical Release, "FRB: H.4.1 Release: Factors Affecting Reserve Balances," September 25, 2014, http://www.federalreserve.gov/releases/h41/20140925/.
10. Simon Potter, *Domestic Open Market Operations during 2013*, Report presented to the Federal Open Market Committee, Federal Reserve Bank of New York, April 2014, http://www.newyorkfed.org/markets/omo/omo2013.pdf.
11. Ben S. Bernake, "What the Fed Did and Why: Supporting the Recovery and Sustaining Price Stability," *Washington Post*, November 4, 2010, http://www.washingtonpost.com/wp-dyn/content/article/2010/11/03/AR2010110307372.html.
12. Federal Reserve Statistical Release, "FRB: H.4.1 Release: Factors Affecting Reserve Balances," September 18, 2014, http://www.federalreserve.gov/releases/h41/20140918/.
13. Jeff Grabmeier, "Household Wealth Still Down 14 Percent since Recession," February 27, 2014, http://researchnews.osu.edu/archive/wealthrecovery.htm.
14. Carmen DeNavas-Walt and Bernadette D. Proctor, "Income and Poverty in the United States: 2013," U.S. Census Bureau, September 2014, http://www.census.gov/content/dam/Census/library/publications/2014/demo/p60-249.pdf.
15. Brian Portnoy, *The Investor's Paradox: The Power of Simplicity in a World of Overwhelming Choice* (New York: Palgrave Macmillan, 2014).
16. Barnes, "Delveraging and the Debt Supercycle."
17. Case-Shiller 20 City Index, S&P Dow Jones Indices LLC, October 2014, http://us.spindices.com/indices/real-estate/sp-case-shiller-20-city-composite-home-price-index/.
18. Charles Gave, "The Euthanasia of Pensioners in Peoria," *Gavekal Dragonomics—The Daily* (2014), March 28, 2014, http://research.gavekal.com/content.php/9914-The-Euthanasia-Of-Pensioners-In-Peoria-by-Charles-Gave.
19. John P. Hussman, "Shifting Policy at the Fed: Good for Long-Term Growth, Bad for Cyclical Bubbles," *Hussman Funds Weekly Market Comment*, March 31, 2014, http://www.hussmanfunds.com/wmc/wmc140331.htm.
20. David Rosenberg, "Breakfast with Dave," *Gluskin Sheff Research*, March 18, 2014.
21. Federal Reserve Board, "Minutes of the Federal Open Market Committee," *FOMC Minutes*, June 21–22, 2011, http://www.federalreserve.gov/monetarypolicy/fomcminutes20110622.htm.
22. Hussman, "Fed-Induced Speculation Does Not Create Wealth."
23. Ibid.

PART VI

UNFINISHED BUSINESS

RETIREMENT SAVING AND HOUSING FINANCE

INTRODUCTION

John G. Taft

Most Americans are in serious financial trouble and don't even know it. Financially, we are like boys and girls proud of their dark sun tans without realizing that in 40–50 years, they will be patients of dermatologists checking for melanomas.

—Charles D. Ellis, guest editorial in the *Financial
Analyst Journal*, March/April 2014

If finance is "the science of goal architecture," as Robert J. Shiller terms it, what two more critical goals does modern society have than to enable its citizens to save enough money to live on for as long as they're alive and to procure acceptable housing? Yet in both cases, as authors Barbara G. Novick and Jeremy Diamond demonstrate, our financial system falls well short of doing the job.

In the case of retirement savings, Charles D. Ellis paints a graphic picture of the consequences of this gap between the retirement savings system we currently have and the expectations of society: "None of us want the United States to be plagued by large numbers of poverty-stricken elderly people who outlived the retirement funds they once thought ample for a comfortable retirement. . . . They will have made their own investment and spending decisions, so nobody else will feel responsible for them. These former workers will be all alone, pleading to the gloom 'Why oh why didn't someone tell me?' If we do not make hard choices now, what pension experts call the 'predictable surprise' will be no surprise at all and it will be nasty."[1]

Contributor Barbara G. Novick describes the problem just as starkly. Retirement, she writes, is "a basic financial goal that unifies us all," yet "most Americans will simply not be able to provide for their own future or their family's future." Novick offers a detailed walk through the patchwork quilt of government, employer-sponsored and personal retirement solutions that currently exists. She demonstrates that none of these individually, nor in combination, is designed to handle the unanticipated challenge of dramatically extended longevity.

Drawing on the work of analysts at the mega-asset manager BlackRock, where she serves as vice-chairman, Novick lays out a series of policy options and recommendations for more comprehensive change than the ineffectual Band-Aids that have been suggested to date. Her urgency is clear and compelling: "The longer the problem remains unaddressed," she writes, "the larger it gets."

The issue of housing finance is a bit thornier. Ironically, the segment of the financial services industry that contributed most to the financial crisis remains unreformed. On one hand, as Jeremy Diamond puts it, our system of housing finance is "a marvel of the modern financial world." Diamond is the former managing director and head of research at Annaly Capital, the largest real estate investment trust that buys mortgage debt. It is an example of what Robert J. Shiller, in chapter 3, terms "the broadly democratic proliferation of insurance, mortgages and pensions—all basic financial institutions—in underwriting the prosperity of millions of people in the past century."

On the other hand, the housing finance system is almost entirely dependent on government support. Almost every mortgage loan made today is guaranteed in some way by the U.S. government, either through the Government National Mortgage Association (known as Ginnie Mae) or the two mortgage finance firms nationalized during the financial crisis: the Federal National Mortgage Association (Fannie Mae) and the Federal Home Loan Mortgage Corporation (Freddie Mac). While Fannie Mae and Freddie Mac have returned to profitability, and in fact have contributed $218.7 billion (and still counting) to the U.S. Treasury in dividends,[2] taxpayers are as exposed to potential problems in the housing finance sector as they were before the crisis.

The question of how to make housing finance sustainable is, ultimately, one of balance. How much should the system rely on private capital, and how much on government support? Setting emotion and ideology aside, designing a system that maximizes access to affordable mortgages with as little risk to taxpayers as possible is an engineering problem. The good news is that serious public discussions and "good faith" policy debates over the best approach are well under way. The bad news, as Diamond points out, is that there seems to be no agreement on any aspect of how to accomplish it. And uncertainty about what it will ultimately look like is actually retarding the return of private capital, a necessary condition for its ultimate repair.

NOTES

1. Charles D. Ellis, "Hard Choices: Where We Are," *Financial Analysts Journal* 70, no. 2 (March/April 2014): 6, http://www.cfapubs.org/doi/pdf/10.2469/faj.v70.n2.4.
2. Joe Light, "Court Throws Out Lawsuits Related to Fannie Mae, Freddie Mac Profits," *Wall Street Journal*, October 1, 2014, http://online.wsj.com/articles/court-throws-out-lawsuits-related-to-fannie-mae-freddie-mac-profits-1412116389.

CHAPTER 14

ADDRESSING AMERICA'S RETIREMENT NEEDS

LONGEVITY CHALLENGE REQUIRES ACTION

Barbara G. Novick

Vice Chairman, BlackRock

A population that is living longer. The lingering effects of the Great Recession. And simply not enough savings. These factors, above all others, have created a retirement funding gap in the United States. One study estimated that gap—the difference between what people have saved and what they will need for retirement—at $6.6 trillion.[1] Despite the deficit, less than 60 percent of workers are saving for retirement. More troubling, 57 percent of those surveyed have less than $25,000 in total savings and investments. And some 28 percent have less than $1,000.[2]

Most Americans will simply not be able to provide for their own future or their family's future. The lack of financial preparedness is evident across the United States. It's time for everyone to rethink today's paradigm of retirement, from policy makers and financial institutions to employers and savers. We need to address America's retirement needs now. Ten thousand baby boomers reach retirement age every day.[3] Americans need access to programs that ensure the blessings of a longer life, without financial hardship.

Retirement security is a complex problem, with lots of legacy components, a wide range of stakeholders and significant financial and fiscal implications inherent in any action—or inaction. On a positive note, there is a growing sense that we may at last gather the courage to take bold steps toward addressing it.

Each of the three pillars of the prevailing retirement funding model have been weakened in recent years, and all three are in urgent need of reinforcement. The three pillars are Social Security, employer-sponsored plans and personal savings. Several components of retirement funding are already sagging under the weight of more retirees living longer with less savings. Based on today's longevity expectations and projected needs in retirement, all three of these critical building blocks need to be strengthened and modified. Ideally, policy makers should take a holistic rather than a piecemeal approach; however, this will require tremendous coordination and cooperation. Retirement savings is a national issue, and the dialogue must begin immediately.

CLEAR INTENTIONS, CONFUSING RESULTS

For many years, legislators have acknowledged and promoted the need to offer U.S. workers the means for a secure retirement. From the Social Security program to tax incentives for employers and individuals to legislation to protect assets and enhance investment returns, retirement planning has been an ongoing focus of policy makers at both the federal and the state levels. This much is clear, and admirable.

But after 75 years of legislative and tax code changes in service of this admirable mission, the result is a complex patchwork of programs covering various groups of Americans (see table 14.1). Each program has its own set of complicated eligibility, funding and other rules. Adding to the complexity are special programs for veterans, changes in existing programs for older workers and retirees versus younger workers, the introduction of new programs and rules over time, and the ability of workers to change jobs and sectors which affects their plan eligibility (see figure 14.1). And what's worse, this confusing patchwork doesn't even come close to addressing today's retirement needs.

ASSESSING THE CURRENT RETIREMENT
FUNDING PARADIGM

Looking past the complexities, let's take a closer look at the three pillars of the U.S. retirement funding paradigm: the federal Social Security program; employer-sponsored plans, both defined benefit (DB) and defined contribution (DC) such as 401(k); and personal savings plans such as Individual Retirement Accounts (IRAs) and similar programs for the self-employed.

TABLE 14.1 RETIREMENT HAS LONG BEEN ON THE PUBLIC AGENDA

1935	Social Security created to provide retirement benefits to American workers; amended in 1939 to include survivor and spousal benefits, and in 1956 to add disability benefits.
1974	Employee Retirement Income Security Act of 1974 (ERISA) enacted to establish minimum standards for pension plans in private industry and to protect the interests of employee benefit plan participants and their beneficiaries by requiring disclosure of financial and other information and establishing standards of conduct for plan fiduciaries. IRAs introduced at the time of ERISA enactment.
1980	401(k) regulations enacted, formally authorizing "salary reduction/savings plans" sparking increased adoption of this type of plan by corporations.
1986	Federal Employee Retirement System/Thrift Savings Plan (TSP) for federal employees enacted.
1991	Congress makes Social Security coverage mandatory for public sector employees not covered by an alternative public pension plan.
2001	Economic Growth and Tax Relief Reconciliation Act enacted many changes to DC plans.
2006	Pension Protection Act (PPA) introduced significant changes in rules governing private sector DB and DC plans.

Source: BlackRock

FIGURE 14.1 A PATCHWORK OF U.S. RETIREMENT PROGRAMS

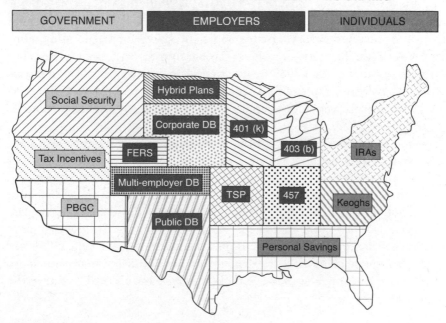

Source: BlackRock

For each program, it is important to understand:

- who funds the savings;
- who selects the investment risk;
- who bears the investment risk;
- who determines the form of the postretirement payout;
- whether the plan includes portability features;
- and whether longevity risks are pooled or individual.

Social Security

Social Security is essentially a DB plan funded by taxes paid by both employers and employees. It promises to pay a defined benefit based on contributions made during an employee's working years. Social Security was never intended to provide a secure retirement by itself. Yet today, for most Americans, Social Security underpins their retirement security. In fact, more than one-third of retirees are getting 90 percent or more of their income from the program.[4]

In addition, the program was designed generations ago, using significantly different demographics and life expectancies than we know today. Five years after Social Security was launched in 1940, a 21-year-old male had roughly a 53 percent chance of living to age 65 and collecting benefits.[5] Today, life expectancies are closer to 80 years, and about one in three Americans who are 65 today will live past 90.[6] Funding this increased longevity puts a strain on the federal budget. As the U.S. population ages, a shrinking number of working-age people are paying for a ballooning number of retirees. The ratio of workers paying into the system to retirees has dropped from 5 to 1 in 1960 to less than 3 to 1 today.[7] By 2033, analysts project only about two people working for each retiree.[8] By that time, Social Security reserves will be depleted and unable to pay scheduled benefits in full.[9]

And that doesn't even count the U.S. government workers who are not eligible for payments under Social Security at retirement. Public employee groups already covered by a plan have the ability to elect whether or not to participate.[10] While civilian employees of the federal government began to participate in 1984, a number of municipalities have opted not to participate in Social Security on the theory that they, and in many cases their employees, contribute to an established DB plan. However, recent events in Detroit and other municipalities illustrate that retirement security can become more tenuous for career public sector workers who have not accrued credits in the Social Security system.

Defined Benefit Plans

DB plans provide more certainty to employees than DC plans. That's because the benefits are generally defined as a certain payout based on years of service, income level, retirement age, vesting and other variables. During the employee's working years, contributions are made by the employer and/or the employee; generally, employees become vested in their benefits by staying at a single employer for many years. In DB plans, the investment risk is borne by the plan sponsor, and longevity risk is managed by the pooling of all covered employees. As such, the employer holds the ultimate risk. In the private sector, the cost and risk associated with this guarantee has increasingly driven sponsors away from providing this form of benefit as corporations seek ways to strengthen their own balance sheets. In the public sector, underfunding issues are threatening benefits, and many municipalities are reevaluating and modifying various aspects of their plans.

Like Social Security, both corporate and public DB plans were created in an era when life expectancies were much shorter and investment assumptions were more optimistic. Today, corporations and municipalities find themselves struggling under the weight of the promised benefits, as discussed in more detail below.

Private Sector Defined Benefit Plans

According to a recent study by Milliman, as of August 2014, the top 100 corporate DB plans (by accrued liability) had aggregate underfunded liabilities of approximately \$281 billion, with a funded ratio of approximately 84 percent.[11] Given corporations' concerns for their own financial health, combined with current accounting rules, many corporations have taken steps to reduce risk. In some cases, this amounts to closing DB plans and shifting to DC plans, essentially transferring investment responsibility and risk to the participant. In other instances, companies have offered participants lump-sum payouts and the option of an annuity purchase.

The closing of DB plans can impact different employees in very different ways. In some cases, existing employees are grandfathered into DB plans, while new employees are excluded, resulting in disparate outcomes for legacy versus new workers. In other plans, all participants are frozen at current levels, and future benefits accrue in a DC scheme. A few companies have transferred full elements of a plan's liabilities to an insurance company at a fixed price. The most notable large companies to have done so are General Motors (for certain retirees) and Verizon. In the cases of shifting to DC plans or providing lump-sum payouts, employees take on the funding and longevity risks, whereas in the insurance transactions, the insurance companies become liable for providing the benefits.

Many of the rules governing the design of DB plans were established in the 1970s and do not reflect today's environment. Unfortunately, the laws are relatively rigid and severely limit employers' abilities to modify benefit structures, despite lower investment returns and dramatically longer life spans. As a result, private sector employers are increasingly exiting DB plans, and the trend toward reducing risk in existing plans continues.

Public Sector Defined Benefit Plans

Public sector DB plans arguably face even greater challenges than those in the private sector. According to Milliman, at the end of 2013, the aggregate underfunding of the largest 100 public pension plans (by accrued liability) was over $1.2 trillion, with an average funded ratio of approximately 67 percent.[12] As recently reported, several states and municipalities have significant pension-funding gaps that are negatively impacting their credit ratings.

In many cases, as municipalities struggled with budgetary and fiscal challenges, pension contributions were delayed, further weakening investment returns. Many state and local governments have taken the initial steps toward pension reform. Some have addressed their liabilities by placing new hires into DC plans, creating hybrid DB/DC plans and/or modifying the payouts for future retirees. Some municipalities have raised the retirement age, increased the service requirement for pension eligibility and increased both employee and employer contributions, to name just a few belt-tightening measures.

But these efforts, while laudable, have had only limited impact on the funding status of public DB plans. Additionally, changes that increase costs to employees or alter benefits have, in certain cases, been challenged in court, delaying implementation. In the extreme case of Detroit, retirement benefit woes (including pension and medical benefits) played a large role in the city's bankruptcy filing; reducing these liabilities will be critical to the long-term fiscal health of the city. Unfortunately, small or deferred changes to pension liabilities can only postpone long-term funding issues. Left unsolved, these changes could result in additional cases of municipal distress.

Defined Contribution Plans

DC plans were first formalized in the 1980 tax code as supplemental savings plans. Employees could voluntarily set aside a percentage of their wages for retirement, with employers offering some type and degree of company match. Often the match was in company stock. While the employee's contributions were immediately vested, the company match generally took several years to vest. The participation rate in these programs varied significantly, with many employees either not participating or opting not to make the maximum allowed contribution. As long as these were supplemental savings plans that augmented traditional DB plans, this worked well.

However, as corporations began freezing DB plans, the role of the DC plan changed significantly. Many newer companies, particularly in the technology sector, have only offered DC plans. Today, the DC plan is the primary or only retirement plan for many U.S. workers. The growth in DC assets among private and public sector employees reflects this more prominent role.

Notably, DC plans shift the investment risk to the participant. Because DC plans most often do not allow for pooled longevity risk, individuals must self-insure against life expectancy. This requires saving for the longest life to ensure each person does not run out of money.

For a mobile workforce, DC plans have an advantage over DB plans, where eligibility rules may limit vesting. DC monies that are accrued (both employee-and employer-vested contributions) are portable. This is significant when you consider that the median number of years a new hire stays with the same employer is approximately 4.6 years.[13] Cliff vesting (the amount of time required at a company to be eligible for some level of benefits) under DB plan rules can be as long as five years. DC plan rules provide for cliff vesting in employer contributions in three years or less.[14]

Over the past three decades, 401(k) plans have grown to be the most common private sector employer-sponsored retirement plan. At year-end 2011, 401(k) plan assets had grown to $3.2 trillion, representing 18 percent of all retirement assets, with an estimated 51 million workers as active participants.[15] Other DC plans (including "457 plans" for state and local government employees, "403(b) plans" for education and tax-exempt employees) are increasingly offered as a supplement or substitute for traditional DB plans. Likewise, beginning in 1986, all new federal civilian employees became eligible to enroll in the Thrift Savings Plan (TSP). As of 2008, federal employees were auto-enrolled in TSP, and by the end of 2013, the TSP had grown to nearly $398 billion, with 4.6 million participants.[16]

The Pension Protection Act (PPA) of 2006 affirmed the growing role of DC plans and the need to increase participation by sanctioning automatic enrollment of employees, meaning employees automatically were enrolled in the plan (unless they affirmatively opted out) and authorizing automatic escalation of contributions.[17] Prior to PPA, the vast majority of employees held a combination of company stock and conservative fixed income funds in their 401(k) accounts. Following the authority granted in the PPA, the Department of Labor issued regulations that authorized a series of asset allocation products, including target date funds, balanced funds and managed accounts, for those participants who fail to make their own investment elections.

Personal Savings Plans

For individual investors, the self-employed and those who are not covered by an employer-sponsored plan, there are a variety of retirement savings programs. IRAs are the most common, holding an estimated $6.5 trillion in assets at the end of 2013.[18] The growth in IRA assets in both absolute and relative terms is staggering. While the overall value of retirement assets has increased, IRAs have grown to represent approximately 28 percent of U.S. total retirement assets as of 2013 compared to 19 percent nearly two decades ago, in 1995.[19]

The second most common personal savings plan is the Keogh plan, named after its congressional sponsor (the late Representative Eugene Keogh of New York) and principally designed for small-business owners. Keogh plans have higher contribution limits than other qualified plans. However, the plan's popularity is constrained somewhat by the fact that it entails considerable paperwork to set up, maintain and calculate payouts.

Self-directed retirement plans, whether employer-sponsored or personal savings plans, raise particular challenges. Do the participants have the ability to make asset allocation and specific investment decisions that are neither too conservative nor too risky? Many participants simply do not have the knowledge, interest or time to manage their own retirement assets. And for those at retirement age, further decisions need to be made about how and when to take distributions to avoid outliving their savings.

Decumulation strategies have become ever more critical as a large portion of the population moves into retirement. This was traditionally a period to use less risky investment strategies. However, assuming retirement at age 65 and longevity estimated at 80-plus, many individuals are facing a retirement investment horizon of 15 years or more. As such, an appropriate amount of risk must be taken to hedge longevity risk (i.e., the risk of outliving your savings). As DC plans become the dominant retirement savings vehicle, these risks are often borne by the individual. The dilemma of what to do with savings postretirement is as real and complex as how to save and invest in the accumulation phase.

REINFORCING AMERICA'S RETIREMENT FUNDING FRAMEWORK

Addressing America's retirement needs means looking at the issue holistically and reinforcing all three pillars of the retirement system: (1) Social Security, (2) employer sponsored retirement plans, and (3) personal savings.

Pillar I: Social Security

Social Security was originally designed to be a safety net only for those who needed it. If Social Security were to be refashioned to this original purpose, policy makers could increase eligibility requirements and cut benefits, thus reducing Social Security liabilities. While politically controversial, serious consideration must be given to increasing the retirement age for those who are currently far from retirement, as this would more accurately reflect changes in health and longevity. As proposed in President Barack Obama's 2013 budget, cost-of-living-adjustment (COLA) calculations need to be altered. Additionally, means testing or a benefits cap for those who have other significant sources of income or savings should be considered. Finally, the issue of funding disability income programs from the same source of tax revenue needs to be reconsidered, as the explosion of disability claimants contributes significantly to Social Security liabilities.

The asset side of Social Security also needs to be reevaluated. Under the current system, employer and employee contributions are invested in U.S. government securities and held in one of two trust funds (one for retirement benefits and the other for disability payments). The system is pay as you go, meaning existing workers help fund benefits for retirees and those collecting disability. As demographics shift and the ratio of workers to retirees declines, the trust funds are being depleted. By investing Social Security tax payments in a wider range of assets, the value of the trusts could be maximized and the reliance on funds from current workers could be reduced.

Reinforcing (and Relieving) Social Security

In order to reinforce the Social Security system, policy makers should consider repositioning Social Security as the "safety net" it was originally designed to be. To relieve the pressure on the Social Security system and decrease liabilities, eligibility requirements must be adjusted to reflect the changes in health and life expectancy that have occurred over the last 75 years. The retirement age should be increased to account for increased longevity and the COLA calculations need to be altered. Furthermore, means testing or a benefits cap for those who have large alternate sources of retirement income should be considered. Social Security liabilities could be further reduced if funding disability income programs did not come from the same pool of tax revenue. To increase the value of Social Security funds, policy makers could invest the tax payments in a wider range of assets to maximize trust values.

Pillar II: Employer-Sponsored Retirement Plans

Despite the wide range of employer-sponsored plans, there are still many employees who are not covered by any plan. All employers, from small to large, should be incentivized to provide retirement benefits to all full-time and part-time employees. This includes evaluating tax incentives, funding requirements and administrative burdens with the intention of encouraging employers to offer defined contribution and/or defined benefit plans.

First, we need to improve the fiscal health of existing DB plans using sound actuarial and investment return assumptions. Under the PPA, corporate plans were to be fully funded by 2015. This seemed highly achievable in 2006, but subsequent market downdrafts and a historically low interest-rate environment (which has kept liability discount rates lower) caused corporate plans to seek further flexibility in calculating corporate pension obligations. Specifically, legislation enacted in 2012 affords corporations the ability to discount liabilities at a higher assumed rate of return, effectively reducing the contribution amount required to reach fully funded status.[20] Legislation enacted in August 2014 extends the funding relief provided in 2012, maintaining the lower funding requirements.[21] While this may have short-term benefits, corporations still need a means to get their DB plans to a fully funded state.

Likewise, states and municipalities must address their underfunding sooner rather than later. Changes and proposed changes to accounting rules for government-sponsored retirement benefits obligations are expected to increase the stated liabilities for these plans and make the funding challenges greater. Moody's recently said that its rating criteria will now factor in discounting these liabilities at a risk-free rate, increasing ratings risks for public plan sponsors.[22] Realistically, more needs to be done to put these plans on a path to fiscal health.

Another important order of business relates to the challenge of lifetime income generation for plan participants. Most initiatives to date, such as automatically enrolling participants and automatically escalating their contributions have focused on bolstering the accumulation stage of retirement funding. But this new decumulation phase requires equal attention. Investors have little guidance when it comes to drawing income from savings in a manner that will ensure their assets are not exhausted while they are still alive.

Meanwhile, cost and complexity for employers is also problematic. Many employers, especially smaller companies, are reluctant to offer pension plans because of their concern about high administrative costs, the risk of compliance errors and fear of litigation. The current system includes a complex set of tax and Employee Retirement Income Security Act of 1974 (ERISA) rules, and creates concerns about potentially large legal exposures. Congress or the Department of Labor should provide clear and simple guidance for plan sponsors to avoid unnecessary liability. For example, so-called excessive fee cases now being brought against DC plan sponsors could be appropriately addressed by providing a safe harbor and an affirmative defense to these cases if the plan sponsor sought bids through a request for proposal, required responses to specific questions and had a robust evaluation process.

A comprehensive review should be conducted of legal/compliance burdens imposed by ERISA and similar state laws to determine what rules are truly necessary to protect participants. Those that are superfluous should be eliminated in order to simplify and streamline the system. This review should include an analysis of all the disclosures and information provided to participants to determine whether they are serving their intended purpose, as the preparation and dissemination of this material imposes a cost on all service providers. Ultimately, these costs reduce the monies available for benefits. We recommend a similar approach to simplifying tax rules and related compliance.

Proposals under consideration by various state legislators are intriguing. In these plans, employers would enroll workers in a DC plan where the assets are pooled and will be managed by the state retirement systems or other investment professionals. These ideas are innovative ways to encourage people to increase their retirement savings. However, the cost to employers and the applicability of ERISA and other legal issues will need to be addressed. "Start-up" tax credits and other incentives should be increased to encourage employers to create plans and to include part-time employees in these plans. The current tax credit of $500 for creating a DC plan significantly understates the true costs to an employer of establishing a plan.

Reinforcing Employer-Sponsored Plans

The fiscal health of existing DB plans must be improved, and funding levels must be restored. There are a variety of tools that should be used to incentivize employers to provide retirement benefits to all employees. Tax incentives would encourage employers to offer DB or DC plans. Decumulation and income distribution should be addressed with enhanced guidance and clarity, and the costs that discourage employers from establishing plans should be assessed and modified. Policy makers need to review the compliance burdens imposed by ERISA and similar state laws in order to retain necessary protections and eliminate unnecessary rules that discourage employers from establishing plans.

Pillar III: Personal Savings

As discussed above, in 2006 the PPA introduced significant changes for DC plans. These changes, as implemented over the last eight years, have generally positioned DC plans to better deliver on the promise of sufficient funds for their retirement. Even with these improvements, 32 percent of employees eligible to participate in an employer-sponsored DC plan fail to do so, or do so only at minimum levels.[23]

One potential solution is to require employees to participate, as long as they have an employer-provided plan. These employees would have a specified minimum contribution level based on their salary. If an employee has retirement savings in the aggregate from other sources (such as a DB plan from a prior employer or an IRA), the minimum contribution could be modified.

Another potential solution is to mandate personal retirement savings for the whole population, as has been done in Australia. Initially required savings would be equal to a small percentage of income, with a small increase each year, accompanied by a tax deferral or other tax incentives. Employers would be encouraged not to drop existing plans, be they DB or DC. A mandated savings program would allow Americans to build wealth over time. Ideally, individuals could accumulate as much as they want; however, the mandatory savings might become voluntary above a specified level. Depending on the program, individuals could be allowed to direct their own investments or invest in government-sponsored pools.

An individual retiring at age 65 today who made the maximum contributions to Social Security will collect annual benefits of roughly $28,500 a year. Based on current tax rules, the retirement saver and his/her employer has to contribute more than 12 percent of eligible yearly income to the Social Security trust fund every year. If that same amount were invested in a diversified portfolio of 90 percent U.S. stocks and 10 percent U.S. bonds when the worker was 30, gradually adjusting to a more conservative mix of 60 percent bonds/40 percent equities over time, the retirement income after 35 years (based on actual historical returns) would be approximately $42,000.[24]

Increasing the level of retirement savings is important, and individuals need information that will help them determine an optimal savings level and how that amount of savings translates into yearly income postretirement. As the focus has begun to turn to decumulation, a number of ways to calculate future potential income have been proposed, and these methodologies continue to evolve.

Reinforcing Personal Savings
There are a number of measures that could increase personal savings levels to improve retirement savings. The establishment of savings targets and the option for individuals to meet such targets through a combination of employer-sponsored savings and personal savings could improve personal savings practices. Another option is mandating personal retirement savings, perhaps via a phased approach that gradually increases income contributions over time. Tax deferrals and other incentives would encourage personal savings participation. Savers should be provided with the option to direct their own investments or participate in government-sponsored pools, and decumulation and income distribution must be addressed with clear guidance.

FIGURE 14.2 RECOMMENDATIONS FOR THREE PILLARS OF RETIREMENT SECURITY

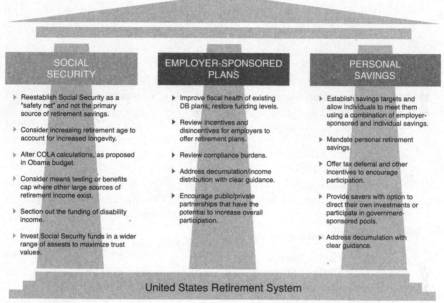

SOCIAL SECURITY

▶ Reestablish Social Security as a "safety net" and not the primary source of retirement savings.

▶ Consider increasing retirement age to account for increased longevity.

▶ Alter COLA calculations, as proposed in Obama budget.

▶ Consider means testing or benefits cap where other large sources of retirement income exist.

▶ Section out the funding of disability income.

▶ Invest Social Security funds in a wider range of assests to maximize trust values.

EMPLOYER-SPONSORED PLANS

▶ Improve fiscal health of existing DB plans; restore funding levels.

▶ Review incentives and disincentives for employers to offer retirement plans.

▶ Review compliance burdens.

▶ Address decumulation/income distribution with clear guidance.

▶ Encourage public/private partnerships that have the potential to increase overall participation.

PERSONAL SAVINGS

▶ Establish savings targets and allow individuals to meet them using a combination of employer-sponsored and individual savings.

▶ Mandate personal retirement savings.

▶ Offer tax deferral and other incentives to encourage participation.

▶ Provide savers with option to direct their own investments or participate in government-sponsored pools.

▶ Address decumulation with clear guidance.

United States Retirement System

Source: BlackRock

CONCLUSION

Most American will retire after their working days are over, making retirement a basic financial goal that unifies us all. Yet the funding of that goal is increasingly strained as life spans increase and the potency of the existing retirement savings paradigm wanes. While steps have been taken and proposals made to address many of the existing programs on the margins, they are mere Band-Aids when compared with the wholesale reinforcement and restructuring that is needed. What is most worrisome is that the longer the problem remains unaddressed, the larger it gets.

Clearly, the Social Security pillar of the U.S. retirement system needs to be preserved, as it provides important disability and survivor protections that all Americans deserve. However, we believe there is a strong case for bolstering the remaining two pillars, particularly the personal savings pillar, to ensure Americans have the financial means to see themselves through many years of retirement.

It is imperative that policy makers consider a holistic approach now— one that bolsters each pillar of retirement savings (see figure 14.2). This is the only way to ensure that all Americans have the opportunity to enjoy their hard-earned longer life spans without the burden of financial hardship.

NOTES

1. "Retirement Income Deficit Fact Sheet," Center for Retirement Research at Boston College, Retirement USA (2010), http://www.retirement-usa.org/retire ment-income-deficit-0.
2. Ruth Helman, Nevin Adams, Craig Copeland, and Jack VanDerhei, "2013 Retirement Confidence Survey: Perceived Savings Needs Outpace Reality for Many," *EBRI Issue Brief*, no. 384 (March 2013), http://www.ebri.org/pdf/briefs pdf/EBRI_IB_03-13.No384.RCS2.pdf.
3. D'Vera Cohn and Paul Taylor, "Baby Boomers Approach 65—Glumly: Survey Findings about America's Largest Generation," Pew Research Center, December 2010, http://www.pewsocialtrends.org/files/2010/12/Boomer-Summary-Re port-FINAL.pdf.
4. "Fast Facts & Figures about Social Security, 2014," Social Security Administration, Office of Retirement and Disability Policy, SSA Publication No. 13-11785 (September 2014) http://www.ssa.gov/policy/docs/chartbooks/fast_facts/2014 /fast_facts14.pdf.
5. "Life Expectancy for Social Security," Social Security Administration, http:// www.ssa.gov/history/lifeexpect.html.
6. "When to Start Receiving Retirement Benefits," Social Security Administration, SSA Publication No. 05-10147 (January 2014), http://www.socialsecurity .gov/pubs/EN-05-10147.pdf .
7. "Ratio of Social Security Covered Workers to Beneficiaries Calendar Years 1940–2010," Social Security Administration, http://www.ssa.gov/history/ratios .html
8. "Social Security Basic Facts," Social Security Administration. (July 2013), http://www.ssa.gov/news/press/basicfact.html.
9. "The 2013 Annual Report of the Board of Trustees of the Federal Old-Age and Survivors Insurance and Federal Disability Insurance Trust Funds," Social Security Administration, May 31, 2013, http://www.socialsecurity.gov/OACT /TR/2013/tr2013.pdf.
10. The election to participate is done by referendum and involves groups of employees by positions (not individual workers); since 1983 a decision to participate cannot be changed—once a position is covered, it remains so. "Social Security: Mandatory Coverage of State and Local Employees," Congressional Research Service Report to Congress (July 2011), http://www.nasra.org/Files /Topical%20Reports/Social%20Security/CRS%202011%20Report.pdf.
11. John Ehrhardt and Zorast Wadia, "Milliman Analysis: Pension Funding Ratio Climbs to 95.2% at Year-End 2013," Milliman, 100 Pension Fund Index (December 2013), http://us.milliman.com/uploadedFiles/insight/2014/pfi-01-2014 .pdf.
12. Rebecca A. Sielman, "2013 Public Pension Funding Study," Milliman (2013). http://www.milliman.com/uploadedFiles/Solutions/Products/public-pension

-funding-study-2013.pdf. Figure represents "recalibrated figures" using market value of assets.

13. "Employee Tenure in 2014," news release, Bureau of Labor Statistics, U.S. Department of Labor, September 18, 2014, http://www.bls.gov/news.release/pdf /tenure.pdf.

14. "What You Should Know about Your Retirement Plan." U.S. Department of Labor, Employee Benefits Security Administration (August 2013), http://www .dol.gov/ebsa/pdf/wyskgreenbook.pdf.

15. Jack VanDerhei, Sarah Holden, Luis Alonso, and Steven Bass, "401(k) Plan Asset Allocation, Account Balances, and Loan Activity in 2011." *EBRI Issue Brief*, no. 380, and *ICI Research Perspective* 18, no. 9 (December 2012), http://www.ebri .org/pdf/briefspdf/EBRI_IB_12-2012_No380.401k-eoy2011.pdf.

16. Thrift Savings Fund Financial Statements. December 31, 2013 and 2012, https://www.tsp.gov/PDF/formspubs/financial-stmt.pdf.

17. "2014 Universe Benchmarks: Measuring Employee Savings and Investing Behavior in Defined Contribution Plans," AON Hewitt (2014). The report finds that auto-enrollment has been shown to increase employee participation rates. The participation rate for employees subject to automatic enrollment was 84.6 percent versus 62.4 percent for those not subject to automatic enrollment.

18. Investment Company Institute, "2014 Investment Company Fact Book: A Review of Trends and Activities in the U.S. Investment Company Industry," 54th ed. (2014), http://www.ici.org/pdf/2014_factbook.pdf.

19. Ibid.

20. Moving Ahead for Progress in the 21st Century Act (MAP-21), July 6, 2012. Full text available at: http://www.gpo.gov/fdsys/pkg/BILLS-112hr4348enr /pdf/BILLS-112hr4348enr.pdf. For more information on MAP-21 and its impact on private plans, see BlackRock's "Corporate Pension Funding Update" (August 2012), http://www.blackrock.com/corporate/en-us/literature/white paper/corporate-pension-funding-update.pdf.

21. Highway and Transportation Funding Act of 2014 (HAFTA), August 8, 2014. Full text available at https://www.congress.gov/113/bills/hr5021/BILLS-113hr 5021enr.pdf.

22. "Adjustments to US State and Local Government Reported Pension Data," Moody's Investor Service, April 17, 2013, http://s3.documentcloud.org/docu ments/686623/moodys-pensions-final-adjustments-sc.pdf.

23. Craig Copeland, "Employment-Based Retirement Plan Participation: Geographic Differences and Trends, 2011," *EBRI Issue Brief*, no. 378 (November 2012).

24. Source: BlackRock. Calculated using price only returns. For more information, see 2013 *ViewPoint*, "Addressing America's Retirement Needs: Longevity Challenge Requires Action," http://www.blackrock.com/corporate/en-us/literature /whitepaper/viewpoint-retirement-needs-092013.pdf.

CHAPTER 15

TO GUARANTEE OR NOT TO GUARANTEE— THAT IS THE QUESTION

Jeremy Diamond

Former Managing Director,
Annaly Capital Management

Many of the causes of the last financial crisis, and potential causes of the next, have yet to be addressed by policy makers. The biggest of these is the U.S. housing finance system.

Housing is a critical economic driver, and the largest and most important financial asset for most Americans. Yet six years after the financial crisis began and Fannie Mae and Freddie Mac were put into conservatorship, many of the main reform issues have yet to be addressed.[1] But in the fall of 2014, with a viable bill in the Senate and other bills making their way through the House, stakeholders in the housing and mortgage markets are welcoming the apparent momentum. Homebuilders, mortgage lenders, realtors, mortgage servicers, consumer groups and investors alike have been part of the process through direct engagement, white papers, advocacy and education.

Yet the stakeholders who will be most affected by Washington decisions—homeowners—have been largely unaware of what is at risk in this policy debate. While all parties say they want to reduce the government's exposure to residential mortgage credit risk and prevent a repeat of the last crisis, the different proposals will have very different consequences for the average American homeowner. Any significant change to the current system will have an impact on mortgage pricing and availability, which will also affect housing values, so it is important to tread carefully.

While the structure of our housing finance system has had some enormous social benefits, such as the relatively democratic access to credit for home buyers, there are also downsides. As we all learned over the past six years, the structure was not only susceptible to housing bubbles and systemic financial crises, but there was an extraordinarily high cost to the socialization of credit risk as a result of poorly designed government involvement. The current system incentivizes the allocation of resources to housing so powerfully that it crowds out other possible uses of those resources. There are also claims of inequality and damage to the environment and public health.[2] Of course, any system that replaces the current one will also have advantages and disadvantages, and the economic effects of any change must be evaluated as well. But in order to fix a system as complex as the American housing finance system, we must first understand how it works and what is broken.

HOW THE SYSTEM WORKS (OR DOESN'T)

Most Americans don't know how a mortgage is made, where the money for a mortgage comes from and how rates are determined. Here's what every American should know: Our housing finance system is a marvel of the modern financial world. Like a national electric grid that can deliver electricity from any power company around the nation to the consumer who flips on a light switch, our mortgage finance system is capable of delivering mortgage funding from mortgage investors around the world to creditworthy American homeowners on essentially the same terms and conditions regardless of where they live in the country, the economic backdrop or the health and lending capacity of their local bank.

There are three foundational elements upon which this modern-day financial miracle is built: (1) securitization, where the mortgage loans from borrowers of similar creditworthiness are pooled into mortgage-backed securities (MBS) and receive the benefits of scale in pricing; (2) the government guarantee—delivered by Fannie Mae, Freddie Mac and Ginnie Mae—to make timely payments of interest and principal on mortgage-backed securities scales the process even further by removing credit risk and making the securities more homogeneous. Fannie Mae and Freddie Mac are known as Government-Sponsored Enterprises (GSEs) and together with Ginnie Mae are called Agencies; and (3) the to-be-announced, or TBA, market,[3] which is what Fannie, Freddie and Ginnie facilitate. It is through the TBA market that the majority of residential mortgages are pooled and sold to secondary market investors, and it enables originators and investors to hedge themselves.

With this structure in place, the U.S. housing finance system has come a long way since the days when taking out a home loan meant going down to the local savings and loan or community bank. Back then, the local bank had a credit officer who checked the borrower's credit, collateral and character, and then made the decision to extend the loan if it had the capacity.[4] The bank would price the loan—based on the borrower's credit risk and the bank's cost of capital—and keep it on its balance sheet, managing the associated credit risk and interest rate risk. Every month, the homeowner would get from the bank a notice to pay principal and interest, and if he or she couldn't make the payment then the bank would have to work it out. It was a bilateral relationship, with its own set of advantages and disadvantages.

Today, all of those steps are still taken, but in most cases they are disaggregated and performed by a variety of specialists, and automated where possible. The loan application is taken by the relationship manager at the bank, mortgage lender or credit union, which may have been chosen by the borrower through an online rate comparison. Documentation of employment and other financial information is collected. The house value is appraised and loans are sized based on cash available for down payment, loan-to-value, debt-to-income levels and the availability of private mortgage insurance, if necessary. The credit evaluation is centralized using Fair Isaac Corporation's (FICO) scores and other credit service bureau information. Credit decisions are determined based on, among other things, the investment criteria of the party providing the capital, such as whether the loan conforms to the Agency guidelines regarding size and credit.

If the loan is approved, it is priced based on interest rates in the secondary market, and that rate can generally be locked-in up to 90 days in advance.[5] It is more than likely that the mortgage is sold by the mortgage banker and placed in a pool with other, similar mortgages in a mortgage-backed security that is bought by and sits in the investment portfolios of secondary market investors here and around the world.[6] These sophisticated secondary market investors shoulder the credit and interest rate risk. Rating agencies evaluate the overall credit quality of the mortgage-backed security if it is not guaranteed by the Agencies. And servicing, including working out a delinquent loan, is probably done by a third-party servicer that specializes in that sort of thing.

This system works well when all of these different specialists do their jobs correctly. But in the buildup to the crisis, they did not. The Financial Crisis Inquiry Commission, which completed its report in January 2011, concluded that "a combination of excessive borrowing, risky investments, and lack of transparency put the financial system on a collision course with crisis."[7] There were execution failures on the part of virtually every mortgage finance player: the borrower, who sometimes lied on his application;

the originator, who had too-easy access to capital to lend; the underwriter, who let standards slip in pursuit of the closed mortgage; the appraiser, who somehow always came up with the right value; the securitization bankers, who packaged and repackaged securitizations with loans they knew would likely not perform; the derivatives geniuses, who designed many of these complex securities that failed; the rating agencies, whose rating models erroneously assumed that home prices only went up; secondary market investors, who outsourced their decisions to the rating agencies; bond counsel, who wrote bond agreements with opaque representations and warranties; and the servicers, who were ill-equipped for the massive numbers of delinquencies and defaults.

Not every one of them was derelict in their duties, and in some parts of the country people were more negligent than others. But enough of them were at fault, and the securities were so well distributed around the world, that the problem became systemic. The party that received the most criticism was the regulators, who were ill-prepared for the complexities of modern mortgage finance and stood by while evidence of the coming crisis was building. "They were hampered," said the Financial Crisis Inquiry Commission, "because they did not have a clear grasp of the financial system they were charged with overseeing, particularly as it had evolved in the years leading up to the crisis."[8]

The result of this breakdown can be seen in the following two graphs. Figure 15.1 shows the issuance of mortgage-backed securities in the United States by the issuing entities—Fannie Mae and Freddie Mac, Ginnie Mae, and non-Agency MBS. Fannie Mae and Freddie Mac issuance boomed during the refinancing wave of 2003 that was brought about by generational lows in interest rates. These same low rates sparked the beginning of a new wave of mortgage origination outside of the Agency market, one in which underwriting standards fell, creative "affordability products" were abused in order to entice borrowers, and investor demand grew. Annual issuance of non-Agency MBS exceeded $1 trillion in both 2005 and 2006, topping annual issuance by Fannie and Freddie for the first time.[9]

Lenders increasingly adopted an "originate to distribute" model, in which they were paid handsomely for the highest-yielding and riskiest mortgages, but retained none of the risk. "The market is paying me to do a no-income-verification loan more than it is paying me to do the full documentation loans," explained William D. Dallas after his company, Ownit Mortgage Solutions, went bankrupt in 2007. "What would you do?"[10] All of the flaws in the private-label, or non-Agency, securitization model resulted in a mortgage debt boom that financed large swaths of the country's housing stock. The home price bubble in the United States was, in reality, a by-product of a mortgage debt bubble. Figure 15.2, which presents the same data from figure

FIGURE 15.1   ANNUAL MBS ISSUANCE BY TYPE, 1996–2013

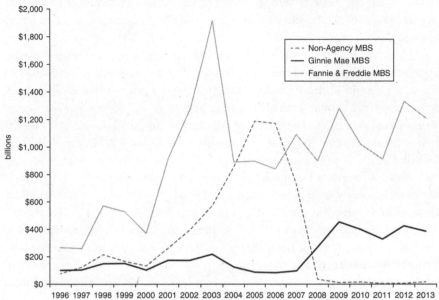

Source: Securities Industry and Financial Markets Association

FIGURE 15.2   MBS ISSUANCE MARKET SHARE, 1996–2013

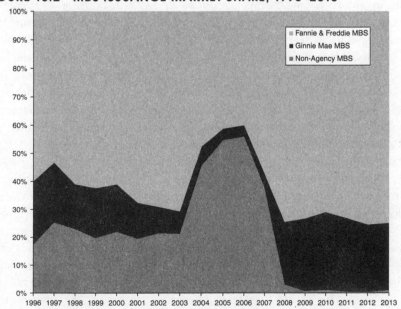

Source: Securities Industry and Financial Markets Association

15.1 on a percentage-of-issuance basis, illustrates quite literally the concept of the mortgage debt bubble that the financial crisis spawned. After inflating in 2005–06, the bubble of non-Agency MBS issuance popped and hasn't recovered.

In addition to not keeping pace with the evolution of mortgage finance, regulators and policy makers did not clearly grasp the pervasive nature of Fannie Mae and Freddie Mac's role in mortgage finance—that is, how those companies function and what their risks are. Born of Depression-era necessity, Fannie Mae, and later Freddie Mac and Ginnie Mae, are the mechanisms by which the government guarantee on Agency MBS are delivered. While Ginnie Mae is a government agency and its mortgage-backed securities carry an explicit full-faith-and-credit guarantee of the U.S. Treasury, the government backing of Fannie and Freddie's guarantee was implied by their government charters and a line of credit from the U.S. Treasury.[11] The government was complicit in perpetuating this gray area—it derived enormous benefits from stimulating housing without the on–balance sheet exposure—so that despite the actual facts to the contrary,[12] every investor in Agency mortgage-backed securities around the world assumed that Fannie and Freddie paper was tantamount to a sovereign credit.[13]

Until they were taken into conservatorship, Fannie and Freddie were unique, hybrid animals—publicly traded companies with government charters. Fannie and Freddie served two masters, and in the end they proved to be disastrous for both. As public companies, they operated as any profit-making entity would, to try to maximize profit by taking advantage of all their opportunities, which included advantageously priced and virtually limitless borrowing thanks to their government relationship. In so doing, they were overleveraged with huge balance sheets and, by the time they were taken into conservatorship, overinvested in some of the riskiest MBS structures.

In a sense, Fannie Mae and Freddie Mac became two of the largest, most levered bond funds in history. The government-backed mortgage guarantee business was their raison d'être, but it was the profits from their portfolios that drove their growth, their share price and their executives' bonuses. When losses on those more risky portfolio investments started piling up, their small slivers of capital were overwhelmed, and the government really had no choice but to take them over; together they had trillions in MBS and senior debt outstanding, all held by investors who trusted in their implied government backstop.[14] The cost to taxpayers to fund those losses in order to honor their senior debt obligations and keep the insurance business going has been over $187 billion.[15] While in conservatorship, the lending that is made possible through that government-backed insurance business has continued as investors understandably shied away from mortgage credit risk. The irony of this situation is that Fannie and Freddie are actually living up to their original government charters by providing market liquidity and a source of funds for mortgage lending during an extended period of market dislocation; if Fannie and Freddie didn't exist, Congress would be trying to create them.[16]

In the aftermath of the financial crisis, the residential mortgage-backed securities market looks like this: The government now touches 9 out of 10 new mortgages, with monthly government Agency origination of mortgage debt running around $100 billion to $150 billion.[17] There is no infrastructure in place for a non-government-guaranteed securitization market that can replace this origination capacity.

Finally, and perhaps most critically for restructuring America's housing finance system: Who is the ultimate funder of residential mortgages? How will they behave in any new system of finance? The next two graphs begin to get at these answers. The financing of the U.S. residential mortgage market is shown in figure 15.3 by the type of entity in which it is held or pooled. Of the approximately $10 trillion of residential mortgage loans outstanding, 61 percent is pooled into Agency MBS and funded by investors in those securities, 28 percent is funded by and sitting on bank balance sheets, and 8 percent is funded by investors in non-Agency MBS. The holders of all senior debt and MBS securities issued by Fannie Mae, Freddie Mac and Ginnie Mae are shown in figure 15.4. The three top holders of these senior Agency obligations—U.S. banks, the Federal Reserve and foreign holders— own these securities primarily because of their near-sovereign status, their capital treatment and their ability to be leveraged. The same can probably be said for most of the other classes of holders—insurance companies, state and local governments, pension funds and money market mutual funds; these are not entities that are likely to be taking on significant amounts of residential mortgage credit risk.

These two graphs together show the importance of the government wrap or guarantee to the financing of America's residential mortgages. While approximately $6 trillion, or 61 percent, of all U.S. mortgages are in pools wrapped by the government guarantee, approximately three-quarters of those investors[18] are unlikely to hold anywhere near the same amount of mortgage-backed securities that are not government guaranteed.

Moreover, the graphs point out a significant difference between the mortgage finance system in our country and those in other countries. While our mortgage finance system is dominated by securitization and secondary market funding, in other developed countries funding from bank deposits still predominates, followed by covered bonds. There is only a minimal amount of securitization in Europe and elsewhere.[19] Thus, while it would be difficult for other countries to replicate our system without developing a functioning securitization market and installed base of secondary market investors, it would be just as unfeasible for the United States to revert back

FIGURE 15.3 COMPOSITION OF RESIDENTIAL MORTGAGE MARKET ON DECEMBER 31, 2013

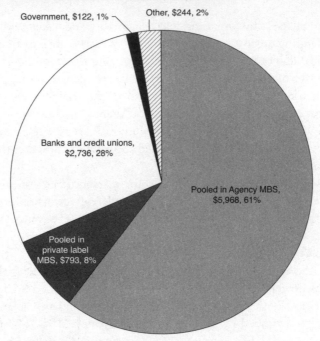

In billions, total $9.863 billion.
Source: Federal Reserve

FIGURE 15.4 HOLDERS OF AGENCY AND GSE-BACKED SECURITIES ON DECEMBER 31, 2013

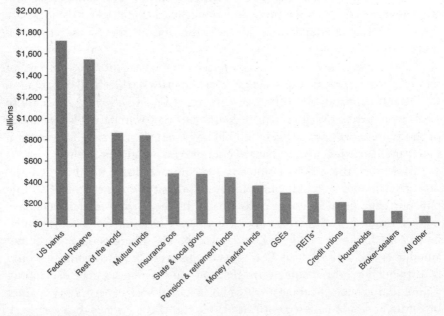

*Real Estate Investment Trusts
Source: Federal Reserve

to a bank-deposit-dominated mortgage finance system. On December 31, 2013, there was approximately $10 trillion in outstanding residential mortgage debt in the United States, while deposits at our country's banks totaled just $11.7 trillion.[20] We just don't have the deposit capacity.

REFORM PROGRESS

Even though no reform legislation has passed, since the beginning of conservatorship of the GSEs in 2008, there have been multiple bills, proposals and white papers issued from the right and the left, from members of Congress, think tanks, trade groups, academics and assorted market participants. Perhaps most important among these, if only for drawing lines in the sand, is the white paper published by the Departments of Treasury and Housing and Urban Development in February 2011. In this document, the Obama administration laid out three possible directions for housing finance reform without stating a preferred outcome.[21] Option 1 calls for a largely privatized system of mortgage finance, with government's role very narrowly targeted to certain disadvantaged groups of borrowers. Option 2 keeps the same narrowly targeted groups receiving government support, while providing for a guarantee mechanism that scales up during economic crises. Option 3 has the same narrowly targeted groups receiving direct assistance, and adds a catastrophic insurance wrap for the conforming mortgage market that stands behind significant private capital.

Aggregating the various proposals issued to date,[22] there is a general consensus on the objectives of a successful system of housing finance going forward: Protect the taxpayer; stabilize the market and facilitate the continued flow of credit to creditworthy residential mortgage borrowers; shrink the government's role in the housing finance system; resolve the future of Fannie and Freddie; and increase the role of private capital in taking on residential mortgage credit risk.

Nevertheless, there remains significant disagreement over how to do it—namely, the amount and form of the first-loss protection by private capital; how to attract sufficient capital dedicated to residential mortgage credit risk to support most plans for taxpayer protection; the structure of the government guarantee delivery system; and the ultimate resolution of Fannie and Freddie.

These points of contention are significant, but Washington is grappling with them. Recent developments have been sufficient to suggest a reform bill could be passed before the next presidential election. This is still probably an aggressively optimistic timetable given the demands of the interim election, the intransigence of ideology and the vicissitudes of a lame-duck presidency, but there are some notable milestones to give us hope.

First, there has been movement in Congress. In the Senate, on June 25, 2013, Senators Bob Corker (R-TN) and Mark Warner (D-VA) of the Senate Banking Committee, along with eight bipartisan cosponsors, introduced a bill entitled the Housing Finance Reform and Taxpayer Protection Act.[23] The bill would wind down Fannie Mae, Freddie Mac and the Federal Housing Finance Agency (FHFA) over a period of five years and replace them with a government-owned guarantor called the Federal Mortgage Insurance Corporation (FMIC). The FMIC would provide catastrophic reinsurance that would stand behind a required first-loss position of 10 percent that would be absorbed by private capital, as well as a mortgage insurance fund that would have reserves of 2.5 percent of the balance of FMIC-guaranteed mortgages outstanding.

In the House, on July 24, 2013, the Financial Services Committee passed the Protecting American Taxpayers and Homeowners Act (PATH Act), sponsored by committee chair Jeb Hensarling (R-TX), Scott Garrett (R-NJ), Shelley Moore Capito (R-WV) and Randy Neugebauer (R-TX), that would eliminate any government guarantee from the mortgage market outside of the Federal Housing Administration (FHA) guarantee (which would also be reduced and limited to the neediest borrowers).[24] It is not a bipartisan bill—voting went strictly according to party lines—and is closest to option 1 from the Treasury's white paper. The PATH Act has three main parts: Title I would wind down Fannie Mae and Freddie Mac within five years and shrink the conforming mortgage loan limits. Title II would spin out FHA from the Department of Housing and Urban Development into a separate agency, capitalize the Mutual Mortgage Insurance Fund (MMIF) at 4 percent and limit the FHA insurance to first-time homebuyers and low- and middle-income borrowers. Title III would establish a National Mortgage Market Utility that would regulate, organize and standardize securitizations for the rest of the mortgage market. Standardization and grouping by credit profile is intended to satisfy the liquidity characteristics that are currently supplied by the government wrap. Title III also sets forth the regulatory framework for a covered bond market. The PATH Act has not come to the full House floor for a vote.

On March 11, 2014, Senate Banking Committee chair Tim Johnson (D-SD) and ranking member Mike Crapo (R-ID) announced a bill that has many of the same features of the Corker-Warner bill.[25] This bipartisan bill has reportedly had input from the White House and, while it was ultimately passed by the committee on May 15, 2014, it is still unclear whether it has enough support to advance to the Senate floor for a vote.

Second, the regulatory front is developing. The FHFA, the regulator of the GSEs, has a new chair, Melvin Watt, who is expected to lean more toward an option 3–type outcome. While Congress has been debating some of the larger policy issues around housing finance reform, FHFA has been pushing to build a new infrastructure for the secondary mortgage market, gradually contract the GSEs' footprint in the market and maintain foreclosure prevention activities and credit availability. One element of the FHFA's plan is to bring more private capital in front of the taxpayer. Both Fannie and Freddie have initiated programs to transfer credit risk to private market participants, and FHFA has also mandated increases in the guarantee fee that the GSEs collect.

Regulators are also getting close to resolving elements of the Dodd-Frank Act designed to address poor underwriting standards and suitability issues. These include definitions for Qualified Mortages (QM), Qualified Residential Mortgages (QRM) and risk retention.[26]

Third, President Obama has stepped up his involvement in the issue. Since the Treasury released its white paper in 2011, the administration has been mostly silent on housing finance reform, choosing instead to let the debate proceed in Congress without executive intervention. Perhaps sensing that the presence of two strong bills in Congress made the time right for more public engagement, on August 6, 2013, Obama delivered a major policy speech on the topic. The president stated that the core principle to drive housing finance reform is that "private capital should take a bigger role in the mortgage market" in an effort to protect American taxpayers.[27] In addition, the president's reform plan is grounded in three other driving principles: ending the Fannie Mae and Freddie Mac business model as we know it; ensuring access to the 30-year fixed-rate mortgage in all economic climates; and preserving affordable homeownership for all. The White House's support of the Johnson-Crapo bill signals its favored direction in the housing finance reform debate.[28]

THE WAY FORWARD

Any discussion of the future of housing finance raises many philosophical and policy questions, such as the value of homeownership as part of the American Dream, the contribution of housing to the economy as a whole and as a builder of household wealth and community strength, and the relative importance of affordable rental housing as a policy goal. Most germane to our current circumstances is the consideration of the appropriate size and scope of the government's involvement in housing and housing finance.

We are not, however, building our housing finance system from scratch. If we were, perhaps the world sketched out by the Republicans on the House Financial Services Committee in the PATH Act would make the most sense. In it, aside from traditional FHA activities, the government would be mostly the setter of rules regarding underwriting standards and credit categories for standardized securitization markets. In other words, the creators of the PATH Act are not trying to find the best mortgage finance system for the United States *given the current mortgage finance system*; instead they solved for the best mortgage finance system for the United States in which the government played a very limited role. While a mortgage market would still exist under those circumstances, it would be a much smaller market, and loans would be more expensive and harder to get.

The world according to the PATH Act completely ignores the current sources of capital for funding residential mortgages, and their motivations for making such investments. Credit Suisse estimated that the mortgage market without a government guarantee would be $3 to $4 trillion smaller.[29] Most of the capital invested in government-guaranteed mortgage-backed securities is only invested in them because of the guarantee and what it makes possible—liquidity, risk-weighting advantages and financeability. Some of these so-called rates investors[30] could cross over, and investors in some other asset classes might be attracted to a deeper non-Agency MBS market, but no one can say for sure how many or at what price or in what time frame. So while a wrap isn't essential for a mortgage market to exist, the future state of housing finance must include a government guarantee if we want to maintain the best features of our current system—such as liquidity, homeowner flexibility, availability and pricing of credit and the TBA market—as well as the well-established base of investors.

In a world without a government guarantee, there would also be the significant problem of transitioning out of our current system. Perhaps the most troubling consequence, and of greatest importance to homeowners, would be the effect on housing values. If there is $3 to $4 trillion less funding available for mortgage loans—a 30 to 40 percent reduction in the size of the market—the value of the homes collateralizing those loans would also have to shrink in proportion.

Consider it this way: Every homeowner today owns and/or financed his or her home in a system in which over 60 percent of all mortgages have a government guarantee. It doesn't even matter if a particular homeowner's loan was itself pooled into an Agency MBS, because *all* mortgages and *all* home values created in this environment have been affected in some way from the larger pool of capital available to fund and hedge all mortgages. If in the future there is no such government involvement in the mortgage finance system, a homeowner will face challenges when trying to refinance or sell. Refinancing will be problematic if the loan is underwater—and we have already seen the lengths to which the government will go in order to assist underwater borrowers.[31] As owners who bought or financed in a market that contains the government guarantee try to sell their homes in one that doesn't, the consequent drop in home values could result in the greatest generational wealth transfer in the history of the country. This may be good or bad, depending on which generation you belong to; regardless, it must be a consciously deliberated concern of the policy equation. So when a representative in Congress announces with pride to her constituents that she has successfully removed the government's involvement in the mortgage market, she must also describe what the potential costs of that policy will be.[32]

From the general movement of the policy discussion in Congress, it is becoming clear that most legislators understand these market truths, and in the future, mortgage finance will likely still have some form of government guarantee. In order for mortgage credit to continue to flow into the U.S. housing market on terms, conditions and availability that are similar to what we have enjoyed in the past, and to protect the taxpayer from the exposure inherent under that guarantee, the following principles should be followed:

1. **Explicit government wrap with significant private capital layers to first absorb losses.** A new system of housing finance should have a government guarantee that is similar to the one currently in place, with a few exceptions. It should be an explicit guarantee of the timely payment of principal and interest on the mortgage-backed securities, but one in which the government incurs a loss only in the event catastrophic market conditions have exhausted the private capital that is in place to absorb the first losses. This principle attempts to strike a balance between an essentially unprotected government guarantee (as historically existed under guarantees provided by Fannie and Freddie) and a fully privatized market. Thus, the government's exposure to loss from the guarantee should have multiple layers of protection in front of it provided by different parts of the private market.
   a. The first layer of private capital protecting the government from loss is the equity provided by the borrower. In order for a mortgage to be eligible for the benefits of pooling into a security with the government guarantee, the maximum loan-to-value will be 80 percent, with a minimum of 5 percent down payment and private mortgage insurance for the balance. (Mortgages that currently qualify for Ginnie Mae backing have different requirements.)
   b. The second layer of private capital protection is provided by the market, either through pool-level insurance, risk-sharing credit notes, simple risk retention, securitization tranching or something similar. Both Fannie and Freddie have been testing the market with these types of programs. The risk-sharing notes generally sell the first 3 percent of risk, while Fannie's

pilot pool-level insurance program bought a 2 percent first-loss piece. The challenge with this layer is that there will be periods in which there is strong demand for this higher-risk/higher-return profile, and there will also be periods where there is low or no demand. Thus, the first-loss piece that is sold in this fashion can be adjusted up or down as market demand dictates.

c. The third layer is also provided by the borrower,[33] in the form of a fee that will be used to capitalize a mortgage insurance fund (MIF) that will ultimately have a reserve ratio of 3 percent. The fee could be sized at 50 basis points to capitalize the fund within six years.[34]

d. The objective of the combination of these three layers is to have in place first-loss protection of 5 percent of the outstanding principal balance of the mortgages outstanding, which would have been sufficient to cover even 2007's loss experience for Fannie and Freddie, the worst year for their Agency MBS pools.[35] With this much protection in front of the government's catastrophic wrap, it is highly unlikely that the taxpayer would have to pay out a dollar to cover losses except in economic conditions that were worse than the Great Recession.

2. **Shrink and wind down Fannie Mae and Freddie Mac.** Fannie Mae and Freddie Mac, despite their flaws as corporate entities, possess valuable assets and technologies as part of their guarantee businesses, and the mortgage market has grown up and now revolves around them. These should be maintained and utilized in the new mortgage finance system.

a. The portfolio activity of Fannie and Freddie should be wound down and legacy assets sold off at a reasonable pace that does not disrupt the market.

b. Profits of the GSEs should be directed into the new MIF during their wind-down as part of the transition to the new system of mortgage finance.

c. The conversion from Fannie Mae and Freddie Mac to the new system should be done over a sufficiently long period of time, during which the legacy GSE mortgage-backed securities would be deliverable into the new securities.

3. **Guarantee delivery system.** The structure of the entity that delivers and organizes the catastrophic guarantee is one of the most challenging for achieving consensus.

a. The path of least resistance would be for the government to internalize Fannie and Freddie and turn conservatorship—which was meant to be temporary—into something permanent, wind down their portfolio activities and at some point merge them into a single entity. Fannie and Freddie would cease to exist as independent companies but would continue to serve their original charter. In this scenario, then, Fannie/Freddie would be an entity similar to Ginnie Mae, with each entity handling its respective portion of the mortgage market. Another option would be to eliminate Fannie and Freddie entirely and expand Ginnie Mae into the ultimate provider of the catastrophic wrap. Ginnie Mae would continue to provide its catastrophic guarantee to its traditional book of business, while the three layers of protection enumerated above would sit in front of the Ginnie Mae wrap that would guarantee what was the old Fannie/Freddie conforming mortgage. U.S. Representatives John Delaney (D-MD), John Carney (D-AL) and Jim Himes (D-CT) introduced a bill that is similar to this proposal in July 2014 called the Partnership to Strengthen Homeownership Act.[36]

b. The structure that is currently under consideration in the Johnson-Crapo bill is complex. It calls for the creation of the FMIC, a new regulator that has many functions. It regulates the mortgage market, provides the explicit catastrophic government backstop, regulates new mortgage bond insurance entities and mortgage aggregators, and organizes both a new mutually owned securitization platform and a small-bank mortgage aggregating cooperative. It has been suggested that this structure will ultimately increase the concentration of lending into a few large banks, thereby ensuring a new generation of too-big-to-fail mortgage giants, but its final form is far from resolved.[37] The Johnson-Crapo structure is feasible, but it has its challenges.[38]

4. **Continue to facilitate the flow of credit to the mortgage market**. The policy objective of a new system of housing finance would be to continue to enable creditworthy borrowers to get a mortgage on essentially the same terms and conditions regardless of where they lived in the country and the economic backdrop. For that to occur, policy makers must take into account the perspective of the providers of mortgage funding.

   a. Maintain the liquidity of the secondary market by preserving the TBA market through the homogeneity that the government wrap provides. This also contributes to preserving the wide availability of the popular 30-year fixed-rate mortgage.

   b. Continue to meet the needs of rates investors, who provide over 60 percent of the funding for residential mortgages.

c. Implement programs and strategies to foster continued support from the secondary market. Fannie and Freddie, and later the Federal Reserve through its monetary policy, were important providers of demand for MBS, particularly in times of market stress. With Fannie and Freddie no longer operating in their traditional role of providing market support, and as the Federal Reserve tapers (and eventually ends) its purchases of Agency MBS, the secondary market will no longer have a government-sponsored participant in the market. This is a healthy market development, but one in which market-based demand for the government-guaranteed MBS would likely have more volatility. Mortgage real estate investment trusts in particular have the ability to step up and play a role in dependably filling this demand. In addition, policy makers should focus on ensuring the safety and soundness of the mortgage insurance and bond insurance industries, because they are likely to grow in importance as vehicles for attracting private capital to take first-loss exposure.

As much of the activity discussed in this essay is occurring in real time, there is a risk that it will no longer be timely after this book's publication. But the many complicating factors involved, and the amount of time that has already passed, suggest it should have a very long shelf life. For example, Fannie Mae and Freddie Mac are generating significant profits now, and their contributions to offsetting budget deficits will be hard for policy makers to give up. There are also court challenges being teed up by investors who have taken positions in those companies' common and preferred securities and want a share of those profits.[39] The first of these cases was decided against the investors, but the issue is still not fully resolved.[40] In addition, Congress has no incentive to legislate. There is no emergency in housing at the moment and conservatorship has no fixed end date. Moreover, absent a significant shift in the makeup of Congress, partisan wrangling and intransigence over ideology will likely stay true to form.

Finally, after lowering the federal funds rate to near zero in December 2008, the Federal Reserve has used several nontraditional tools to execute monetary policy, including the purchase of Agency MBS in its quantitative easing program. The size of this program, along with its purchases of Treasuries, has suppressed yields on mortgage-backed securities, lowered mortgage rates and distorted the pricing of virtually every security in the marketplace. It has gone on for such a lengthy period of time that it remains to be seen what effect tapering will have on the markets, not to mention the eventual raising of rates, but it would be dangerous to draw any specific conclusions about the market ramifications of policy decisions (i.e., mortgage rates, market demand, housing prices) while the Fed is still leaning heavily on the markets.[41]

While Congress works through its process, many of the flaws in the system are already being addressed, both by regulators and the markets. The new qualified mortgage rules should help reduce the number of unsuitable loans being made. New appraisal rules are tightening that process. Frameworks for improving lender representations and warranties are being developed in Washington and in the industry. Rating agencies have improved their models for evaluating mortgage pools. Servicing standards are tighter, and servicers are under much closer scrutiny. Underwriting standards have gotten more prudent (perhaps even overly stringent for a lengthy portion of the postcrisis period), leading to much improved credit performance on newer vintage loans. The higher guarantee fees that are currently and prospectively going to be charged better reflect the risk of the government's exposure under the guarantee, although they don't address the moribund private-label securities market. Fannie and Freddie's risk-transfer pilot programs are growing and market acceptance is building. These will help price risk more appropriately and, as they grow, protect the taxpayer.

Our system of housing finance is a modern financial market marvel, but certain flaws in that system helped produce one of the worst economic crises in American history. The two dominant entities in housing finance are currently operating in a limbo of conservatorship. Uncertainty over the outcome inhibits the participation of stakeholders, particularly the private label securitization market, which only foments the need for more government involvement. Housing finance reform is necessary, but reform that is ill-designed could wreak more damage than the status quo. The markets will adapt to whatever policies come out of Congress, but an understanding of how they will adapt is critical to the success of whatever system exists in the post–Fannie and Freddie world of housing finance. As FHFA entitled its 2012 strategic plan for the GSE conservatorships, the debate over housing finance reform is the "story that needs an ending."[42] Americans—homeowners, taxpayers, voters—are waiting.

NOTES

1. Under the Housing and Economic Recovery Act of 2008, Fannie Mae and Freddie Mac were placed into conservatorship on September 6, 2008. Since that time they have conducted their business under the direction of their regulator, the Federal Housing Finance Agency, or FHFA.
2. Michael Milken, "How Housing Policy Hurts the Middle Class," *Wall Street Journal*, March 5, 2014, http://online.wsj.com/news/articles/SB10001424052702 304610404579401613007521066.
3. TBA is a contract for the purchase or sale of Agency mortgage-backed securities, to be delivered at a future, specified date. At the time of the trade, only six criteria are agreed upon by the buyer and seller: issuer, maturity, coupon, face value, price and settlement date. The exact mortgage pools, number of pools and loans composing the pools are not known, but investors know enough to make the forward purchase commitment. The fungibility and homogeneity of the conforming loan product, the characteristics that make Agency MBS homogeneous, are made possible by the government guarantee.
4. Capacity is dictated by the amount of a bank's funding, such as deposits and bank capital, both equity and debt, and its loan commitments. Think of the speech delivered by James Stewart as George Bailey of Bailey Savings & Loan, trying to stave off a bank run in *It's a Wonderful Life:* "The money's not here. Your money's in Joe's house . . . right next to yours. And in the Kennedy house, and Mrs. Macklin's house, and a hundred others. Why, you're lending them the money to build, and then, they're going to pay it back to you as best they can." In order for George Bailey to keep making loans, he needed not only more deposits, but he also needed existing mortgage borrowers to pay their loans back.
5. The TBA market has contracts for purchasing conforming mortgages 60 or 90 days (or beyond) in advance at a particular interest rate or yield, and that rate is the basis upon which the rate lock is made. Without the secondary market investors' forward commitment to buy in the TBA market, forward rate locks would be much harder and more expensive (for the borrower) to come by.
6. Unlike George Bailey, these modern-day mortgage lenders in essence recycle their capital through securitization, enabling them to make many more loans by selling them to the secondary market for a small profit and, sometimes, retaining the servicing fee stream.
7. The Financial Crisis Inquiry Commission, "The Financial Crisis Inquiry Report," January 2011, xix, http://cybercemetery.unt.edu/archive/fcic/20110310173 545/http:/c0182732.cdn1.cloudfiles.rackspacecloud.com/fcic_final_report_full .pdf.
8. Ibid., xxi.
9. Securities Industry and Financial Market Association, U.S. Mortgage-Related Issuance and Outstanding, http://www.sifma.org/research/statistics.aspx.
10. Vikas Bajaj and Christine Haughney, "Tremors at the Door," *New York Times*, January 26, 2007, http://www.nytimes.com/2007/01/26/business/26mortgage .html?_r=0.
11. Fannie Mae, then known as the Federal National Mortgage Association (FNMA), was founded in 1938 during the Great Depression. In 1968, Congress partitioned FNMA into Fannie Mae and Ginnie Mae; Fannie became a

privately held corporation and supported the conventional mortgage market, while Ginnie remained a government organization and supported the FHA and VA markets, among others. Freddie Mac was created by Congress in 1970 to compete with Fannie Mae. The $2.5 billion lines of credit that were available to Fannie and to Freddie were, at the end, purely symbolic.

12. Even today, in conservatorship, the title page of every Fannie Mae single-family MBS prospectus carries the following warning for potential investors: "We guarantee to each trust that we will supplement amounts received by the trust as required to permit timely payments of principal and interest on the certificates. We alone are responsible for making payments under our guaranty. The certificates and payments of principal and interest on the certificates are not guaranteed by the United States and do not constitute a debt or obligation of the United States or any of its agencies or instrumentalities other than Fannie Mae." Freddie Mac MBS offering documents carry a similar legend.

   Fannie Mae MBS prospectus: http://www.fanniemae.com/syndicated/documents/mbs/mbspros/SF_October_1_2014.pdf.

   Freddie Mac MBS prospectus: http://www.freddiemac.com/mbs/docs/pcoc_040314.pdf.

13. A sovereign credit is a debt obligation of a sovereign country, like a U.S. Treasury, and therefore backed by the full faith, credit and taxing power of that country's government.

14. Needless to say, the common equity and preferred shareholders of Fannie Mae and Freddie Mac were not treated in the same manner as the senior creditors; these junior capital securities holders were all but wiped out in conservatorship. Some investors have purchased these securities for pennies postconservatorship in the hope and belief that there will be some value to them once the futures of Fannie Mae and Freddie Mac are resolved. Whether this is true remains to be seen, and may only be settled through the courts.

15. There are many sources for this number, including the Federal Housing Finance Agency, the regulator of Fannie Mae and Freddie Mac, and it refers to the amount of financial support provided by the U.S. Treasury to enable the GSEs to fund their losses and continue to operate. http://www.fhfa.gov/Conservatorship/Pages/History-of-Fannie-Mae–Freddie-Conservatorships.aspx.

16. Michael A. J. Farrell, founder of Annaly Capital Management, first developed this idea, articulated in his "Letter from a Washington Conference Room," August 20, 2010, https://www.creditwritedowns.com/2010/08/letter-from-a-washington-conference-room.html.

17. Securities Industry and Financial Market Association, U.S. Mortgage-Related Issuance and Outstanding.

18. The sum of the holdings of U.S. banks, the Federal Reserve, foreign holders, insurance companies, state and local governments, pension and retirement funds, and money market funds as a percentage of all holdings of Agency and GSE-backed securities.

19. European Mortgage Federation, Policy Issues, Mortgage Funding, http://www.hypo.org/Content/default.asp?PageID=448.

20. Source: Federal Reserve, Z.1. Financial Accounts of the United States. Table L.100 for mortgage total, Table L.109 for deposits. Includes checkable deposits, small time and savings deposits and large time deposits at U.S.-chartered depository institutions, foreign banking offices, banks in U.S.-affiliated areas and credit unions. http://www.federalreserve.gov/releases/z1/Current/z1r-4

.pdf. This is why mortgage-backed securities and other market-based financing sources such as money market funds are sometimes called shadow banks, because they replace what had traditionally been within the purview of banks. Once that disintermediation has occurred, it is difficult to reverse. In the case of bank deposits moving to money market funds as well as mortgage loans moving from bank balance sheets to mortgage-backed securities pools, reversing those trends would require significantly more capital in the banking system. Thus, calls for the U.S. system to become more like a European system or a Danish system—which have similar homeownership rates but have nothing similar to Fannie and Freddie or our securitization markets—miss two important points. First is the extent to which the housing finance models of Europe, Denmark and Canada are bank-centric and therefore unfeasible in the United States today: in the United States, the mortgage debt-to-deposit ratio is much higher than in European countries. Second is that such a bank-centric model does, in fact, have implicit government support because bank deposits are guaranteed and many banks were nationalized or otherwise supported during the financial crisis.

21. U.S Department of the Treasury and the Department of Housing and Urban Development, "Reforming America's Housing Finance Market: A Report to Congress," February 2011, http://www.treasury.gov/initiatives/Documents /Reforming%20America%27s%20Housing%20Finance%20Market.pdf. The three options aren't necessarily mutually exclusive and could have been meant for sequential implementation. The white paper was unclear.

22. "The $5 Trillion Question: What Should We Do with Fannie Mae and Freddie Mac: Comparison of 27 Plans to Reform Fannie Mae and Freddie Mac," The Center for American Progress, February 2014. The Center for American Progress has put together a handy table of 27 different plans to reform Fannie Mae and Freddie Mac and the American housing finance system, updated through February 2014. http://www.americanprogress.org/wp-content/uploads /2014/02/GriffithHousingTable-revised.pdf.

23. Housing Finance Reform and American Taxpayer Protection Act, http://www .corker.senate.gov/public/index.cfm/housing-finance-reform.

24. Protecting American Taxpayers and Homeowners (PATH) Act, http://finan cialservices.house.gov/uploadedfiles/bills-113hr-pih-path-ss.pdf.

25. Technically Johnson-Crapo is considered an "amendment in the nature of a substitute" to Corker-Warner, and thus carries the same name and bill number (S. 1217). Consider Johnson-Crapo as a revised Corker-Warner that provided key changes and necessary detail. After all, Corker-Warner's draft was only 160 pages, while Johnson-Crapo is some 450 pages long. http://www.banking .senate.gov/public/index.cfm?FuseAction=Files.View&FileStore_id=512757b1 -e595-4b85-8321-30d91e368849.

26. The Wall Street Reform and Consumer Protection Act, commonly known as the Dodd-Frank Act after its sponsors, Congressman Barney Frank and Senator Chris Dodd, was signed into law by President Obama on July 21, 2010. The re-published rule for QRM actually has two proposals for comment: One is QRM = QM, and the other is QM + 30% down payment. See Bingham for a summary: http://www.bingham.com/Alerts/2013/09/~/media/Files/Docs/2013/A-guide -to-the-Re-proposed-Credit-Risk-Retention-Rules.ashx. The latter proposal is not viable.

27. "Helping Responsible Homeowners," President Barack Obama, August 6, 2013. http://www.whitehouse.gov/economy/middle-class/helping-responsible-ho meowners.

28. The administration supported Johnson-Crapo in a public statement from its communication office: "We support this effort and believe it is a workable bipartisan approach to complete the biggest remaining piece of post-recession financial reform," http://www.latimes.com/business/money/la-fi-mo-fannie-mae-freddie -mac-senate-housing-finance-reform-20140311,0,2529598.story#axzz2xbO33lBs.

29. Bethany McLean, "Taking Government out of the Mortgage Business Is Harder Than It Looks," Reuters, August 20, 2013, http://us.mobile.reuters.com /article/topNews/idUSBRE97J0N220130820.

30. Rates investors buy debt securities that are principally exposed to interest rate risk, such as Treasuries and Agency paper. Credit investors, on the other hand, invest in securities that also have credit risk.

31. The Making Home Affordable Program was announced in February 2009 in an effort to stabilize the housing market and provide relief for homeowners who were underwater, which is when the value of the home has fallen to below the principal amount of the mortgage that financed it. MHA has two components, the Home Affordable Refinance Program (HARP) and the Home Affordable Mortgage Program (HAMP). HARP helps borrowers who have been unable to get traditional refinancing to lower their interest rate due to a decline in home value, while HAMP focuses on principal reduction. According to the January 2014 FHFA Refinance Report, over 3 million HARP refinances have been completed since inception, approximately 16 percent of all GSE refinances.

32. And if she does, unless she represents a district of renters or millennials, she will likely find herself voted out of office.

33. We can say that the fee is paid by someone else in the mortgage finance cycle, like the lender, but ultimately all such fees and added expenses get passed on to the borrower.

34. Urban Institute, "Housing Finance at a Glance," March 2014, p. 20. http:// www.urban.org/UploadedPDF/413061-Housing-Finance-At-A-Glance-March -2014.pdf.

35. Laurie S. Goodman and Jun Zhu, "The GSE Reform Debate: How Much Capital Is Enough?" Urban Institute, October 24, 2013, http://www.urban .org/UploadedPDF/412935-The-GSE-Reform-Debate-How-Much-Capital -Is-Enough.pdf.

36. "Delaney, Carney, and Himes Introduce Housing Finance Reform Legislation," July 10, 2014, http://delaney.house.gov/news/press-releases/delaney-car ney-and-himes-introduce-housing-finance-reform-legislation.

37. Josh Rosner, "The Wrong Remedy for Fannie and Freddie," *Wall Street Journal*, March 28, 2014, http://online.wsj.com/news/articles/SB1000142405270230441 8404579462962749649106?KEYWORDS=josh+rosner&mg=reno64-wsj.

38. The principal flaw in the Johnson-Crapo bill is the poorly designed first-loss piece structure. In the bill, private entities would either originate or buy mortgages and sell securities eligible for the government wrap only after first arranging for a first-loss layer of private capital equal in size to 10 percent of the outstanding principal balance of the mortgage pool. This 10 percent would be further backed by a mortgage insurance fund with a reserve ratio of 2.5 percent. The 10 percent prerequisite is pro-cyclical—without the 10 percent there is no

FMIC wrap for the MBS, and the times during which there is likely to be low or no demand for that risk exposure are exactly the times when the mortgage finance system must be able to continue to facilitate the flow of mortgage credit. Moreover, the combined 12.5 percent (on top of a 20 percent equity cushion from the borrower) is far in excess of the amount of insurance required compared to the cumulative historical loss rates (see Goodman and Zhu, "The GSE Reform Debate"). It would be like buying $500,000 of insurance on a house that was only worth $150,000.

39. Jody Shenn, "Hedge Funds Bet on Fannie and Freddie May End Up Worthless," *Bloomberg Businessweek*, March 13, 2014. The legal case notwithstanding, there is not a lot of support in Congress for hedge fund investors or others to profit from their positions in these securities, most of which were typically taken postconservatorship for pennies on the dollar. Expressing a sentiment held by many, Senator Bob Corker stated that Fannie and Freddie would "be generating not one dime of revenue if it weren't for the federal government," http://www.businessweek.com/articles/2014-03-13/hedge-funds-big-bet-on-fannie-freddie-may-end-up-worthless#p2.

40. Joe Light, "Court Throws Out Lawsuits Related to Fannie Mae, Freddie Mac Profits," *Wall Street Journal*, October 1, 2014, http://online.wsj.com/articles/court-throws-out-lawsuits-related-to-fannie-mae-freddie-mac-profits-14121 16389?KEYWORDS=fairholme.

41. Federal Reserve chair Janet Yellen expressed concerns about the state of the housing recovery in her May 7, 2014, remarks before Congress. Continuing concern could certainly play a role in the process and execution of tapering its current quantitative easing program of Agency MBS buying. http://federal reserve.gov/newsevents/testimony/yellen20140507a.htm.

42. Federal Housing Finance Agency, "A Strategic Plan for Enterprise Conservatorships: The Next Chapter in a Story that Needs an Ending," February 21, 2012. http://www.fhfa.gov/Media/PublicAffairs/PublicAffairsDocuments/2012 letterStrategicPlanConservatorshipsFINAL.pdf.

PART VII

THE TRANSFORMATIONAL IMPACT OF LONG-TERM INVESTORS

INTRODUCTION

John G. Taft

Long-Term Thinking: 1800–2013

Long-Term Thinking died on Tuesday. His last true friend, Vanguard founder Jack Bogle, was at his side. He was 213 years old. Long-Term Thinking lived an illustrious life since the start of the Industrial Revolution. . . . But poor incentives and 24/7 media chipped away at his health. The final blow came Monday, when a trader on CNBC warned that a 10% market pullback—which has occurred on average every 11 months over the last century—could be "devastating" for investors. "That's it," Long-Term Thinking whispered from his hospital bed. "There's no more room for me." He died soon after . . .

—Mock obituary by Morgan Housel in
The Motley Fool online, January 13, 2014

The contributors to this part take aim at the phenomenon of short-termism in financial markets, a subject Roger L. Martin also addressed in chapter 11. Short-termism refers to the focus by actors in the market economy on near-term results, whether corporate earnings or investment performance, rather than on sustainable long-term performance. This dynamic, the authors believe, is leading to outcomes that are not in the long-term interests of society: slower GDP growth, higher unemployment, lower returns for savers and degradation of the environment. Both chapters that follow suggest that one way to change this dynamic of short-termism lies in the growing size and influence, and the changing character, of long-term investors.

In chapter 17, which was first published in the *Harvard Business Review*, Dominic Barton and Mark Wiseman suggest "a crucial breakthrough would occur" if "big asset owners"—including sovereign wealth funds and pension funds, like the Canada Pension Plan Investment Board, which Wiseman runs—were "acting like [true] owners"—in other words, if they were to engage the management of companies they own as active investors, influencing them to maximize their long-term performance rather than trying to win at the game of "quarterly capitalism." Barton and Wiseman show how this could lead the way to a new "kind of balanced, long-term capitalism that ultimately benefits everyone." In 2013, Barton and Wiseman, and their respective companies, cofounded the "Focusing Capital on the Long Term" initiative. Today, they cochair the initiative, which develops practical structures, metrics, and approaches for longer-term behaviors in the investment and business worlds.

Former CFA Institute president and CEO John Rogers goes a step further. In one of the most original pieces in the book, Rogers introduces the concept of "universal owners." Like Barton and Wiseman, Rogers's focus is on big asset owners, which he terms "super-fiduciaries"—like pension funds and sovereign wealth funds.

Rogers's insights are about the unique nature of funds such as the Government Pension Fund of Norway, which have a direct (unmediated) fiduciary responsibility to their constituencies. These constituents not only include the people of Norway who are living today, but also those in future generations, in perpetuity. These funds have grown so large (and are getting even larger) that through their investing activities, they own "virtually every economic and social outcome of what the world's corporations and governments are doing." The Government Pension Fund's assets are more than $840 billion, and because of their size and their "universal owner" status, there are no externalities that do not end up impacting these funds. As Rogers puts it, they have "no place to hide." As a result, these long-term owners have a fiduciary obligation to ensure that the corporations and governments in which they invest act in ways that produce positive, long-term outcomes for society. In this way, they have a fiduciary obligation to be a force for good.

To the extent these universal owners and super-fiduciaries are able to act in concert to influence corporations and governments on behalf of their constituents, Rogers envisions the dawn of an age of "fiduciary capitalism." And with it, a better system of finance, "measured and managed to the needs of people today and for as long as we continue as a species."

At a time when systemically important banks increasingly resemble utilities, regulators are bogged down in the complexities of rule making, politicians are stuck in gridlock, many asset managers are chasing benchmarks and many corporations are managing quarterly earnings, long-term investors are the stirring giants in the world of finance. They hold in their hands the power to redefine financial capitalism.

CHAPTER 16

THE DAWN OF FIDUCIARY CAPITALISM

John Rogers

Former President and CEO, CFA Institute

What does nuclear energy have to do with finance? When Robert Oppenheimer, known as the father of the atomic bomb, witnessed the first test detonation of the weapon, he uttered the words, "Now I am become death, destroyer of worlds."[1] He and his colleagues in the Manhattan Project harnessed the insights of Albert Einstein, a pacifist, to win a brutal war. The bomb created the potential to destroy life on Earth and led Einstein to later note, "I do not know how the Third World War will be fought, but I can tell you what they will use in the Fourth—rocks!"[2]

The destructive nature of atomic energy doomed its peaceful use. Despite its tremendous potential as a clean energy source, repeated accidents have frightened capital away from the sector. The risks of atomic technology have rendered it an orphan industry, a utility to be tightly controlled. Heavy government regulation is the industry norm. It holds little attraction and is reluctantly tolerated rather than welcomed in the economic landscape.

While it may be unfair to compare the dangers of the finance industry with reactors and cooling towers, the fact is that financial firms have, over the past century, created two significant social and economic crises—the first in 1929 and the second in 2008. For all the good finance brings to society, it has also created significant dislocations and human suffering. It is an industry that is now widely distrusted, and in many cases barely tolerated. Despite intense lobbying of politicians and policy makers by financial interests, it is threatened with increasing regulation. The repercussions of the 2008–09 global financial crisis will be with us for years. In an era when finance is widely mistrusted, despite its power as a positive force, what is the way forward? Does the industry succumb to regulations, assert a market solution to clean things up, or is there a third way?

This chapter outlines a source of inspiration for the future of finance. Fiduciary capitalism is a promising concept that better connects the pragmatic, enabling and market-oriented nature of finance with the hopes and needs of society. The legal and moral basis for this is already in place, and technology and globalization are giving fiduciary capitalism a chance to thrive. In fact, the recent crisis may prove to be the impetus for its spread. But of course, there are obstacles: among them, lack of scale among fiduciary capitalists, insufficient resources where they are truly needed and sheer inattention to the long-term opportunities.

Finance exists to serve social and economic progress. It exists as a means, rather than as an end unto itself. The etymology of the industry's name dates to the Old French words *fin* and *finir*, which mean (and continue to mean in several languages) "to complete, to enable, to end." Finance is a medium through which real economic activity takes place. Finance dates from earliest times, established as a superior means of exchange compared to barter and other simple transactions.[3] Concepts such as debt financing, joint ownership, insurance, forward contracts and syndication of risk are at the heart of finance's many contributions to economic and social progress. These are all essential tools for people, organizations and governments. In building the future of finance, consider that an era of fiduciary capitalism could feature progressive, long-term-oriented leadership in financial markets. This could lead to more productive and less harmful resource allocation, with less probability of episodic chaos in the finance sector itself.

In the following sections, I will first address the need for a new model of finance, then explain the concept of fiduciary capitalism, discuss universal owners and super-fiduciaries, and finish with a review of the merits and obstacles to an era of fiduciary capitalism.

THE CASE FOR A NEW MODEL OF FINANCE

The staff at the Dallas branch of the U.S. Federal Reserve estimate that the global financial crisis cost the United States between $6 trillion to $14 trillion, the equivalent of $50,000 to $120,000 for every U.S. household.[4] The U.S. unemployment rate rose from 5 percent in 2008 precrisis to 10 percent by late 2009—in other words, from approximately 7 million people in 2008 to 15 million by 2009.

In the aftermath of the global financial crisis, entire financial systems, mainly in the banking sector, have been taken down by market forces and governments. They've since been rebuilt in Greece, Iceland, Ireland, Belgium and the United Kingdom, to name a few. How many more accidents can finance handle before its institutions become pariahs to taxpayers, voters, politicians and investors? When I meet with groups of students in financial centers, I am often asked *why* they should pursue a career in finance.

Another critical consideration is the cost of many years of shortsighted financial markets to the global economy. As will be described later, our investment and accounting practices have created countless incentives for short-term thinking, at great expense. Decades of environmental degradation, accompanied by weak or nonexistent accounting for the resource costs associated with our industrial and agricultural output, are beginning to come due in stark terms. The world's 3,000 largest public companies caused $2.15 trillion in environmental damage, primarily through air and water pollution, in 2008.[5] The United Nations Environment Program Finance Initiative and Principles for Responsible Investment (PRI) estimate this figure as 35 percent of the total cost of all such damage created by humans on the planet.[6] Much of these costs are estimated to come from outsourced activities in supply chains. The horrific carnage in Bangladeshi textile factories in 2013, the worst of which killed 1,129 in a single building collapse, is just one graphic example of this cost.

These environmental and human damages are largely unrecognized in corporate earnings and valuations. When they occur in a supply chain, the vendor usually absorbs them. When they are hidden across time—through gradual environmental degradation, for instance—future generations pay, resulting in an intergenerational tax. National accounts treat the revenues accruing from resource depletion as current income, and generally fail to account for more than a fraction of the human and environmental costs. A more complete way to account for this would be to recognize the costs of natural resource depletion and environmental damage as a global depreciation expense.[7] Finance as an industry has largely failed to address these issues. Within the agency chain of financial services, there are no incentives for comprehensively accounting for long-term (i.e., 10-year-plus) outcomes.

If the scientific and economic data regarding environmental damage aren't of interest, perhaps avoiding market crashes will be. The same factors are at work here, but they better tend to capture the attention of those in positions of power. The global financial crisis of 2008–09 is an example of off-balance-sheet and unrecognized consequences of leverage coming home to roost. "Lack of transparency surrounding subprime mortgage lending debts, structural disequilibrium and conflicts of interest contributed to risk management failures."[8] Economic agents failed to recognize or model externalities and amplified systemic reactions that unfolded in 2008.[9] Unlike the earlier environmental and social examples, a market crash is an event where financiers have a great deal of self-interest. Yet it has largely been left to regulators, politicians and nonparticipants to demand better disclosure and more safeguards with respect to the risks being taken within the global financial system.

While environmental problems often lead people to change their consumption habits, financial crises appear to influence savings habits. There is evidence that the collapse in trust in financial markets and financial institutions is influencing younger individuals to make poor long-term investment decisions by investing defensively in short-term strategies. Young people whose retirement needs are 30 or 40 years hence should not be engaging in defensive investment strategies. The resulting retirement gap is a side effect that creates social dislocation and political and economic instability.

WHAT IS FIDUCIARY CAPITALISM?

A fiduciary is an individual or entity to which another individual has entrusted something of value through a formal relationship. Common law in the United States and United Kingdom, among others, as well as the codes of conduct of many professional bodies, has much to say about the fiduciary duty. The fiduciary owes a duty of loyalty, care and prudence to the beneficiary and must place the beneficiary's interests above all other considerations.[10]

The term *fiduciary capitalism* was first used extensively by James P. Hawley and Andrew T. Williams in their book *The Rise of Fiduciary Capitalism*.[11] Author Paul McFedries has a crisp definition of fiduciary capitalism: he calls it "a capitalist model in which corporations are influenced and guided by shareholders, particularly large institutional shareholders—such as pension funds and mutual funds—that act on behalf of many smaller investors."[12] Robert Monks, widely considered a father of corporate governance, was one of the first to use the term. For reasons to be explained, I will offer some minor amendments to McFedries's terms.

I define fiduciary capitalism as having three major elements: (1) an economic system of allocating financial resources, which we can think of as investment decisions; (2) these decisions are based on the long-term interests of the ultimate beneficiaries of pools of savings, including pension funds, endowments, sovereign funds, permanent funds and foundations; (3) these decisions are made primarily by the boards and employees of these entities, who are fiduciaries, bound often legally and always morally to act solely in the interest of the funds' beneficiaries.

The next few pages will flesh out this skeletal definition and perhaps provide a picture of the likely result.

The "Super-Fiduciary"

Due to a variety of factors, there is now a group of "super-fiduciaries" who have extraordinary size, growing sophistication and economic clout. Because of their size and highly diversified investments, they are also universal owners of virtually every economic and social outcome of what the world's corporations and governments are doing. There will be more on this theme later. To frame up the size of these investors, the top 1,000 fiduciary capitalists account for $25 trillion in assets. With these funds, they could own more than half the world's listed companies. A 1 percent portfolio allocation from just these top 1,000, or a sum of $250 billion, would buy almost all of Microsoft.

When these institutions act together, as they increasingly do in matters of corporate governance and market structure, they can reshape the financial markets and significantly impact economic activity. An era of fiduciary capitalism could be one in which this group of investors drives a set of norms and behaviors in the financial markets and broader economy. In fiduciary capitalism, the dominant players in capital formation are the institutional asset owners. Fiduciary capitalism has some attractive traits, most notably because it encourages long-term thinking. As universal owners, fiduciaries have an obligation to foster engagement with companies' management teams and public policy makers on governance and strategy. In textbook terms, they should seek to minimize negative externalities and reward positive ones.

Some super-fiduciaries have publicly defined their mission and vision beyond a simple statement of return maximization. A good example of this is the Ontario Municipal Employees' Retirement System (OMERS), which at over $65 billion is in the top 50 pension funds globally. Its public statement of purpose announces:

> OAC [OMERS Administration Corporation] believes that well-managed companies are those that demonstrate high ethical and environmental standards and respect for their employees, human rights, and the communities in which they do business, and that these actions contribute to long-term financial performance.
>
> Corporations should account for their behaviour and its implications for the creation of value. OAC supports the view that companies should maintain policies and procedures with respect to ESG [environmental, social and governance] issues that materially affect long-term shareholder value. . . .
>
> OAC participates in various investment initiatives through its Investment Entities that provide broader benefits to our economy while generating the returns necessary to meet the obligations to the Primary Plan members.[13]

At the community level, the International Corporate Governance Net-work (ICGN) was established in 1995 to promote best practices in the field. Recognizing that the potential for double standards, where fiduciaries de-manded a level of transparency without holding themselves to the same rules, the ICGN offered this call to action:

> Institutional investors' obligations to their beneficiaries or clients and their scope for influence of companies in which they invest bring important re-sponsibilities . . . extending from formal rights to exercise votes or to put matters formally in front of other investors, to informal scope for exercis-ing influence on management and boards across a range of key matters. . . . Ultimate owners cannot delegate these underlying responsibilities; even when they employ agents to act on their behalf. . . . As sophisticated inves-tors with influence, often including voting rights, institutional investors have a unique leadership opportunity to encourage appropriate behaviours by their investee companies.[14]

By defining fiduciary capitalism around large, not-for-profit investors who are only one step away from their beneficiaries, I have left out large pieces of the financial services industry that also act as fiduciaries: mutual funds and other collective trusts, private wealth managers, trust banks, hedge funds, financial advisors and others. For the purposes of this chapter, I'll call these entities the for-profit financial services industry. There is no question that these entities and the people in them also owe a duty of care and loyalty to their clients.

In fiduciary capitalism, however, the for-profit financial services indus-try plays only a supporting role. Money managers of collective investment vehicles such as mutual funds, exchange-traded funds and investment trusts almost always are managing against a market benchmark, as opposed to a requirement to pay pensions or support social security. Their constituents can come and go freely, and these managers tend to compete against one another for assets. While they can be quite large and a driving force in capi-tal formation (which counts for half the definition of fiduciary capitalism), their fiduciary duty is closely related to their investment strategy, not to the underlying owners themselves.

These for-profit organizations' behavior can be influenced by a variety of forces, including economic incentives (pay for performance), social pres-sure (divestment campaigns) and governance leaders (for example, proxy ad-visory firms). In that sense, the investment behavior of leading fiduciaries can have a ripple effect on the trillions of dollars invested in for-profit investment vehicles.

Private wealth managers and advisors are also fiduciaries; unlike col-lective vehicle managers, they are extremely close to their clients, have an intimate sense of their needs and are generally not benchmark-driven. They qualify for a piece of the fiduciary capitalism definition (proximity to the ultimate owner), but due to their dispersed and relatively small asset sizes, they are rarely drivers of capital formation or corporate behavior at a macro level.

THE SUPER-FIDUCIARIES

With their enormous size, the super-fiduciaries have the potential to drive global economic change. To understand more about how this might take place, we need to understand what motivates these investors. It helps to look at how some of them describe themselves. Some of the largest funds in this cohort are sovereign wealth, or permanent funds. These entities typically have an economic role that enables a social agenda. While often couched in the dry language of finance, the raison d'être for many large funds is focused on securing retirement for citizens of a country, state or region. The Abu Dhabi Investment Authority (ADIA), which is estimated to be the world's second-largest sovereign wealth fund (official data on assets under management are not disclosed), describes its mission this way: "ADIA's mission is to sustain the long-term prosperity of Abu Dhabi by prudently growing capital through a disciplined investment process and committed people who reflect ADIA's cultural values."[15]

The Government Pension Fund of Norway, valued at $840 billion and the world's largest sovereign wealth fund, issues an annual report that runs to 100 pages. It states that "the purpose of the Fund is to facilitate government savings to finance rising public pension expenditures, and support long-term considerations in the spending of government petroleum revenues."[16] Its disclosure of investment results includes 1-, 3-, 5-, 10-year and since-inception performance on several levels, including gross, after inflation, net of management costs and "double net" of those two factors. Its cost of management of the global fund, including all internal and external fees and charges, was .07 percent (7 basis points) in 2013.[17] It has 336 employees, a number that has risen due to the insourcing of asset management. It benchmarks its costs against other similar funds, using a third-party service.

The next group of super-fiduciaries is public pension funds, which provide for the long-term security of groups of employees, usually in the government sector. Here's what some of them say about their mission: ABP (Algemeen Burgerlijk Pensioenfonds), the Dutch pension fund ranked number 1 by size, describes its purpose and mission in this way: "The ABP brand has always been associated with the target group for which it administers the pension scheme. The Board of Trustees made that relationship even more explicit by stating that: ABP exists for the people who serve the public, and the public is all of us. . . . ABP aims to be a sustainable and dependable pension fund for its participants that is able to meet its financial liabilities now and in the future."[18]

CalPERS, the California Public Employees' Retirement System, is the second-largest retirement system in the world, serving the state of California's public employees. It states that its mission is to "provide responsible and efficient stewardship of the System to deliver promised retirement and health benefits, while promoting wellness and retirement security for members and beneficiaries."[19]

The final group includes endowments and foundations, often connected with higher education or a social mission. The Bill & Melinda Gates Foundation, at $34 billion, describe its mission this way: "Guided by the belief that every life has equal value, the Bill & Melinda Gates Foundation works to help all people lead healthy, productive lives."[20]

Regardless of category, these fiduciary capitalists share several common agenda points:

- Their asset bases are established to serve today's and tomorrow's generations, possibly in perpetuity. Deferring today's problems represents a disservice to future generations.
- The income and returns generated by the funds support human life and society. The economic role of these organizations does not exist in a vacuum.

These mission-driven super-fiduciaries are not what the public imagines when it conjures up images of Wall Street. Their needs, with an emphasis on the very long term, patient investing and their individual liability profile, aren't what brokers and bankers are set up to provide. Much of the financial industry, serving in an agency capacity, has business models geared toward transactions, complexity and intermediation. The main interaction between fiduciaries and the financial industry has historically been asset managers. These agents, themselves charged with fiduciary obligations toward their clients, are generally paid to deliver a slice of market returns, or beta, and generally some excess return, or alpha, relative to a market benchmark. It is true that the sum of the parts, if every agent is doing what it is paid for in terms of generating returns, should equal a whole return that meets the super-fiduciary's needs. The question is whether those needs should be redefined more specifically to address the two major agenda items above.

There are indications that this reframing exercise is gathering momentum. Their massive size alone has forced super-fiduciaries to rethink what they are trying to achieve with capital markets. Like Gulliver tied down by the smaller natives in the land of Lilliput, these funds are too large to trade in and out of individual assets, held down by their own weight and in some cases too large even to tactically move in and out of many asset categories themselves. Many asset owners seek to beat the law of averages (and some achieve this) by hiring specialists, often by the dozens, to invest in alternative and exotic assets, or by engaging in active asset allocation. Most have struggled at this attempt, due to a combination of high fees and expenses, underperformance or excess volatility, or the complexity of administering a large stable of specialists. Having learned this lesson themselves, or having seen it happen to others, leading super-fiduciaries have refocused on their funds' unique set of needs and accepted that they will be fortunate to do as well or a bit better than the total economic return of the world's capital markets.

When we combine our three key themes thus far—the fiduciary duty across generations, the Gulliver Factor (constraints caused by size) and the permanent nature of super-fiduciaries' asset pools—we have a pretty good description of a universal owner. This name describes a long-term, all-inclusive approach to equity ownership and to a wider range of economic and social responsibilities.[21] We will explore universal ownership a few pages down, as it is central to fiduciary capitalism.

FORCES SUPPORTING FIDUCIARY CAPITALISM

Pension funds, endowments and foundations have been around for a long time. But it is only in recent years that they have become big enough to assume a leadership role in the global economic framework. In addition to the first factor of size, I will discuss three more factors: technology, globalization and universal ownership that have created these super-fiduciaries.

Technology and Globalization

The digital revolution has helped level the playing field in finance. Cheap computing power has given super-fiduciaries access to the same information that was once available only to deep-pocketed brokers, bankers and money managers. The term *information asymmetry* is widely used to describe the advantage many professions have over their clients.[22] For decades, there was an asymmetric information advantage confronting fiduciaries, large and small. These "principals," to use the language of principal-agent theory, had no choice but to rely heavily on agents for information and access to the markets where they needed to invest. Today, that information gap is largely gone.

For example, BlackRock, the world's largest commercial asset manager, offers clients a data-hosting and analytics service that boasts $15 trillion of client assets on the platform. This service puts highly sophisticated tools in the hands of fiduciaries themselves, but does not tie them to using the hosting organization for transactions or other agency roles. Powerful decision tools—such as portfolio optimization, simulations, scenario analysis and risk management—are available off-the-shelf to investors.[23]

Technology has also freed large institutional investors from traditional capital marketplaces. There are now a plethora of private trading platforms, often called dark pools, where institutions do business on a peer-to-peer basis, away from public market noise and potentially false signals created by rapid-trading robots and their transient liquidity.[24] In less liquid assets such as private equity and real estate, investing with agents (asset managers) was once the only way to obtain access. We now read of increasing numbers of direct placements by fiduciaries. In one of many examples, the magazine *Pensions and Investments* reported that large Canadian public pension funds now prefer direct investments in commercial real estate and are bypassing investment managers and purchasing properties and portfolios of real estate holdings as principals.[25]

In the public markets, technological advances and new product structures open up indexation in almost any permutation imaginable. This means that there are now many low-cost index strategies that put most of the public capital markets in the category of commodity products. There is ample evidence that it is difficult for active managers to outperform equity markets with consistency, and after fees and expenses.[26]

This challenge, and the availability of very-low-cost index strategies, has spurred many fiduciaries to move to in-house management of large portions of their assets. CalPERS, for example, has 83 percent of its equity portfolio managed internally.[27] This has changed the money management industry, and will continue to drive margins for agents down for some years to come. This has added many new promising and interesting jobs in finance: working for endowments, foundations and other institutional asset owners. These organizations provide stable, long-term platforms for investment professionals to build their careers and invest globally. In Singapore, for example, the estimated $300 billion GIC Private, formerly known as the Government Investment Corporation, has over 500 investment professionals, and may rival even the largest asset management firm or brokers' research department for depth and breadth.

The next enabling factor for fiduciary capitalism is globalization. Less than a generation ago, it was quite difficult for managers of fiduciary funds to gather and share information, and collaborate across time zones and borders. The digital age and global wealth trends have changed that dramatically. Super-fiduciaries are globe-trotting investors who know their peers and are prepared to collaborate with them when their agendas coincide.

The Promise and Burden of Universal Ownership

The term *universal ownership* was first used extensively by Robert Monks and Nell Minow in 1996, and it is a linchpin in the concept of fiduciary capitalism. It is an investment philosophy that is embraced by some super-fiduciaries, and in many cases other financial entities. The preconditions for universal ownership include: (1) a fiduciary duty to intergenerational equity, for example, treating tomorrow's beneficiaries as well as we do those of to-day;[28] (2) scale, meaning these investors can't easily trade in and out of hold-ings and therefore must express their investment opinions in other ways, such as engagement in governance; and (3) liabilities that afford it a long investment time horizon.

Universal owners are concerned about the impact of externalities and have a mandate to reduce harmful externalities. Universal owners do this by pushing to improve a company's corporate governance and government's policies. Externalities are the often-hidden negative and positive costs of our economic activity. Here's how one group, the United Nations' PRI, which counts over $34 trillion in signatories' assets under management, defines a classic negative externality: "When the costs of environmental damage, such as pollution, are excluded from the transaction between a buyer and seller, they are largely 'external' to the company causing damage and are borne by third parties."[29]

The best-known example of a negative externality is pollution. When a cement manufacturer, for example, creates its product, the damage caused by carbon dioxide emissions, water pollution and other variables is not fully recognized in the cost of production. This overstates profits for the current owner of the company. Over time, those costs will usually be borne by other parties or future owners of the company, for example, in the cost of respira-tory illness, water treatment costs, contaminated site remediation, et cetera. Universal owners—being permanent in nature, large and heavily diversi-fied—must understand that they "own" the externalities generated across their investment portfolio and also through time.

To take the above example, these investors may hold shares in the ce-ment maker without incident for 30 years only to have its value destroyed suddenly when its profits are slashed due to a requirement forcing it to bear the cost of its environmental damage. At a high level, the costs to society of water and air remediation are a form of wealth transfer from investment to deferred maintenance. These costs will be a drag on overall returns for the universal owner's portfolio. Such negative externalities are likely to be internalized to the fund's performance in the future. For a universal owner, there is no place to hide from externalities that rebound as taxes, insurance premiums, inflated input prices and disaster recovery.[30]

While an investor may benefit for the short term from a single investee company's ability to externalize costs, the same investor may experience a reduction, over time, in total returns on its portfolio due to the cost of those externalities coming back in other ways.[31] Most thinking investors understand the link between social and economic progress as a whole and their beneficiaries' long-term financial security. Fiduciaries who find themselves in the category of universal owners (and arguably any long-term investor) will seek to reduce negative externalities like pollution and corruption and increase positive externalities such as good governance and employee training, across their portfolios.[32]

Table 16.1 lists of some of the major positive and negative categories of externalities, with a sense of the attendant investment benefits and risks:

TABLE 16.1 POSITIVE AND NEGATIVE SIDE EFFECTS OF INVESTMENTS

Externality	Indirect Cost to Investor	Direct Cost to Investor
Pollution	Taxes, health care	Direct costs of remediation, business interruption/cease and desist
Unsafe working conditions	Health-care system, social insurance expenses	Safety upgrades, fines, boycotts
Resource extraction	Environmental remediation, water/air pollution	Cleanups, fines, protests/stoppages
Corruption	Higher cost of capital, increased market volatility	Management turmoil, strategic discontinuity, lower profits, loss of business contracts, fines
Inadequate employee benefits	Higher social welfare costs	High attrition, low productivity
High-quality training	Increased productivity, higher value-added workforce, lower social costs	Low attrition, high productivity, innovation
Attractive employee benefits/safe working environment	Lower social welfare costs, lower unemployment	Low attrition, high productivity, innovation
High governance standards	Lowered costs of capital, higher profitability, reduced volatility, lower enforcement costs, higher confidence in financial markets	Lower cost of capital, lower volatility, stable shareholder platform, lower compliance costs

Source: John Rogers

Externalities can explode into public view without notice, causing losses and crises for management teams, boards of directors and the investors who have backed these firms. A few notable examples include the 2006 explosion of BP's Deepwater Horizon drilling platform, the 2013 Bangladeshi textile factory fires and building collapses, the 2014 sustained cutoff of water in West Virginia due to insufficient maintenance, and the collapse and nationalization of Iceland's banking sector in 2008. These events destroy value, raise volatility and uncertainty in asset prices, and in turn hike the cost of capital required in the respective sectors involved.

Universal owners, therefore, must attempt to understand the potential costs of unrecognized externalities in their portfolios, and they need to take steps to mitigate them. The environmental, sustainable and governance (ESG) movement is the catchall category for investors and users of capital alike seeking to define this responsibility and express it in investment behavior through values, beliefs and norms. We can see this concept has momentum due to the very large amount of assets from many sources, not just super-fiduciaries, who have subscribed to the UN's PRI, and the fact that there is reportedly over $1 trillion committed to pooled vehicles with an ESG mandate in some form. The motivating forces behind dealing with externalities are hard-headed economics and finance, and are entirely consistent with the fiduciary duty of care to beneficiaries.[33] Pollution is one of the biggest unrecognized externalities, with enormous costs that significantly affect investment returns, not to mention quality of life. The PRI Universal Ownership Report concluded that five industry groups account for a high concentration of man-made pollution.[34] The good news is that there should be leverage in terms of accounting for and then mitigating pollution. Shareholders are collectively pressuring a relatively small number of industries in order to have a significant impact. The concept of "stranded assets" has emerged in the investment industry recently. This holds that universal owners will incorporate downstream externalities in their valuation of energy firms' hydrocarbon reserves and demand such a valuation discount that these reserves can't be extracted economically, leaving them "stranded" and excluded from investment consideration.[35] The nuclear energy industry, which cannot obtain private financing without government guarantees, is an example of a stranded asset today.

The three main benefits of incorporating externalities into the investment process are (1) higher productivity due to higher returns on investment from more efficient capital allocation; (2) higher GDP, as this higher productivity feeds through corporate profits and adds to economic growth; and (3) reductions in risk at the investee firm and possibly sector level, reflected in a lower cost of capital.[36] These salubrious outcomes can trigger a permanently higher level of equilibrium growth and return on invested capital.[37]

By raising economic growth and capital returns, incorporating externalities into the investment process creates permanent positives and should be reflected in higher asset prices.

The Government Pension Fund of Norway offers a model for putting these concepts into practice. It defines its strategy as a universal owner (my terms) as follows: "The Ministry emphasizes the Fund's role as a responsible investor. Good long-term financial return is assumed to depend on sustainable development in economic, environmental and social terms, and on well-functioning, efficient and legitimate markets. The . . . Fund has a very long investment horizon. The Fund has no clearly defined liabilities, and it is unlikely that the State will need to withdraw large amounts from the Fund over a short period of time."[38] In addition, the fund established specific mandates for environment-related investment strategies in 2009. As of the end of 2012, it had funded ten of these, seven of which were invested in companies within renewable energy and related technology, and the remaining three were in water and waste management.

To recap, super-fiduciaries don't compete with one another and are all invested in the positive, and negative, outcomes of corporate behavior and government policy. The impact of trillions of dollars speaking with one voice has yet to be fully seen, but could be enormous. Super-fiduciaries are coming to understand that as they will basically have to own most companies' shares and debt "forever," they have a responsibility to become involved with their long-term problems as well. The next section shows how that engagement process with private companies and public policy makers can occur.

CORPORATE GOVERNANCE AND
FIDUCIARY CAPITALISTS

From the beginning of this chapter, I have asserted that fiduciary capitalism can help support more effective corporate decision making by forcing focus on the long term. My conclusion is that the super-fiduciary is obliged to engage in governance at many levels, including with the investee firm itself, the industry in which it operates and the public policy environment in which the fiduciary's beneficiaries exist. This can be incredibly complicated, but it equally holds great promise in terms of impact on returns and risk.

A legal basis for engagement by U.S. pension funds was established in the well-known Avon letter of 1988. The U.S. Department of Labor found that fiduciaries, in this case pension funds and their agents, had a fiduciary obligation to vote the proxies of forms they owned.[39] While proxy voting is perhaps the weakest form of corporate governance engagement, it at least establishes a floor on fiduciary responsibilities. The Avon letter helped spark a new niche industry: the proxy advisory firm. For most asset owners, the process of researching and coming to an independent and informed decision on governance issues for the thousands of companies they may own is impossible. The proxy advisory firm does that work in order to provide guidance on votes to its clients. These firms have become quite powerful, and work for both investors and issuers in some cases.

In the wake of the 2007–08 global financial crisis, a number of countries have sought to raise the standards of investor accountability in their role as shareholders. A recent example was Switzerland, where regulators announced in 2013 that all local pension funds must vote in all the annual general meetings of Swiss companies in which they hold a stake.[40]

The purpose of engagement is to encourage decision-making processes and investments that are consistent with the concepts behind fiduciary responsibilities. Engagement is a process in which fiduciaries, as the source of capital, can better align their agendas with the agendas of those seeking their funds. This engagement takes many forms, from proxy voting, to campaign to withhold votes, to publicity, to lawsuits.

The ICGN describes proactive engagement as follows: "Institutional investors should engage intelligently and proactively as appropriate with investee companies on risks to long term performance in order to advance beneficiary or client interests."[41]

When it comes to collaboration and collective action, nonprofit super-fiduciaries have some advantages compared to other shareholders. Corporate pensions, insurance companies and fund managers need to worry about angering corporate issuers who may also be their clients. An example would be the possible blowback from joining class action lawsuits where a corporate parent does business with the defendant. This is a topic that is rarely discussed publicly, but is certainly a consideration for many corporate shareholders.[42] But super-fiduciaries don't have these conflicts of interest. In addition, since these entities do not compete with each other, collective action is less awkward than for organizations that are potential competitors.[43]

The current debate is about how to measure super-fiduciaries' governance impact. Recall that universal ownership behavior is expected to create three types of long-term gains: a productivity effect from more efficient capital allocation, a growth effect from this higher productivity and reduced volatility, which should result in a lower cost of capital.[44] In addition, the traditional approach for institutions to hold shares over a long holding period has given way to less engaged forms of ownership, such as technical and/or high-frequency trading and indexation. Today, many investors behave like renters rather than owners. As a consequence, corporate leaders around the world bemoan the impersonal and short-term orientation of owners of their companies. This focus on short-term profits and share prices can compress the strategic decision making of corporate executives to a tactical rather than strategic time horizon. This can lead them to forgo longer-term (and often riskier-in-the-shorter-term) projects in order to keep earnings moving over the next quarter or two.

Today, the leaders of the biggest for-profit institutions are acknowledging the universal ownership philosophy. Laurence Fink, chairman and CEO of BlackRock, recently sent a letter to the chairs and CEOs of America's largest public companies. He wrote, "To meet our clients' needs, we believe the companies we invest in should similarly be focused on achieving sustainable returns over the longer term. . . . Corporate leaders can play their part by persuasively communicating their company's long-term strategy for growth. They must set the stage to attract the patient capital they seek."[45]

The economic returns from corporate engagement look even better when you consider the limited options available for super-fiduciaries. They hold sufficiently large positions in most companies that trading their holdings will cause price disruptions, making it unlikely they will get a fair price when they sell their stake. The returns from successful governance should be higher than those available through seeking to trade in shares. For fiduciaries who hire third parties to manage part of their assets, as do most, it is increasingly common to provide these external money managers with investment mandates that incorporate ESG and related topics.[46] In taking this form of engagement to the next level, best practice would be to review with potential and current money managers exactly how they analyze, incorporate, engage and report on these topics of interest to fiduciaries.

FROM WORDS TO ACTION: THE PROMISES AND BARRIERS TO FIDUCIARY CAPITALISM

Super-fiduciaries have the potential to improve the capitalist system, and they can do so without going against their own self-interest. Nonetheless, there are three major obstacles on the road to fiduciary capitalism: (1) the topic of disclosure and transparency; (2) the need for continuous improvement in fiduciaries' governance and understanding of universal ownership; and (3) reporting standards for measuring results.

Many super-fiduciaries are secretive and do not disclose enough about their activities. Sovereign wealth funds, in particular, generally say virtually nothing about their investment activities, governance philosophy or other details of their organizational lives. Their beneficial owners (including citizens and voters in the case of sovereign funds) need more information in order to make reasonable judgments about their operations. For decades, proponents of investor rights have pushed for higher standards of accounting and corporate reporting transparency in order to make better-informed long-term investment decisions. Fiduciaries, as part of their investment program, have an obligation to seek high levels of disclosure and transparency from their investees. Should they not be held to similar standards by their beneficiaries?

A simple illustration of this is to look at the Global Investment Performance Standards (GIPS). This is an industry standard for asset managers in communicating investment performance to clients, and it is very widely adopted by institutional asset management firms worldwide. However, only a handful of super-fiduciaries report that they prepare their own investment performance data in conformance with GIPS.[47] Similarly, there needs to be more transparency in the true costs of managing these pools of assets. Investment management fees and other expenses often go undisclosed. There is also an opportunity in many cases to change the language of relative performance, from one focused on how they have fared versus market benchmarks toward how they have fared compared to their liabilities, or against such measures as retirement adequacy ratios.

An example of the movement toward holding fiduciaries accountable is Detroit, the largest bankruptcy in U.S. municipal history. Its pension fund was reported to have been in relatively strong fiscal condition prior to the city's bankruptcy; however, further analysis revealed that it was several billion dollars underfunded. To prevent this lack of transparency, a panel of the U.S. Society of Actuaries recommended that pension actuaries report to a public pension board and to the public the fair value of pension obligations and annual cash outlays required to achieve them.[48]

For fiduciary capitalism to take root, the governance function, starting with super-fiduciaries, must respond to new challenges. As many fiduciaries become large, complex organizations, governance needs have grown to encompass a wide range of skills and experience. Some large fiduciaries have complex governance structures that make the job of managing investments an even bigger challenge.

As much as super-fiduciaries can do to usher in a more sustainable form of capitalism, there is great fragmentation in the ranks of smaller fiduciaries. Pension funds, foundations and endowments are widely dispersed, often limited in resources. These organizations may have the same basic agendas as super-fiduciaries, but they lack the internal capabilities to act on them. This reality tends to limit the follow-through factor that can support deep change. It also represents a major business opportunity. These same, smaller-asset owners rely heavily on agents to manage their money and governance and fiduciary responsibilities. Firms that can provide services fully aligned with universal ownership and fiduciary capitalism offer an important value proposition.

The third major obstacle is how to measure success in a move toward fiduciary capitalism. Today's corporate and governmental accounting standards reward current consumption and income and ignore, minimize or defer downstream costs of human and environmental resource usage.[49] A more inclusive approach is being developed, consistent with the values of universal owners. This approach is based on "true cost accounting" principles, which seek to capture the externalities of economic activity and account for them at their source. While no accounting system is perfect, the concept of true cost is a major step in the right direction.

It is also a challenge to measure performance at the corporate and investor level. The investment management industry has an incentive system geared mainly toward performance versus market benchmarks. When money managers get measured and paid against a given yardstick, they will quite rationally focus in on it with singular intensity. Until these benchmarks better reflect the needs of universal owners, the investment management industry will ignore them.[50]

SUMMARY

Finance is a powerful tool. The impact of investment decisions changes lives, nations, our physical environment and social structure. In the aftermath of the global financial crisis, a reevaluation of the role and purpose of finance is under way, with a view toward a more sustainable and longer-term approach. The notion of fiduciary capitalism answers many of the criticisms of finance leveled over the past decade. With the commitment of large fiduciary institutions and engagement with corporate and civic leaders, a better financial system can emerge. This approach is based on matching capital with good ideas and long-term objectives, embracing the concept of universal ownership and considering externalities. It promotes the creation of value through transparency and good governance, and holds its proponents to the same standards. Fiduciary capitalism incorporates everything we have learned about investing over the past decades, but goes beyond to recognize that financing takes place in a societal context. The financial system and its impact are human activities and must be measured and managed to the needs of people today and for as long as we continue as a species.

NOTES

1. James A. Hijiya, "The Gita of Robert Oppenheimer," *Proceedings of the American Philosophical Society* 144, no. 2 (June 2000).
2. Albert Einstein, in an interview with Alfred Werner, *Liberal Judaism* 16 (April-May 1949), 12. Einstein Archive 30-1104, as sourced by Alice Calaprice, in *The New Quotable Einstein* (Princeton, NJ: Princeton University Press and The Hebrew University of Jerusalem (2005), 173.

3. Sydney Homer and Richard Sylla, *A History of Interest Rates*, 3rd ed. (New Brunswick, NJ: Rutgers University Press, 1991), chapter 1.

4. Tyler Atkinson, David Luttrell, and Harvey Rosenblum, "How Bad Was It? The Costs and Consequences of the 2007–09 Financial Crisis," *Staff Papers* at Federal Reserve Bank of Dallas, No. 20 (July 2013), 3, www.http://dallasfed.org/assets/documents/research/staff/staff1301.pdf.

5. PRI, "Universal Ownership: Why Environmental Externalities Matter to Institutional Investors," PRI Association and UNEP Finance Initiative 2011, 3.

6. Ibid., 25.

7. Ibid., 19.

8. Ibid.

9. M. J. Dwight, "Catastrophe Insurance and Regulatory Reform after the Subprime Mortgage Crisis," cited in ibid., 9.

10. CFA Institute, *Standards of Practice Handbook*, 10th ed. (2010), 70, http://www.cfapubs.org/doi/pdf/10.2469/ccb.v2010.n2.1.

11. James P. Hawley and Andrew T. Williams, *The Rise of Fiduciary Capitalism: How Institutional Investors Can Make Corporate America More Democratic* (Philadelphia: University of Pennsylvania Press, 2000).

12. Paul McFedries, *Word Spy: The Word Lover's Guide to Modern Culture*, Paul McFedries and Logophilia Limited. Posted on May 13, 2004, http://wordspy.com/words/fiduciarycapitalism.asp.

13. Ontario Municipal Employees' Retirement System, "Enterprise Statement of Investment Policies and Procedures—Primary Plan," December 23, 2013, 6, http://www.omers.com/pdf/SIPandP.pdf.

14. International Corporate Governance Network, "ICGN Statement of Principles for Institutional Investor Responsibilities," 2013, 4, https://www.icgn.org/images/ICGN/files/icgn_main/Publications/best_practice/SHREC/ICGN_Principles_Investor_Responsibilities_Guidance_Sept_2013_print.pdf.

15. Abu Dhabi Investment Authority, "About ADIA," website accessed September, 2014, http://www.adia.ae/En/About/Mission.aspx.

16. Government of Norway, Ministry of Finance, "The Government Pension Fund," website accessed June 2014, http://www.regjeringen.no/en/dep/fin/Selected-topics/the-government-pension-fund.html?id=14.

17. "Report no. 19 to the Storting," 5, www.regjeringen.no.

18. ABP, website accessed June 2014, http://www.abp.nl/en/about-abp/about-us/.

19. CalPERS Official Site, website accessed June 2014, http://www.calpers.ca.gov/index.jsp?bc=/about/strategic-business/home.xml.

20. Bill and Melinda Gates Foundation, "Foundation Fact Sheet," website accessed June 2014, http://www.gatesfoundation.org/Who-We-Are/General-Information/Foundation-Factsheet.

21. Roger Urwin, "Pension Funds as Universal Owners: Opportunity Beckons and Leadership Calls," *Rotman International Journal of Pension Management* 4, no. 1 (June 2011): 26–33.

22. George A. Akerlof, "The Market for 'Lemons': Quality Uncertainty and the Market Mechanism," *Quarterly Journal of Economics* 84, no. 3 (1970): 489.

23. "BlackRock: The Monolith and the Markets," *The Economist*, December 7, 2013, http://www.economist.com/news/briefing/21591164-getting-15-trillion-assets-single-risk-management-system-huge-achievement.

24. Scott Patterson, *Dark Pools: The Rise of the Machine Traders and the Rigging of the U.S. Stock Market* (New York: Crown Business, 2012).

25. Pensions & Investments, "Canadian Funds Prefer Direct Route for Investment," December 23, 2013, 6, http://www.pionline.com/article/20131223/PRINT/131229980/canadian-pension-funds-prefer-direct-route-for-investment.

26. John C. Bogle, "The Arithmetic of 'All-In' Investment Expenses," *Financial Analysts Journal* 70, no. 1 (January/February 2014): 13–21.

27. Randy Diamond, Pensions & Investments, "CalPERS Ponders Taking More Equities In-House," April 1, 2013, http://www.pionline.com/article/20130401/PRINT/304019984/calpers-ponders-taking-more-equities-in-house.

28. Roger Urwin, "Pension Funds as Universal Owners: Opportunity Beckons and Leadership Calls," *Rotman International Journal of Pension Management* 4, no. 1 (June 2011).

29. PRI, "Universal Ownership."

30. Adam Seitchik, "Climate Change from the Investor's Perspective," Civil Society Institute, Newton, MA, 2007, 5, http://trilliuminvest.com/pdf/climate-change-from-the-investor-perspective.pdf.

31. Raj Thamotheram and Helen Wildsmith, "Putting the Universal Owner Hypothesis into Action," presentation to Rotman International Center for Pension Management, June 2006 workshop. Available at www.rijpm.com, 1.

32. Ibid.

33. Urwin, "Pension Funds as Universal Owners."

34. PRI, "Universal Ownership."

35. MSCI, "Options for Reducing Fossil Fuel Exposure," ESG Issue Brief, December 2013, www.msci.com/resources/research_papers.

36. Thamotheram and Wildsmith, "Putting the Universal Owner Hypothesis into Action."

37. Ibid.

38. Government of Norway, Ministry of Finance, Meld. St.27, Report to the Storting "The Management of the Government Pension Fund in 2012," 10, www.rejgeringen.no.

39. Center on Executive Compensation, "A Call for Change in the Proxy Advisory Industry Status Quo: The Case for Greater Accountability and Oversight," January 2011, 2, http://www.execcomp.org/Docs/c11-07a%20Proxy%20Advisory%20White%20Paper%20_FULL%20COLOR_.pdf.

40. Barbara Ottowa, Investment & Pensions Europe, "Swiss Pension Funds Forced to Vote in AGMs after Government Volte-Face," November 26, 2013, http://www.ipe.com/swiss-pension-funds-forced-to-vote-in-agms-after-government-volte-face/10000482.fullarticle.

41. International Corporate Governance Network, "ICGN Statement of Principles for Institutional Investor Responsibilities," 2013, 7, www.icgn.org/images.

42. Personal interviews with investment management firm executives, France and Belgium, February 2014.

43. Thamotheram and Wildsmith, "Putting the Universal Owner Hypothesis into Action."

44. Ibid.

45. Letter sent by Laurence D. Fink, March 21, 2014, accessed from the *Wall Street Journal* Online, June 2014. http://online.wsj.com/public/resources/documents/blackrockletter.pdf.

46. PRI, "Universal Ownership."

47. Discussions with colleagues at CFA Institute, January-February 2014.

48. Society of Actuaries, "Expert Public Pension Panel Recommends Improved Financial Management, Increased Disclosures and Stronger Actuarial Standards," February 2014, https://www.soa.org/News-and-Publications/Newsroom/Press-Releases/Expert-Public-Pension-Panel-Recommends-Improved-Financial-Management,-Increased-Disclosures-and-Stronger-Actuarial-Standards.aspx.
49. PRI, "Universal Ownership."
50. Discussion with PRI executives, London, February 2014.

CHAPTER 17

FOCUSING CAPITAL ON THE LONG TERM

Dominic Barton

Global Managing Director, McKinsey & Company

Mark Wiseman

President and CEO, Canada Pension
Plan Investment Board

Since the 2008 financial crisis and the onset of the Great Recession, a growing chorus of voices has urged the United States and other economies to move away from their focus on quarterly capitalism and toward a true long-term mind-set. This topic is routinely on the meeting agendas of the Organisation for Economic Co-operation and Development (OECD), the World Economic Forum, the G30 and other international bodies. A host of solutions have been offered—from "shared value" to "sustainable capitalism"—that spell out in detail the societal benefits of such a shift in the way corporate executives lead and invest. Yet despite this proliferation of thoughtful frameworks, the shadow of short-termism has continued to advance—and the situation may actually be getting worse. As a result, companies are less able to invest and build value for the long term, undermining broad economic growth and lowering returns on investment for savers.

The main source of the problem, we believe, is the continuing pressure on public companies from financial markets to maximize short-term results. And although some executives have managed to ignore this pressure, it's unrealistic to expect corporate leaders to do so over time without stronger support from investors themselves. A crucial breakthrough would occur if the major players in the market, particularly the big asset owners, joined the fight—something we believe is in the best interests of their constituents. In this chapter we lay out some practical approaches that large institutional investors can take to do this—many of which are already being applied by a handful of major asset owners.

THE INTENSIFYING PRESSURE FOR SHORT-TERM RESULTS

One of us (Dominic Barton) previously wrote about the need to "fight the tyranny of short-termism" (see "Capitalism for the Long Term," *Harvard Business Review*, March 2011), and over the past few years both our organizations have been monitoring the debate on short-termism. Early in 2013, McKinsey and the Canada Pension Plan Investment Board (CPPIB) conducted a *McKinsey Quarterly* survey of more than 1,000 board members and C-suite executives around the world to assess their progress in taking a longer-term approach to running their companies. The results are stark:

- 63 percent of respondents said the pressure to generate strong short-term results had increased over the previous five years.
- 79 percent felt especially pressured to demonstrate strong financial performance over a period of just two years or less.
- 44 percent said they use a time horizon of less than three years in setting strategy.
- 73 percent said they should use a time horizon of more than three years.
- 86 percent declared that using a longer time horizon to make business decisions would positively affect corporate performance in a number of ways, including strengthening financial returns and increasing innovation.[1]

What explains this persistent gap between knowing the right thing to do and actually doing it? In our survey, 46 percent of respondents said that the pressure to deliver strong short-term financial performance stemmed from their boards—they expected their companies to generate greater earnings in the near term. As for those board members, they made it clear that they were often just channeling increased short-term pressures from investors, including institutional shareholders.

That's why we have concluded that the single most realistic and effective way to move forward is to change the investment strategies and approaches of the players who form the cornerstone of our capitalist system: the big asset owners.

PRACTICAL CHANGES FOR ASSET OWNERS

The world's largest asset owners include pension funds, insurance firms, sovereign wealth funds and mutual funds (which collect individual investors' money directly or through products like 401(k) plans). They invest on behalf of long-term savers, taxpayers and investors. In many cases their fiduciary responsibilities to their clients stretch over generations. Today they own 73 percent of the top 1,000 companies in the United States, versus 47 percent in 1973.[2] So they should have both the scale and the time horizon to focus capital on the long term.

But too many of these major players are not taking a long-term approach in public markets. They are failing to engage with corporate leaders to shape the company's long-range course. They are using short-term investment strategies designed to track closely with benchmark indexes like the MSCI World Index. And they are letting their investment consultants pick external asset managers who focus mostly on short-term returns. To put it bluntly, they are not acting like owners.

The result has been that asset managers with a short-term focus are increasingly setting prices in public markets. They take a narrow view of a stock's value that is unlikely to lead to efficient pricing and collectively leads to herd behavior, excess volatility and bubbles. This, in turn, results in corporate boards and management making suboptimal decisions for creating long-term value. Work by Andrew Haldane and Richard Davies at the Bank of England has shown that stock prices in the United Kingdom and the United States have historically overdiscounted future returns by 5 percent to 10 percent.[3] Avoiding that pressure is one reason why private equity firms buy publicly traded companies and take them private. Research, including an analysis by CPPIB, which one of us (Mark Wiseman) heads, indicates that over the long term (and after adjustment for leverage and other factors), investing in private equity rather than comparable public securities yields annual aggregate returns that are 1.5 percent to 2.0 percent higher, even after substantial fees and carried interest are paid to private equity firms.[4] Hence, the underlying outperformance of the private companies is clearly higher still.

Simply put, short-termism is undermining the ability of companies to invest and grow, and those missed investments, in turn, have far-reaching consequences, including slower GDP growth, higher unemployment and lower return on investment for savers. To reverse this destructive trend, we suggest four practical approaches for institutional investors serious about focusing more capital on the long term.

1. Invest the Portfolio After Defining Long-Term Objectives and Risk Appetite.

Many asset owners will tell you they have a long-term perspective. Yet rarely does this philosophy permeate all the way down to individual investment decisions. To change that, the asset owner's board and CEO should start by defining exactly what they mean by long-term investing and what practical consequences they intend. The definition needs to include a multiyear time horizon for value creation. For example, Berkshire Hathaway uses the rolling five-year performance of the S&P 500 as its benchmark to signal its longer-term perspective.

Just as important as the time horizon is the appetite for risk. How much downside potential can the asset owner tolerate over the entire time horizon? And how much variation from the benchmark is acceptable over shorter periods? Short-term underperformance should be tolerated—indeed, it is expected—if it helps achieve greater long-term value creation. Singapore's sovereign wealth fund, GIC, takes this approach while maintaining a publicly stated 20-year horizon for value creation. The company has deliberately pursued opportunities in the relatively volatile Asian emerging markets because it believes they offer superior long-term growth potential. Since the mid-2000s GIC has placed up to one-third of its investments in a range of public and private companies in those markets. This has meant that during developed-market booms, its equity holdings have underperformed global equity indexes. While the board looks carefully at the reasons for those results, it tolerates such underperformance within an established risk appetite.

Next, management needs to ensure that the portfolio is actually invested in line with its stated time horizon and risk objectives. This will likely require allocating more capital to illiquid or "real" asset classes like infrastructure and real estate. It may also mean giving much more weight to strategies within a given asset class that focus on long-term value creation, such as "intrinsic-value-based" public equity strategies, rather than momentum-based ones. Since its inception in 1990, the Ontario Teachers' Pension Plan (OTPP) has been a leader in allocating capital to illiquid long-term asset classes as well as making direct investments in companies. Today real assets such as water utilities and retail and office buildings account for 23 percent of OTPP's portfolio.[5] Another believer in this approach is the Yale University endowment fund, which began a self-proclaimed "revolutionary shift" to nontraditional asset classes in the late 1980s. Today the fund has just over 35 percent in private equity and 22 percent in real estate.[6]

Finally, asset owners need to make sure that both their internal investment professionals and their external fund managers are committed to this long-term investment horizon. Common compensation structures like a 2 percent management fee per year and a 20 percent performance fee do little to reward fund managers for long-term investing skill. A recent Ernst & Young survey found that although asset owners reported wanting annual cash payments to make up only 38 percent of fund managers' compensation (with equity shares, deferred cash, stock options and other forms of compensation accounting for the rest), in practice they make up 74 percent.[7] While many institutions have focused on reducing fixed management fees over the past decade, they now need to concentrate on encouraging a long-term outlook among the investment professionals who manage their portfolios. CPPIB has been experimenting with a range of novel approaches, including offering to lock up capital with public equity investors for three years or more, paying low base fees but higher performance fees if careful analysis can tie results to truly superior managerial skill (rather than luck), and deferring a significant portion of performance-based cash payments while a longer-term track record builds.

2. Unlock Value through Engagement and Active Ownership.

The typical response of many asset owners to a failing corporate strategy or poor environmental, social or governance practices is simply to sell the stock. Thankfully, a small but growing number of leading asset owners and asset managers have begun to act much more like private owners and managers who just happen to be operating in a public market. To create value, they engage with a company's executives—and stay engaged over time. BlackRock CEO Laurence Fink, a leader in this kind of effort, tells companies not to focus simply on winning over proxy advisory firms (which counsel institutional investors on how to vote in shareholder elections). Instead, says Fink, companies should work directly with BlackRock and other shareholders to build long-term relationships. To be clear, such engagement falls along a spectrum, with varying levels of resources and commitment required (see table 17.1). But based on their in-house capabilities and scale, all asset owners should adopt strategies that they might employ individually or collaboratively.

Some asset owners are large enough to engage on their own by formally allocating dedicated capital to a relationship-investing strategy. This could involve taking a significant (10 percent to 25 percent) stake in a small number of public companies, expecting to hold those for a number of years and working

TABLE 17.1 THE EQUITY ENGAGEMENT SPECTRUM

Asset owners are developing a range of approaches to engage with companies in which they have equity investments. As the size of their stakes rise, they move from monitoring and coalition building to acting like owners, often with board representation.

	Ownership Stake in Company	
<2%	*1–5%*	*>10%*
Ongoing Engagement	*Active Ownership*	*Relationship Investing*
• Continuously monitors companies, with a mix of active and reactive engagement • May build microcoalitions with other investors • Often does not pursue any additional investment beyond an index-weighted holding	• Owns a meaningful position in a handful of companies • Usually remains below the 5% threshold for public disclosure of holdings • Tries to build microcoalitions with other investors • Works publicly or privately to persuade the board and management to change long-term strategy	• Takes a significant minority ownership • Often has board seats • Works collaboratively with management on long-term strategy

Source: McKinsey & Company and Canada Pension Plan Investment Board

closely with the board of directors and management to optimize the company's direction. For smaller asset owners, independent funds like ValueAct Capital and Cevian provide a way to pool their capital in order to influence the strategies of public companies. The partners in such a coalition can jointly interact with management without the fixed costs of developing an in-house team.

Engaging with companies on their long-term strategy can be highly effective even without acquiring a meaningful stake or adopting a distinct, formal investment strategy. For example, the California Public Employees' Retirement System (CalPERS) screens its investments to identify companies that have underperformed in terms of total stock returns and fallen short in some aspect of corporate governance. It puts these companies on its Focus List—originally a published list but now an internal document—and tries to work with management and the board to institute changes in strategy or governance. One recent study showed that from 1999 to mid-2013, the companies targeted through the Focus List collectively produced a cumulative excess return of 12 percent above their respective industry benchmarks after five years.[8] Other studies have shown similar results, with companies doing even better in the first three years after going on the Focus List. Interestingly, the companies CalPERS worked with privately outperformed those named publicly, so from 2011 onward, CalPERS has concentrated on private engagement.

Despite the evidence that active ownership is most effective when done behind the scenes, there will inevitably be times when public pressure needs to be applied to companies or public votes have to be taken. In such cases, asset owners with sufficient capacity should go well beyond following guidance from short-term-oriented proxy advisory services. Instead they should develop a network with like-minded peers, agree in advance on the people and principles that will guide their efforts, and thereby position themselves to respond to a potentially contentious issue with a company by quickly forming a microcoalition of willing large investors. Canadian Pacific Railway is a recent example where a microcoalition of asset owners worked alongside long-term-oriented hedge funds to successfully redirect management's strategies.

Transparency makes such collaborative efforts easier. In the United Kingdom, major institutions are required to "comply or explain" their principles of engagement under the U.K. Stewardship Code. Elsewhere, big asset owners and managers should also publish their voting policies and, when a battle is joined, disclose their intentions prior to casting their votes. Smaller asset owners or those less interested in developing in-house capabilities to monitor and engage with companies can outsource this role to specialists. Hermes Equity Ownership Services, for example, was set up by the BT Pension Scheme in the United Kingdom to provide proxy voting and engagement services to 35 global asset owners that together have some $179 billion under management.[9]

Finally, to truly act as engaged and active owners, asset owners need to participate in the regulation and management of the financial markets as a whole. With some exceptions, they have largely avoided taking part publicly in the debates about capital requirements, financial market reform and reporting standards. Some of the biggest players in the game are effectively silent on its rules. As long-term investors, asset owners should be more vocal in explaining how markets can be run more effectively in the interests of savers.

3. Demand Long-Term Metrics from Companies to Change the Investor-Management Conversation.

Making long-term investment decisions is difficult without metrics that calibrate, even in a rough way, the long-term performance and health of companies. Focusing on metrics like 10-year economic value added, R&D efficiency, patent pipelines, multiyear return on capital investments and energy intensity of production is likely to give investors more useful information than basic Generally Accepted Accounting Principles (GAAP) accounting in assessing a company's performance over the long haul. The specific measures will vary by industry sector, but they exist for every company.

It is critical that companies acknowledge the value of these metrics and share them publicly. Natura, a Brazilian cosmetics company, is pursuing a growth strategy that requires it to scale up its decentralized door-to-door sales force without losing quality. To help investors understand its performance on this key indicator, the company publishes data on sales force turnover, training hours per employee, sales force satisfaction and salesperson willingness to recommend the role to a friend. Similarly, Puma, a sports lifestyle company, recognizes that its sector faces significant risks in its supply chain, and so it has published a rigorous analysis of its multiple tiers of suppliers to inform investors about its exposure to health and safety issues through subcontractors.

Asset owners need to lead the way in encouraging the companies they own to shift time and energy away from issuing quarterly guidance. Instead they should focus on communicating the metrics that are truly material to the company's long-term value creation and most useful for investors. In pursuing this end, they can work with industry coalitions that seek to foster wise investment, such as the Carbon Disclosure Project, the Sustainability Accounting Standards Board, the investor-driven International Integrated Reporting Council and, most broadly, the United Nations–supported Principles for Responsible Investment.

But simply providing relevant, comparable data over time is not enough. After all, for several years, data sources including Bloomberg, MSCI and others have been offering at least some long-term metrics—employee turnover and greenhouse gas intensity of earnings, for example—but uptake has been limited. To translate data into action, portfolio managers must insist that their own analysts get a better grasp on long-term metrics and that their asset managers—both internal and external—integrate them into their investment philosophies and their valuation models.

4. Structure Institutional Governance to Support a Long-Term Approach.

Proper corporate governance is the critical enabler. If asset owners and asset managers are to do a better job of investing for the long term, they need to run their organizations in a way that supports and reinforces this. The first step is to be clear that their primary fiduciary duty is to use professional investing skill to deliver strong returns for beneficiaries over the long term—rather than to compete in horse races judged on short-term performance.

Executing that duty starts with setting high standards for the asset owner's board itself. The board must be independent and professional, with relevant governance expertise and a demonstrated commitment to a long-term investment philosophy. Board members need to have the competencies and time to be knowledgeable and engaged. Unfortunately, many pension funds—including many U.S., state and local government employee pension plans—are not run this way; they often succumb to short-term political pressure or lack sufficient expertise to make long-term investment decisions in the best interests of beneficiaries.

However, successful models do exist. For example, the New Zealand Superannuation Fund is overseen by a board of "guardians" whose members are selected for their experience, training and expertise in the management of financial investments. The board operates at arm's length from the government and is limited to investing on what it calls "a prudent, commercial basis." The board is subject to a regular independent review of its performance, and it publishes its progress in responding to the recommendations it receives.[10] Two other exemplary models are the Wellcome Trust, a U.K.-based global charitable foundation, and Yale University's endowment fund; each delegates strategic investment implementation to a committee of experienced professionals.

Professional oversight needs to be complemented by policies and mechanisms that reduce short-term pressures and promote long-term counter-cyclical performance. These could include automatic rebalancing systems to enforce the selling of equities during unsustainable booms, liquidity requirements to ensure there is cash available to take advantage of times of market distress, and an end to currency hedging to reduce the volatility of short-term performance. Such policies need to be agreed to in advance of market instability, because even the best-governed institutions may feel the heat during such periods.

A case in point is Norges Bank Investment Management (NBIM), which invests Norway's revenue from surplus petroleum (more than $814 billion) in the country's global government pension fund. In 2007 the Ministry of Finance and NBIM set a long-term goal: to raise the equity content of the fund from 40 percent to 60 percent. Yet when the financial crisis hit, NBIM lost over 40 percent of the value of its global equity portfolio, and it faced significant external pressure not to buy back into the falling market. Its strong governance, however, coupled with ample liquidity, allowed it to continue on its long-term path. In 2008 it allocated all $61 billion of inflows, or 15 percent of the fund's value, to buying equities, and it made an equity return of 34 percent in the following year, outperforming the equity market rebound. In similar circumstances a few years later, NBIM kept to its countercyclical

11134434552111

strategy and bought into the falling equity market of mid-2011, turning an equity loss of nearly 9 percent that year into an 18 percent return in 2012.[11]

A final imperative for the boards and leadership of asset owners is to recognize the major benefits of scale. Larger pools of capital create more opportunities to invest for the long term by opening up illiquid asset classes, making it cost-effective to invest directly and making it easier to build in-house engagement and active ownership capabilities. According to analysts such as William Morneau, the Ontario Ministry of Finance's pension investment advisor, these opportunities are often cost-effective once an asset owner has at least $50 billion in assets under management.[12] That suggests that savers, regulators and board members of smaller asset owners should be open to these institutions pooling assets or even merging.

LEADING THE WAY FORWARD

Today a strong desire exists in many business circles to move beyond quarterly capitalism. But short-term mind-sets still prevail throughout the investment value chain and dominate decisions in boardrooms.

We are convinced that the best place to start moving this debate from ideas to action is with the people who provide the essential fuel for capitalism—the world's major asset owners. Until these organizations radically change their approach, the other key players—asset managers, corporate boards, and company executives—will likely remain trapped in value-destroying short-termism. But by accepting the opportunity and responsibility to be leaders who act in the best interests of individual savers, large asset owners can be a powerful force for instituting the kind of balanced, long-term capitalism that ultimately benefits everyone.

NOTES

1. Jonathan Bailey, Vincent Berube, Jonathan Godsall and Conor Kehoe, "Short-termism: Insights from business leaders, findings from a Global Survey of Business leaders commissioned by McKinsey & Company and CPP Investment Board," *CPPIB and McKinsey & Company*, January 2014, http://www.fclt.org/content/dam/fclt/en/ourthinking/20140123%20McK%20Quarterly%20Survey%20Results%20for%20FCLT.org_FINAL.pdf.
2. Matteo Tonello and Stephan Rahim Rabimov, "The 2010 Institutional Investment Report: Trends in Asset Allocation and Portfolio Composition" November 11, 2010, The Conference Board Research Report, No. R-1468-10-RR, 2010.
3. Andrew Haldane and Richard Davies, "The Short Long," speech presented at the 29th Société Universitaire Européene de Recherches Financières Colloquium: *New Paradigms in Money and Finance?*, Brussels, May 2011, http://

www.bankofengland.co.uk/publications/Documents/speeches/2011/speech495
.pdf.

4. Robert S. Harris, Tim Jenkinson, and Steven N. Kaplan, "Private Equity Performance: What Do We Know?" *Journal of Finance*, 69 (October 2014): 1851–1882. doi: 10.1111/jofi.12154.

5. "An Evolving Plan," 2012 Ontario Teachers' Pension Plan Annual Report, http://www.otpp.com/documents/10179/686250/-/39482a3d-435c-40d1-96cf-cd6a38d6880a/Annual%20Report.pdf.

6. Yale Investments Office, "2012 Yale Endowment Update," Yale Corporation Investments Committee, http://investments.yale.edu/images/documents/Yale_Endowment_12.pdf.

7. Ernst & Young, Global Hedge Fund Investor Survey, 2012, http://www.ey.com/Publication/vwLUAssets/Global-hedge-fund-and-investor-survey_2012/$FILE/CK0582_Global-HF-Survey-2012.pdf.

8. Andrew Junkin, "Update to the 'CalPERS Effect' on Targeted Company Share Prices," September 24, 2013, http://www.calpers-governance.org/docs-sof/focus list/2013-focus-list-study.pdf; CalPERS press release, June 9, 2004, http://www.businesswire.com/news/home/20040609005667/en/CalPERS-Releases-2004-Corporate-Governance-Focus-List.

9. Hermes Equity Ownership Services, http://www.hermes-investment.com/eos/en-gb/overview.aspx.

10. New Zealand Superannuation Fund, https://www.nzsuperfund.co.nz/nz-super-fund-explained/governance.

11. Based on publicly available information in Norges Bank Investment Management (NBIM) Annual Reports, http://www.nbim.no/en/, and at NBIM website, http://www.nbim.no/en/the-fund/history/.

12. "Facilitating Pooled Asset Management for Ontario's Public-Sector Institutions: Report from the Pension Investment Advisor to the Deputy Premier and Minister of Finance," 2012, http://www.fin.gov.on.ca/en/consultations/pension/recommendations-report.pdf.

PART VIII

RETOOLING THE FINANCIAL SYSTEM FOR SUSTAINABILITY

INTRODUCTION

John G. Taft

The contributors to this part are David Blood, a cofounder (with former vice president Al Gore and five others) of Generation Investment Management, and John Fullerton, founder of the Capital Institute. Fullerton is a veteran J. P. Morgan banker who is now reimagining the role of finance in society. Both he and Blood are refugees, of sorts, from the traditional investment banking and asset management world. They are working through how to untether finance from the basic assumptions that have governed capitalism for the last century. Both perceive that we are between paradigms. We are shifting away from "financial capitalism"—which itself replaced the previous system of "industrial capitalism"—to what Blood calls "Sustainable Capitalism" and Fullerton calls "Regenerative Capitalism":[1] that is, a system in which consistent GDP growth, regardless of negative social and environmental side effects, is no longer the "primary metric of prosperity."[2]

What does this new form of capitalism look like? And how does the financial system need to evolve to support it? These are the seminal questions Blood and Fullerton address.

Returning to concepts discussed in part I, the premise is that the corporate social contract is undergoing radical change. One indication is the evolving attitudes of high-net-worth investors. According to a 2014 survey by Capgemini and RBC Wealth Management, over 60 percent of high-net-worth investors globally rate "positive social impact" as "very important" or "extremely important" to their capital allocation decisions.[3]

It is clear, Blood believes, that the long-term best interests of society will no longer be served by a capitalist system that is "driving our economies and our planet into liquidation," in the words of ecological economist Herman Daly.[4] Or as Blood also puts it, society no longer desires economic practices that "do not incorporate sufficient regard for [their] impact on people and the planet."

While Blood's focus is more on financial investment and Fullerton's more on "real investment"—that is, investments that directly impact economic activity, such as the construction of a building—both contributors echo many of the themes running throughout this book, namely:

- We live in a world today that is so globally interconnected that it can no longer be argued that any private action does not in some way impact someone else, somewhere else. As a result, externalities—the impact of private actions on the public commons such as pollution or secondhand smoke—must not be ignored.
- We may be entering an era of limited, resource-constrained growth. We may be living at an inflection point in human history when increasing scarcity of material resources and the planet's inability to sustain billions of additional inhabitants have introduced to capitalism constraints that never existed before. We may have reached the point where exponential growth may not only be unachievable, it may not be desirable.
- There is an urgent need for long-term thinking to replace short-termism when it comes to making decisions about both where to invest portfolios and where to invest corporate cash. Otherwise we may not be able to avoid outcomes that society surely does not want.

NOTES

1. John Fullerton, "Beyond Sustainability: The Road to Regenerative Capitalism," *The Future of Finance* (blog) Capital Institute, http://capitalinstitute.org/blog /beyond-sustainability-road-regenerative-capitalism/.
2. "Sustainable Capitalism," v. 1.1 (January 2012), Generation Investment Management LLP, February 15, 2012, http://www.generationim.com/media/pdf -generation-sustainable-capitalism-v1.pdf.
3. "Importance of Social Impact for HNWIs, Q1 2014," World Wealth Report 2014, Capgemini, RBC Wealth Management and Scorpio Partnership Global HNW Insights 2014, 27. A PDF of the report is available for download from https://www.worldwealthreport.com/.
4. "Sustainable Capitalism."

CHAPTER 18

SUSTAINABLE CAPITALISM

David Blood

Cofounder and Senior Partner,
Generation Investment Management

Capitalism has great strengths and is fundamentally superior to any other system for organizing economic activity. It is more efficient in allocating resources and in matching supply and demand. It is demonstrably effective in wealth creation. It is more congruent with higher levels of freedom and self-governance than any other system. It unlocks a higher fraction of the human potential with ubiquitous, organic incentives that reward hard work, ingenuity and innovation. These strengths are why it is at the foundation of every successful economy.

Yet while the present form of capitalism has proven its superiority, it is nevertheless abundantly clear that some of its manifestations do not incorporate sufficient regard for its impact on people and the planet—and those manifestations are now posing a number of fundamental challenges that require attention, particularly in a resource-constrained world of 7 billion (soon to be 8 to 10 billion) people.

The challenges facing the planet today are unprecedented and extraordinary: climate change, water scarcity, poverty, disease, growing inequality of income and wealth, demographic shifts, transborder and internal migration, urbanization and a global economy in a state of constant dramatic volatility and flux, to name but a few. While governments and civil society will need to be part of the solution to these massive challenges, ultimately it will be companies and investors that will mobilize the capital needed to overcome them.

To address these sustainability challenges, we advocate for a paradigm shift to Sustainable Capitalism. For some time, we and others have argued for this longer-term, more responsible form of capitalism. Sustainable

Capitalism is more than corporate social responsibility or impact investing, which are worthwhile endeavors compatible with the precepts of Sustainable Capitalism but narrower in focus.

Sustainable Capitalism is a framework that seeks to maximize long-term economic value creation by reforming markets to address real needs, while considering all costs and integrating environmental, social and governance (ESG) metrics into the decision-making process. Specifically, Sustainable Capitalism internalizes negative externalities through appropriate pricing, such as putting a price on carbon so that global warming pollution can be accounted for.

Sustainable Capitalism applies to the entire investment value chain, from entrepreneurial ventures to publicly traded large-cap companies, from investors providing seed capital to those focused on late-stage growth-oriented opportunities, from company employees to CEOs, from activists to policy makers and standard setters. Sustainable Capitalism transcends borders, industries, forms of ownership, asset classes and stakeholders.

What does Sustainable Capitalism look like in practice? For companies, it means internalizing the business case for sustainability and adapting business models accordingly, with C-suite and board support. For asset owners, it means embracing a longer time horizon and sustainability as value-creating tools. For asset managers, it means investing for the long term and adopting incentive structures that reward such behavior. For governments, it means understanding that there are serious and ongoing fundamental market failures that threaten not only the future of our companies and investments, but also the sustainability of our planet. For nongovernmental organizations, it means clearly defining their roles in the economic system and developing a better understanding of the motivations of companies and investors and identifying ways to encourage them to change through appropriate methods of impactful engagement. And for the media, it means challenging companies—and commentators—to do more than just talk about sustainability and to hold companies to a high standard when evaluating their actions.

However, we believe that global progress toward the mainstreaming of sustainability in financial markets has reached a plateau. This is because of a number of factors, including a widely shared failure to rigorously make and reinforce the economic case for Sustainable Capitalism.

FIVE KEY RECOMMENDATIONS FOR
MAINSTREAMING SUSTAINABLE CAPITALISM

We recognize these ideas are not exhaustive and that they are necessary but not sufficient to achieving our goal of mainstreaming Sustainable Capitalism by 2020.

1. Identify and Incorporate Risks from Stranded Assets

A stranded asset is one that loses significant economic value well ahead of its anticipated useful life as a result of changes in legislation, regulation, market forces, disruptive innovation, societal norms or environmental shocks. Stranded assets have the potential to result in significant reductions in the long-term value of entire sectors ranging from oil and gas to pharmaceuticals, and not just the value of particular companies. Until there are policies that establish a fair price for widely understood externalities, academics and financial professionals should strive to quantify the impact of stranded assets and analyze the subsequent implications for assessing investment opportunities.

Stranded carbon assets are an example of this idea in practice. As the case for curbing carbon emissions continues to gain support on economic and scientific grounds, the commercial viability of carbon-intensive assets—particularly fossil fuels—will be increasingly threatened, creating stranded carbon assets. While investors who hold carbon-heavy assets may benefit in some ways in the short term from continued inaction, the growing effects of the climate crisis will inevitably harm them elsewhere. In short, either investors strand carbon assets today or impair real estate infrastructure, farmland, forestry and other assets down the line.

2. Mandate Integrated Reporting

Despite an increase in the volume of information made available by companies and the frequency with which it is produced, access to more data for public equity investors has not necessarily translated into more comprehensive insight into companies. Integrated reporting addresses this trend by encouraging companies to integrate both their financial and ESG performance into one report that includes only the most salient or material metrics. This will enable both companies and investors to make better resource allocation decisions about how ESG performance can contribute to sustainable, long-term value creation. While voluntary integrated reporting is gaining momentum, it must be mandated in order to ensure swift and broad adoption.

3. End the Default Practice of Issuing Regular Earnings Guidance

Regularly issuing earnings guidance, either quarterly or annually, can create incentives for executives to manage for the short term and encourage some investors to overemphasize the significance of these measures at the expense of the longer-term, more meaningful measure of sustainable value creation. Ending this default practice in favor of only issuing guidance as deemed appropriate by the company (if at all) would encourage a long-term view of the business rather than the current focus on short-term results. More thoughtful issuance of earnings guidance is compatible with enhanced standards of disclosure.

4. Align Compensation Structures with Long-Term Sustainable Performance

Presently, most compensation schemes emphasize short-term actions disproportionately and fail to hold asset managers and corporate executives accountable for the ramifications of their decisions over the long term. Instead, financial rewards should be paid out over the period during which these results are realized, and compensation should be linked to fundamental drivers of long-term value, employing rolling multiyear milestones for performance evaluation.

5. Encourage Long-Term Investing

The dominance of short-termism in the market, often facilitated and exacerbated by algorithmic trading, is correlated with stock price volatility[1] and fosters general market instability as opposed to useful liquidity and undermines the efforts of executives seeking long-term value creation. Companies can take a proactive stance against this growing trend of short-termism by attracting long-term investors through a communication strategy focused on highlighting long-term value creation and potentially using financial instruments that reward patient capital.

We also believe that there are five broader ideas that merit ongoing support and attention. Specifically, there is a need to:

1. reinforce sustainability as a fiduciary issue;
2. create advisory services for sustainable asset management;
3. expand the range and depth of sustainable investment products;
4. reconsider the appropriate definition for growth beyond GDP; and
5. integrate sustainability into business education at all levels.

WHAT COMPANIES CAN DO

There has been significant work done to identify the many ways in which embracing sustainability enables a company to create value. Through our own investment research we have seen firsthand the positive effect that sustainability can have on the continued profitability of a company. As others have noted, "Leading companies are using sustainability to create operational and strategic long-term advantages."[2] Typically, the adoption of sustainability within a corporation has three distinct phases as executives discover the multilayered benefits.

- **Strategic advantage.** Developing sustainable products and services can increase a company's profits, enhance its brand, strengthen public trust[3] and improve its competitive positioning as the market increasingly rewards this behavior.[4]
- **Operational effectiveness.** Sustainable capitalism can also help companies save money by reducing waste and increasing energy efficiency in the supply chain and by improving human-capital practices so that retention rates rise and the costs of training new employees decline (subsequently improving corporate culture, which has been shown to generate superior long-term returns[5]).
- **Compliance and risk management.** Focusing on ESG metrics allows companies to achieve higher compliance standards and to better manage risk since they have a more holistic understanding of the material issues affecting their business.

As companies undergo the transformation to becoming more sustainable through these stages, it usually becomes evident within the company that sustainability does not involve a trade-off between profitability and improving the environment and society. Rather, it can in fact improve operations and inspire innovation. The benefits outlined above can clearly yield top-line growth, cost reductions and enhanced profitability through strategic competitive advantage. By integrating sustainability into the company's strategy and operations, executives are simply running the business better and are positioning the company for greater long-term success.

There is also empirical evidence to show that sustainable business practices are associated with financial benefits. For example, work by Bauer and Hann has demonstrated that proactive environmental practices are associated with a lower cost of debt.[6] They also find that the effect is not limited to companies that are operating in sectors that are traditionally considered environmentally sensitive, such as oil and gas.

Work by Cheng, Ioannou and Serafeim finds that companies with strong ESG performance also face lower capital constraints.[7] As they also confirm, companies that suffer from capital constraints are associated with poorer stock returns. These authors find that one of the reasons for the improved access to capital is precisely the companies' greater transparency and stakeholder engagement. Greater transparency around ESG performance reduces information asymmetries in the capital market, where improved stakeholder engagement reduces agency costs that can cause significant contracting costs. Both effects lower capital constraints and allow companies to invest more efficiently.

Those who advocate Sustainable Capitalism often find themselves having to argue why integrating sustainability adds value. Yet the question that should be asked of those who are skeptical is why an absence of sustainability does not damage both the company and wider society. Whether there is a formal licensing requirement or not, society ultimately does require, in one way or another, that a company earns the right to operate. When managers do not consider the impact of their decisions on all stakeholders, not just shareholders, we believe that they are putting this license to operate at risk.

The consequence of not maintaining this societal license to operate can be, and often is, damaging to companies in a variety of ways.

- Popular disapproval of a company's actions may lead to boycotts or reduced sales and brand degradation.
- Government and regulatory pressure may restrict the company's freedom to operate.
- Investor flight may increase the company's cost of capital.
- Staff may be unwilling to remain at the company and top talent deterred from joining.
- Potential business partners and suppliers may be less willing to trade with the company.
- Lack of confidence in management may lead to a decline in the valuation of the company and the risk of a takeover.

Most companies will not get to the point of actually losing their license to operate because shareholders and boards will eventually intervene. However, companies have a duty to monitor these issues in order to avoid value destruction.

Building a sustainable company is not straightforward, even with a committed board of directors, CEO and executive team. Just as an executive team cannot embed a culture of innovation in an established company without a major multiyear change program, the same is true for sustainability.

WHAT INVESTORS CAN DO

The pressure for short-term returns that investors are placing on companies is leading to dramatically inefficient capital allocation. Aside from the damage this short-termism is doing to our planet and to society, it is also reducing returns for investors. Haldane and Davies (at the Bank of England) show that across the public markets, long-term investment opportunities are routinely missed because cash flows are inappropriately discounted.[8] In their paper, they show that cash flows five years out are routinely discounted as if they were eight years out, and cash flows 30 years out are scarcely valued at all. They also document evidence that this pattern has been accelerating since the mid-1980s. Since it is investors who ultimately set the discount rate for companies through the returns they expect on their capital, it is therefore investors who have the ability to redress this market failure.

In addition, there are several other compelling reasons why this short-term approach does not necessarily maximize economic value and why the alternative of Sustainable Capitalism provides investors with opportunities for greater wealth creation.

The Financial Performance of Sustainable Companies

A study by Eccles, Ioannou and Serafeim indicates that sustainable companies outperform a matched group of firms in the long term.[9] The authors identified 90 companies that adopted a substantial number of environmental and social policies in the early 1990s. They then created a second sample of 90 companies that adopted almost none of these policies during the same period. The two samples exhibited almost identical size, capital structure, operating performance and growth opportunities in the early 1990s.

The study found that $1 invested in a value-weighted portfolio of sustainable firms at the beginning of 1993 would have grown to $22.60 by the end of 2010. In contrast, $1 invested in a value-weighted portfolio of unsustainable firms at the beginning of 1993 would have grown to $15.40 by the end of 2010. The difference in annual abnormal stock market performance, after taking into account four risk factors (market, size, book-to-market, and momentum) was 4.8 percent. Moreover, the study found that the portfolio of sustainable firms exhibited less volatile performance relative to the portfolio of unsustainable firms. This empirical evidence suggests that investors who spend resources identifying companies that embed sustainability into their strategy can earn substantial returns while experiencing low volatility.

More Comprehensive Valuation Criteria

Studies have shown the materiality of ESG factors for business[10] and have demonstrated that, encouragingly, "investors are increasingly interested in nonfinancial information."[11] However, most investors are still not considering ESG factors in their valuation processes; they operate with incomplete information about the companies in which they invest, routinely ignoring key, highly relevant aspects of performance when assessing companies' value propositions and relative competitive advantages. According to Aviva Investors, "While there is clearly value in estimating near-term company earnings, the majority of a company's value is derived from its ability to generate long-term earnings. Therefore, it is important for investors to identify factors that influence long-term earnings and integrate them into their analysis."[12]

As such, asset managers and financial analysts should move to a more comprehensive valuation methodology. Developing the skills necessary to analyze ESG metrics in addition to traditional financial performance indicators will be critical, as will incorporating appropriately priced externalities to develop a more complete view of a company's long-term value. While not all ESG issues are easy to quantify as line items in a model, it is nonetheless true that acknowledging and considering the impact of material ESG metrics to a company, even qualitatively, is an important first step. Factoring ESG issues into traditional investment analysis may not be a guaranteed way to create wealth; however, it is a helpful dimension in evaluating the long-term viability of a business.

Matching Investment Liabilities to the Appropriate Investment Time Horizon

Pension funds, sovereign wealth funds, foundations, endowments and other investors with long-term liabilities need to match the performance of their assets to the maturation of those liabilities. As such, the integration of ESG issues that have a material impact on the long-term viability of companies clearly should be an essential step in their valuation and investment process, and thus the ability to manage the integration of ESG issues clearly should be a key consideration for these investors when selecting an asset manager.

Avoid Losing the License to Operate

Dividing the investor group into asset owners and asset managers reveals that, like companies, asset managers face the threat of losing their license to operate if they engage in unsustainable practices, such as the disregard of key relevant factors in investing including ESG, excessive exposure to unsustainable industries, high portfolio turnover and short-term trading practices that could be subject to regulation and taxation.[13] Therefore, asset managers should proactively adopt sustainable practices if for no other reason than to avoid a funding vacuum left by asset owners who seek to avoid these looming risks.

Ultimately, what Sustainable Capitalism requires is for investors to be good investors: to fully understand the companies they invest in, to believe in their long-term value and potential and to engage with management to ensure that they are behaving in the interest of continuous value creation.

WHAT GOVERNMENT CAN DO

Government is too often left with the task of cleaning up the wreckage left by the short-term and unsustainable practices of both companies and investors. The recent example of the global financial crisis highlights a sad reality: government is the backstop to serious blunders by businesses. As such, the widespread practice of Sustainable Capitalism would have a profound, positive impact on government and across all sectors.

To encourage Sustainable Capitalism, governments can, among other things, develop key infrastructure and policy frameworks. Programs related to human rights, public health and education are just some of the essential pillars necessary to help support the private sector's transition to a more sustainable model. Governments can also foster public-private partnerships, create appropriate regulation to level the playing field among businesses in relation to sustainability (e.g., mandate integrated reporting) and serve as an active and collaborative stakeholder in the investment value chain. According to Peck and Gibson, "Governments that lead [in sustainability] will be in a strong position to set the agenda and establish advanced positions for their industries and their citizens. Countries that lag behind will inevitably face increasing competitive disadvantage and lost opportunity."[14]

Ultimately, government is often the biggest "business" of all and therefore must lead by example. As noted in the *Business Magazine for a Sustainable Government*: "A sustainable society needs local and central government to lead the way by consuming differently, and by planning effectively and efficiently in order to integrate sustainable practices in the services it provides to citizens, and throughout its estates and workforce."[15] Governments must also strive for the same tenets of sustainability—the prudent management of financial and ESG resources. In doing so they will create a platform on which stable and prosperous societies can grow.

BARRIERS TO OVERCOME

Our thoughts and advocacy work around Sustainable Capitalism date back to the founding of Generation Investment Management. Building on our earlier efforts and our deepening conviction, we realized that to make a more significant and immediate impact on mainstreaming Sustainable Capitalism, we needed to identify and better understand the obstacles we faced. To achieve this, we collaborated with McKinsey in the summer of 2010 to convene a range of experts and practitioners in the Sustainable Capitalism field. Through those sessions we identified five barriers to mainstreaming Sustainable Capitalism.[16]

1. **Short-termism and misaligned incentives.** The often-misaligned incentives of company executives and investors, compared to those of their stakeholders, fuel short-termism. For example, reporting and managing to quarterly results clearly restricts the ability to create more favorable long-term results.
2. **Market fundamentalism.** An engrained fear of alternatives to currently prevailing approaches to capitalism plagues investors, and a complacent inertia persists among a majority of people who are waiting to be convinced of the opportunities Sustainable Capitalism presents.
3. **Obsession with numbers.** Investors value most highly that which can be measured most easily and frequently. Given that ESG-related issues can be difficult to quantify, they are often ignored. Abraham Maslow famously quipped, "If the only tool you have is a hammer, every problem begins to look like a nail." In the same way, if the only tool you use for measuring value is a price tag, business factors with no price tag conveniently attached may seem to have no value.
4. **Complexity of the challenge.** The adoption of Sustainable Capitalism is a highly complex problem requiring sophisticated and comprehensive cross-sector solutions. Although many businesses have already solved this problem, there is as yet a lack of widespread awareness of the success stories of businesses and leaders driving this change.
5. **Lack of competencies.** There is a dearth of education on Sustainable Capitalism. The skill sets of business leaders, investors and asset owners need to be informed by Sustainable Capitalism.

Overcoming these barriers will be essential to mainstreaming Sustainable Capitalism, and we are under no illusions about the effort necessary to achieve this goal.

Ben Franklin famously said, "You may delay, but time will not, and lost time is never found again." We have the opportunity to rebuild for the long term and an obligation to seize it. Sustainable Capitalism will create opportunities and rewards, but it will also mean challenging the pernicious orthodoxy of short-termism. Now is the time to accelerate the transition.

This chapter is based on the Generation Investment Management white paper, "Sustainable Capitalism," originally published in 2012.

NOTES

1. Frank X. Zhang, *The Effect of High-Frequency Trading on Stock Volatility and Price Discovery* (New Haven, CT: Yale University School of Management, 2010).
2. PwC's Deals Webcast Series, "Private Equity & Environmental Sustainability—Creating Long-Term Value," June 30, 2011, http://www.pwc.com/us/en/transaction-services/webcasts.
3. Edelman, 2011 Edleman Trust Barometer, http://www.edelman.com/trust/2011.
4. Robert G. Eccles, Ioannis Ioannou, and George Serafeim, "The Impact of a Corporate Culture of Sustainability on Corporate Behavior and Performance," Working paper, Harvard Business School, 2011.
5. Alex Edmans, "Does the Stock Market Fully Value Intangibles? Employee Satisfaction and Equity Prices," *Journal of Financial Economics*, January 20, 2010, http://ssrn.com/abstract=985735
6. Rob Bauer and Daniel Hann, "Corporate Environmental Management and Credit Risk," Maastricht University, European Centre for Corporate Engagement, 2010.
7. Cheng Beiting, Ioannis Ioannou, and George Serafeim, "Corporate Social Responsibility and Access to Finance," Working paper no. 11-130, Harvard Business School, 2010.
8. Andrew Haldane and Richard Davies, "The Short Long," Speech presented at the 29th Société Universitaire Européenne De Recherches Financières Colloquium: New Paradigms in Money and Finance?, Brussels, Belgium, May 2011, http://www.bankofengland.co.uk/publications/speeches/2011/speech495.pdf.
9. Eccles, Ioannou, and Serafeim, "The Impact of a Corporate Culture of Sustainability."
10. Ibid.
11. Robert G. Eccles, Michael P. Krzus, and George Serafeim, "Market Interest in Nonfinancial Information," Working paper no. 12-018, Harvard Business School, 2011.
12. Jason Josefs, Aviva Investors Thought Leadership, Integrating ESG, accessed October 2011, http://www.avivainvestors.co.uk/markets_and_views/thought_leadership/investors-journal-v2/integrating-esg/index.htm.
13. Graham Bowley, "Clamping Down on Rapid Trades in Stock Market," *New York Times*, October 8, 2011.
14. Steven Peck and Robert Gibson, "Pushing the Revolution," *Alternatives Journal* 26, no. 1 (Winter 2000); cited in David V. J. Bell, "The Role of Government in Advancing Corporate Sustainability," Working paper, March 27, 2002.
15. "Public Sector Sustainability under the Spotlight," *Government Sustainability* (April 2009), http://www.governmentsustainability.co.uk.
16. Generation Investment Management and McKinsey, "Mainstreaming Sustainable Capitalism by 2020: Seize the Opportunity," Unpublished internal study, 2010.

CHAPTER 19

REAL INVESTMENT IN THE ANTHROPOCENE

John Fullerton

Founder and President, Capital Institute

The true nature of the international system under which we were living was not realized until it failed.

—Karl Polanyi, *The Great Transformation*

"Welcome to the Anthropocene." So reads the title of the May 26, 2011, cover story of the *Economist* magazine. The article describes, in purely scientific terms, our exit from the relatively placid Holocene era into a new geological period, wherein human activity is altering the health of the living system we call the Earth. It warns that business as usual will lead, inevitably, to irreversible damage to the life-supporting systems of the planet.

Absent from the exposition, however, is any discussion of the critical role finance plays in shaping those impacts. Einstein said, "It is the theory which decides what can be observed." Devoid of any connection to ecological systems in the real world, finance theory blinds us from the crises it facilitates. The *Economist* missed a golden opportunity to provide insight into how our relentless pursuit of the exponential growth of financial capital, hardwired into our economic system, will bring us to the brink of collapse if we don't change course.

In fact, since the negative impacts of human activity that characterize the Anthropocene era are manifesting largely through the material flows of the real economy—raw materials drawn into the economic system and wastes discarded out of it—the *Economist* article should have seized the opportunity to declare that the emergence of the Anthropocene requires a seismic shift in the way we *observe* economics and the human economy. Critically, we must now understand that there is, in fact, nothing out of the system. Instead, the economy is literally embedded in the biosphere—a closed system (other than the life-enabling constant inflow of solar energy) that obeys the laws (not theories) of thermodynamics. In the current era of finance capitalism, we must also understand that it is finance that is driving most of the dominant material flows of the global economy (for good and bad). It then follows that connecting finance to the realities of the Anthropocene is essential. Those realities must set the context for the governance of our financial system and, in particular, for the decision making that drives *real investment*—in plant and equipment and large-scale infrastructure. They must also be the point of reference for public policies that support an economic system that serves people without damaging the planet's life-supporting functions over the long run.

Currently, the realities that the Anthropocene represents are rarely the subject of public discussion, even within the sustainable investment community. Instead, financial market commentators and policy makers preoccupy themselves, understandably, with the now all-too-apparent connection between irresponsible banking and short-term-obsessed and speculative capital markets on one hand, and real economy health on the other: unemployment, fiscal deficits and growing inequality in particular. Indeed, the egregious offenses of modern finance need little elaboration. The finance-induced Great Recession—still a depression in parts of the European Union—is causing oppressive human pain and suffering, with multigenerational consequences, including public sector fiscal distress, worsened structural unemployment and increased wealth inequality within nations, all cascading throughout the global economy.

However, if we can peer beyond the wreckage, we may glimpse a silver lining: the lingering economic crisis has moved even mainstream economists to question as never before the very foundations of our finance-driven economic system, *the theories that determine what we can observe* and through which we interpret events and structure policy responses. The time is ripe for the exploration of a fully integrated approach to grappling with the systemic challenges of our era.

More dangerous over the long run than rogue banks too big to fail or govern, or the predatory casino finance that has become their stock-in-trade, is the *undifferentiated* and therefore unsustainable growth that drives the modern economy beyond the resource and waste sink limits of the biosphere. Not all growth is economic, when real costs are considered. Climate change is but the most pressing symptom of this *systemic crisis*, which will define the twenty-first century. How we rise to this challenge will determine our legacy on this planet.

The sustainability challenge to finance is quite distinct from, although interconnected to, the mainstream agenda for financial reform after the financial crash of 2008. Financing the transition to a sustainable and inclusive economic system will demand a much deeper inquiry into the practice of finance and, in particular, long-term decision making affecting the flow of trillions of dollars of real investment in the decades ahead. It is not merely a matter of regulating the financial system more effectively to avoid a Great Depression, or to avoid another socialization of the costs of reckless behavior and failed leadership on Wall Street. We must also focus on the link between finance and our *real investment choices* at the macrosystemic level, not just excessive financial speculation in capital markets, in response to the new context of the Anthropocene. The Anthropocene changes everything.

SUSTAINABLE FINANCE

Practitioners are making tangible progress in the all-important measurement and transparency initiatives of the environmental, social and governance (ESG) framework, and in the related quest for integrated reporting that fully addresses the impacts of enterprise activities on all stakeholders, across multiple kinds of capital: human capital (intellectual, experiential), social capital (reputational, community) and natural capital (nature and the priceless ecosystem services we depend on) in their many forms. It is noteworthy and instructive that Michael Bloomberg and Mary Schapiro are the new chair and vice-chair, respectively, of the Sustainability Accounting Standards Board (SASB).[1] With a growing awareness of the reality that climate change is upon us now, our minds have turned to the enormous challenge of identifying who will fund the $44 trillion of clean energy investment the International Energy Agency estimates will be needed through 2050 if we are to have even an 80 percent chance of limiting warming to 2 degrees Celsius.[2] And then there is necessary water infrastructure investment, also measured in trillions. Together, this infrastructure replacement and upgrade represents both a massive opportunity and a herculean financing challenge.

Unfortunately, lacking a holistic approach grounded in this changed context, some of the well-intended regulatory responses to the financial collapse have made financing the transition to a sustainable economic system much more difficult. Bank management's inability to "stop dancing," to paraphrase the infamous words of Citigroup CEO Chuck Prince, have led to undifferentiated liquidity limits aimed at reining in reckless credit and liquidity mismatch practices, but unintentionally have also limited banks' appetites to do the critical long-term project finance associated with renewable energy infrastructure needs. Instead, we have bloated too-big-to-fail bank balance sheets clogged with speculative trading positions that serve no real economic purpose and short-term loans to hedge fund speculators when we need that balance sheet capacity and more for infrastructure lending.

This real investment imperative is unprecedented. In addition to the tens of trillions of dollars for energy and water infrastructure, there are the infrastructure demands of new megacities to accommodate the urbanization desires of a global population that is expected to grow by another 2 to 3 billion people before it levels off. As we contemplate this flow of real investment at a macrosystemic level, we must at the same time hold it within the context of the unprecedented realities of the Anthropocene. To do that, we will now turn to the concept of planetary boundaries.

PLANETARY BOUNDARIES

In 2009, Johan Rockström led a group of internationally renowned scientists in identifying nine planetary boundaries within which humanity can continue to develop and thrive well into the future.[3] It is a framework to identify and understand the critical thresholds of biophysical systems such as the carbon cycle and the water cycle, which are intrinsic to the healthy function of the Earth's life support system, upon which the human economy depends.

The report highlights that climate change (carbon cycle out of balance) was already well past the "safe operating space" in 2009. The rate of biodiversity loss was even more worrying if we accept (as is now the scientific consensus) that the sixth "great extinction" already under way is a direct threat to human prosperity and even survival. Similarly, the nitrogen cycle was out of balance well beyond its safe operating space, creating dead zones at the mouths of all major river systems on the planet, with feedback loops we don't fully comprehend.

Increasingly, policy makers grappling with the sustainability challenge of the Anthropocene are working from this conceptual framework. Yet remarkably, few mainstream economists of either political persuasion, and even fewer financial system regulators or leaders, acknowledge its relevance to their work, or are even aware of the study. This must change.

Science tells us that our planet, along with all of its complex, interconnected biochemical systems that enable life to exist, is fixed in scale. Yet our dominant economic theories—*theories that determine what we observe*—assume, in conflict with the laws of physics, that our path to prosperity requires limitless, undifferentiated, exponential growth of the economy's metabolism—raw materials in and waste out of the system, otherwise known as material throughput.

Of course the material throughput per unit of GDP is not fixed, and technological advances in materials and energy productivity, and closed-loop production systems in which waste becomes raw material, are quite promising, if slow to penetrate the global economy. However, these same efficiency improvements often stimulate more demand from the savings they create, what is called, in science, the rebound effect. Critically, unless we simply assume, against all the current evidence and common sense, that we can continue generating exponential material throughput growth indefinitely into the future while at the same time achieve *greater* material efficiencies every year indefinitely, then the possibility of shrinking the economy's footprint on the planet is an illusion. And the science is clear that we are already well beyond the "safe operating space" of the planet and getting worse every year.

We must now rein in speculative finance that serves no social purpose while harming overall system resilience, and redeploy it as a tool to realign our economy with the earth's biophysical constraints. Finance's most important practical function in the real economy is the transformation of savings into *productive* investment and the credit creation process of the banking system. The reorientation of the flow of real investment (not to be confused with the sideshow of financial asset speculation) is the bridge to, and the steering mechanism for, the great transition to an economy that serves the needs of people while respecting the Earth's physical limits.

Since real investment fuels economic growth, the same planetary boundaries that dictate both qualitative and quantitative limits to growth also imply qualitative and quantitative limits to investment at the system level.

This is new. No economic system in the history of civilization has ever had to contemplate such a constraint. How much, and where, large economic actors like multinational corporations and nation-states invest—as well as where and how they forgo investment—will significantly determine the quality and sustainability of the future global economy and our collective well-being and security. As a consequence, real investment choices, right alongside other common interests like providing national security, must become a central concern of global governance, notwithstanding the many failings of governing institutions and our justifiably reduced confidence in them.

THE IMPACT OF INVESTMENT

The economy, as measured by gross national product (GNP), includes consumption, investment, government spending and net exports, often rendered as a simple equation:

$$GNP = C + I + G + netX$$

Concern for sustainability has typically focused on consumption since it represents the largest share of the economy (70 percent in the United States, less in emerging economies like China and India). However, capital invest-ment has a disproportionately large impact because of the long-term impli-cations it has on future consumption through technology lock-in and the embedded feedback loops of business enterprise. For example, if an automo-bile company constructs a factory to build SUVs, then its advertising and sales efforts will focus on increasing the demand for these SUVs for years to come, which will impact consumer behavior.

The distinction between financial investment and real investment is critically important. The former has attracted considerable attention in the investment community: witness the debates about the impact of ESG factors on corporate behavior and investment performance. Yet financial investors and speculators—groups that increasingly blur together—are typically far removed from the *real capital investment* decisions of the large public corpora-tions that, to a significant extent, drive and shape the material economy. Even some leading practitioners of ESG and sustainable investment acknowledge that ESG is primarily a risk mitigation strategy for financial investment portfolios, rather than a transformational strategy for the real economy.[4]

The top 1,000 global corporations represent half of the total market value of the world's 60,000 public companies and, undoubtedly, an even greater share of capital investment budgets.[5] What demands our attention, therefore, are the decades-long impacts of the capital expenditure decisions of these largest corporations, together with the impacts of large government capital expenditures like investments in infrastructure. Corporate reporting on social and environmental performance, however, tends to focus on supply chain impacts rather than the initiating impact of the capital expenditures that create these supply chains. To take one of the world's largest corpora-tions as an example, Wal-Mart's continued investment in new superstores matters much more than its subsequent efforts to "green" its supply chain, notwithstanding the importance of that work.

Shareholder engagement that focuses on capital investment decisions will inevitably confront pushback rooted in concerns about long-term growth, competitiveness and share price. Corporations generally make their invest-ment decisions using an internal rate of return framework that compares a project's expected financial return with the firm's cost of capital. Because of the way finance discounts the future, corporations approve capital expendi-tures that achieve financial return targets with time horizons that rarely ex-ceed ten years and typically ignore externalities, including those with serious long-term risks. Concerns about the systemic impact on social and natural capital rarely enter the investment analysis. They are managed afterward, if at all. This short-termism is compounded by the even shorter-term horizon of financial investors and speculators preoccupied with quarterly earnings and share prices.

Policy responses, moreover, rarely occur until after enterprise investment decisions have already been made. In the name (and current theory) of "free market capitalism," companies are free to build a cigarette industry, and only afterward does society respond with labeling and advertising policies that, at best, partially mitigate the damage. Today, unprecedented and potentially catastrophic ecological risks make this reactive approach unacceptable. Many forward-thinking CEOs and policy makers fully understand this new reality yet feel powerless to change it.

FROM THE FIRM TO THE SYSTEM

An adequate response to the challenge of a world at risk requires turning from the firm-level investment decisions to the economic system as a whole.[6] Along with genuine contributions to human progress, our economic system has produced staggering growth in financial wealth. Financial assets in the United States have doubled as a percentage of GDP since 1980 alone.[7] This should give us pause, rather than reason for celebration.

The drive for exponential returns on financial capital pushed finance to shorter-term and more speculative—at times predatory—activity at the same time as physical resource limits began to impose constraints on growth. This confluence has an alarming cost. Of the 20 largest countries in the world, constituting nearly three-quarters of global GDP, all but Japan (which experienced little if any real growth in the relevant period) suffered per capita losses in their natural capital stocks between 1990 and 2008.[8] Although natural capital can be eroded for decades, we already appear to have passed safe limits, most notably the atmosphere's limit to absorb carbon waste, as the previous discussion makes clear.

Notwithstanding essential improvements in material productivity now on the horizon, enabled by regenerative practices and circular economy technologies, in the full-world context in which we now find ourselves, qualitative and quantitative limits to aggregate material growth logically imply similar limits to investment at the system level (remember, the economy is embedded in the biosphere, not separate from it). Our challenge is to determine *where* we invest, *what* we grow and *how* we grow it. A distributed renewable energy system, material productivity improvements in the industrialized world and leap-frogging technology investments in support of healthy lives with dignity for the less-developed economies are obviously top priorities.[9] Investments in carbon-intense energy, fossil-fuel-hogging luxury yachts and indoor skiing in the Dubai desert are not. But who gets to decide?

Of course, for those without material sufficiency, growth in financial capital will continue to be essential. However, for those with a surplus of both material and financial wealth, other forms of wealth must be pursued, while effectively recycling financial capital back into social and natural capital. This *systemic requirement* of a sustainable system fits nicely with our broadly shared moral belief that those who reap the greatest benefit from the system have the most responsibility to give back. Like many before them, the Buffett and Gates Giving Pledge is powerful evidence of this belief in practice. Our challenge, at this pivotal time, is to radically scale up and accelerate these actions, given present imbalances where 85 people control as much wealth as the bottom half of the global population, and when our stocks of natural capital are being severely degraded, creating catastrophic consequences for the next generations. And we need to expand our conventional thinking beyond charity, to the proactive regeneration of both social capital *and* natural capital.

Thriving individual enterprises—particularly the ones needed to drive the transition to a truly sustainable economy—can and will continue to grow and deliver exponential returns to private investors, at least for a while. However, even accounting for unanticipated efficiency gains in the energy and material intensity of the economy, the *aggregate* stock of financial capital will need to pass through a critical inflection point to declining rates of growth as represented in figure 19.1.[10] We may even need to contemplate a peak (financial) capital stock given planetary boundaries for a given level of technologies in operation.

This transition can occur through some combination of the following developments, many of which are already under way:

- a declining aggregate rate of return on invested capital;
- a systematic financial asset devaluation;
- the debasing of currencies through inflation;

FIGURE 19.1 PATHWAYS FOR THE GROWTH OF FINANCIAL CAPITAL

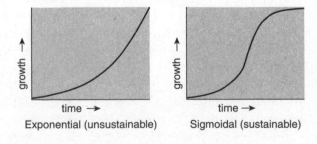

Source: John Fullerton

- defaults leading to voluntary or involuntary debt extinguishment;
- an unprecedented scale of private philanthropy to recycle financial capital back into social and natural capital;
- a large-scale voluntary or policy-induced reinvestment of profits by the corporate sector into natural and social capital; and
- an increase in taxation to allow the public sector to recycle financial capital back into natural and social capital on behalf of vital public security interests.

We can choose to lead this seemingly unnatural transition to reduced growth in the aggregate stock of financial capital while augmenting the stocks of social and natural capital. This would mean investing in education, health care, social safety nets, reforestation, reversing desertification to replenish vital natural carbon sinks and truly sustainable agriculture, to name a few. The flow of capital into such investments would be catalyzed by getting prices more right, most notably by putting a price on carbon and eliminating fossil fuel subsidies so markets can do what they do so well. Alternatively, we risk an uncontrolled reduction in the stock of aggregate financial capital—financial asset collapse—forced upon us by nature's limits, social upheaval or—most likely—both at the same time. As the saying goes, "nature bats last."

THE WAY FORWARD

The scale and complexity of the necessary shift in thinking is unparalleled, and time is not on our side. Not only are we in ecological overshoot, drawing down our life-sustaining stock of natural capital, and not only are we putting social cohesion at risk because of grotesque and growing inequality and related social stresses, but we are no doubt in "financial overshoot" as well.[11] This is because financial assets—both stocks and bonds—are valued by a marketplace that has not yet fully accounted for the multidecade adjustment process ahead, in which honest pricing of externalities and the real resource constraints of planetary boundaries constrain aggregate growth rates below current market expectations. Stranded asset risk—that is, the risk that assets such as fossil fuel reserves should become uneconomic under future governance regimes—is the most obvious example of the many complex risk exposures lurking in the near future.[12] If this transition is left unmanaged, as is the case today, the feedback loops of asset valuation adjustments into the real economy could unleash chaos. Only the timing remains unknown; but markets often adjust violently once new expectations appear, long before the new reality takes hold.

Three interconnected solutions are apparent, all immensely challenging. First, we can work within the current neoliberal economic paradigm to shift the flow of investment by getting prices right—internalizing the costs of the externalities that we currently ignore. Second, business, government and large pools of private capital can begin leading, through enlightened real investment and integrated philanthropy, even before a world of true costs and accurate accounting is realized. Third, the public can demand a new set of rules and regulations—some local, some regional, some global—to establish the necessary guardrails and mandates to force the transition. Let us briefly consider each approach.

1. Getting prices right. Commercial enterprises must begin to pay the true social and environmental cost of their operations and pass these costs on to consumers. Establishing sound measurement procedures and mandatory transparency is an essential first step. Integrated reporting initiatives such as the International Integrated Reporting Council and standards-setting bodies such as the SASB are developing rapidly. Enforced disclosure will soon be a foregone conclusion.[13] Critically, however, the presumption that getting prices right alone is a solution, that we actually can put a correct price on many of these costs—this is naive and dangerous. Some costs represent harms that can be mitigated, while others represent wrongs that never can. The value of a life in a life insurance policy is certainly not the true value of that life. This same principle applies to the value of healthy ecosystem functioning—not "a life," but "life"—which is literally priceless. Getting prices "right" to the extent possible is a crucial, but insufficient, response. There is a danger that current economic theory—*which determines what we are allowed to observe*—will blind us to the limitations of using markets, even fair and transparent markets, as our only tools for all contexts. Social capital and natural capital are inherently different from financial capital, necessitating different tools—for example, caps and quotas to deal with planetary boundaries—for their safe management.

2. Enlightened private behavior. Progress is under way as smart, leading companies, institutions and communities are investing in resource productivity and alternative energy to save money and accelerate the shift to a regenerative economy. Experimentation with forms of enterprise that better align all stakeholder interests, from long-established partnerships and cooperatives to innovative forms of for-benefit corporations and social enterprise, is accelerating.[14] A small group of entrepreneurs and enlightened stewards of capital are leading the way, albeit at a pace too slow and a scale too small. Could a group of institutional-scale actors including businesses, governments, sovereign wealth funds, pension funds, foundations and endowments and high-net-worth families—unshackled from speculative capital markets no longer fit for the purpose and using innovative investment methods such as Evergreen Direct Investing[15]—work collectively to alter the course and quality of the economy through their aggregate real investment decisions and approaches? Or will the emergent bottoms-up, distributed innovation fueled by crowd-sourced funding scale to such a degree that it impacts aggregate investment flows in the global economic system?

The answer remains unclear. On one hand, climate stabilization demands that we not burn the vast majority of known fossil fuel reserves already sitting on company balance sheets, yet the energy industry continues to invest hundreds of billions of dollars per year in search of more.[16] On the other hand, real progress is afoot within progressive corporations, without which meaningful and peaceful economic transition would be difficult, if not impossible. A growing community of wealthy families, foundations and sovereign wealth funds are engaging in "impact investing" and strategic philanthropy to harmonize ecological and social impact with financial returns. But the critical large-scale (measured in the hundreds of billions and eventually trillions of dollars) expansion of this integrated approach, particularly the explicit recycling of financial capital back into social and natural capital, has yet to emerge.

3. Public policy responses. No realistic assessment of the transition ahead, even by the most steadfast advocates of technology-driven and market-based solutions, can fail to see the primacy of the public sector's role in catalyzing this unprecedented shift. We will need to streamline outdated regulations and call aggressively for new regulatory frameworks, incentives and financing mechanisms to redefine the playing field of the Anthropocene and help steer an economic transition more profound than the Industrial Revolution. Economically obvious but politically difficult policies like carbon caps and/or taxes must contribute to a portfolio of tools for curbing greenhouse gas emissions along with expanded research and development in clean technology and the use of public procurement to drive demand for clean technologies, driving down costs in the process. Action to remove subsidies from fossil fuel–based energy and agriculture and shift them to drive improved resource productivity and accelerated growth of renewable energy and sustainable agriculture is long overdue.

However, a larger and more uncomfortable requirement looms. In the full world of the Anthropocene, our notions of freedom will need to adjust to new realities.[17] Simply encouraging so-called green investment will not be enough if we do not curtail investment that has negative and even catastrophic impacts. Deciding the qualitative choices and the absolute scale of investment must become a matter of the public interest, and subject to a functional democratic process. Logic then points to a fresh and expanded need for governance, even though our confidence in government at the moment is low because of valid concerns about competence and corruption.

History teaches us that societies that concentrate too much power lead to corrupt governance and eventual collapse. New and effective approaches to global and regional governance, likely using cities and regions as the central nodes of coordinating power, are essential.

In the complex and interconnected crises ahead, the seemingly impossible will become the inevitable. The previously unchallenged belief in the unencumbered freedom of large corporations and other large economic actors to make investment decisions that may have catastrophic and irreversible consequences for all must now be challenged. Activists fighting deforestation in the Amazon and the construction of the Keystone XL pipeline are showing the way forward. We must begin to accept as vital to our national and interdependent global security interests some form of public interest influence over both the scale and direction of private and public investment capital flows. The U.S. military understands this, even if the political class and the diehard free market zealots do not.[18]

We can look to the public utility sector's (imperfect) permitting process for precedents of regulatory engagement in capital investment decisions at regional scale.[19] Numerous state and multilateral actors, such as the World Bank and other international development banks, already influence the course of investment capital flows. The idea is not new, but the potential scale and scope are, particularly in regard to the need to curtail certain investments, such as the continued, unrestrained extraction of coal and tar sands oil.

Central banks are obvious candidates for radical institutional reform to encompass this new imperative, although not without challenges. Central banking in the Anthropocene might well entail *qualitative* mandates to differentiate investment and credit flows, in addition to conventional inflation and full-employment mandates. Will we see qualitative easing (and qualitative tightening) in the future? Turns out, it already exists with specific social objectives in mind, both in Japan and Bangladesh, and perhaps other countries as well.

We must also tackle thorny questions regarding the public and private nature of banking institutions, the credit creation function that the banks now manage under a fractional reserve system, and the alignment of the mission of banks with public purpose rather than private speculation at public expense. Member banks in the Global Alliance for Banking on Values, collectively representing $75 billion in assets, are at the cutting edge of values-driven private sector banks whose purpose is to serve the transition to a sustainable economy. It's noteworthy that they perform better financially than too-big-to-fail, subsidized behemoths.[20] The well-managed State Bank of North Dakota is a state-owned bank with a public purpose that collaborates with the private banking sector in the state and provided stability to the state's economy through the recent recession. And even mainstream commentators such as Martin Wolf of the *Financial Times* and researchers at the International Monetary Fund (IMF) are now openly discussing radical ideas like the Chicago Plan (a set of bank reforms originally proposed by a group of University of Chicago economists following the Great Depression), which would remove the money-creation function from private sector banks and return it to the public sector.[21] These are just some of the issues that warrant our attention in the Anthropocene.

We will achieve our greatest impacts on capital flows if we concentrate our regulatory capabilities in order to rein in and influence the capital investment decisions of just the very largest corporations and the G-20 governments, as well as the credit decisions of the 50 largest global banks and financial intermediaries. Supporting public policies can achieve this while allowing more decentralized and generally less potentially destructive entrepreneurial energies and associated capital flows to flourish at appropriate scale within a new macro framework. If megafirms in the private sector fail to act in accordance with this overriding public interest, or prove to be ungovernable, we may have no alternative but to nationalize and manage them in the public interest, as Milton Friedman's mentor and teacher H. C. Simmons well understood in his own context.[22]

Can such unprecedented global oversight, even if limited to the most critical economic actors, be practical without harming the global economy? We have no choice but to try, for business-as-usual will lead eventually to social and ecological collapse—and, of course, the collapse of the financial system and real economy as well. There will inevitably be short-term efficiency and growth trade-offs in exchange for system resilience. But it is resilience that we are lacking at this time.

The careful, holistic management and monitoring of aggregate real investment flows are inevitable parts of the economy of the future and the challenging transition to it. They will require new global oversight mechanisms, informed by the best scientific understanding of critical ecosystem boundaries and empowered by sovereign nation-states and global corporations, to define and enforce a "safe operating space" within which our innovation-driven, free enterprise system can thrive.[23]

Large-scale investment decisions simply must be considered a vital part of the public interest and on the agenda of an informed, democratic process. The sooner we acknowledge the implications of this immense challenge, the better.

NOTES

1. "Michael R. Bloomberg and Mary Schapiro Appointed to SASBS Board Leadership," PR Newswire, May 1, 2014, http://www.prnewswire.com/news -releases/michael-r-bloomberg-and-mary-schapiro-appointed-to-sasbs-board -leadership-257486101.html.

2. International Energy Agency, "Energy Technology Perspectives 2014: Pathways to Clean Energy System" (Paris: OECD.IEA, 2014), http://www.bloomberg .com/news/2014-05-11/power-decarbonization-cost-rises-22-to-44-trillion -iea-says.html.

3. Johan Rockström et al., "A Safe Operating Space for Humanity," *Nature* 461 (September 2009): 472–75.

4. Private communications.

5. Robert G. Eccles and George Serafeim, "Top 1,000 Companies Wield Power Reserved for Nations," *Bloomberg*, September 11, 2012, http://www.bloomberg .com/news/2012-09-11/top-1-000-companies-wield-power-reserved-for-na tions.html.

6. Although the focus here is on large firms, nurturing decentralized, low-capital enterprises will be vital to building a sustainable economy.

7. Charles Roxburgh et al., *Global Capital Markets: Entering a New Era* (New York: McKinsey Global Institute, 2009), http://www.mckinsey.com/insights /global_capital_markets/global_capital_markets_entering_a_new_era.

8. International Human Dimensions Programme on Global Environmental Change, *Inclusive Wealth Report: Measuring Progress Toward Sustainability* (Cambridge: Cambridge University Press, 2012).

9. Hunter Lovins and Boyd Cohen, *The Way Out: Kick-Starting Capitalism to Save Our Economic Ass* (New York: Hill and Wang, 2012).

10. Of course, the abstract sigmoidal curve leaves key questions unanswered—what grows, what shrinks, what impact will technology have, who decides, how do we manage the adjustment and so on.

11. John Fullerton, "Financial Overshoot," *The Future of Finance* (blog), Capital Institute, July 23, 2012, http://www.capitalinstitute.org/blog/financial-overshoot.

12. http://www.carbontracker.org/report/wasted-capital-and-stranded-assets/.

13. International Integrated Reporting Council, *Consultation Draft of the International <IR> Framework* (London: IIRC, 2013), http://www.theiirc.org /wp-content/uploads/Consultation-Draft/Consultation-Draft-of-the-Interna tionalIRFramework.pdf; "SASB Principles," Sustainability Accounting Standards Board, last modified 2013, http://www.sasb.org/approach/principles.

14. Marjorie Kelly, *Owning Our Future: The Emerging Ownership Revolution* (San Francisco: Berrett-Koehler, 2012).

15. http://fieldguide.capitalinstitute.org/evergreen-direct-investing.html.

16. Bill McKibben, "Global Warming's Terrifying New Math," *Rolling Stone*, July 19, 2012, http://www.rollingstone.com/politics/news/global-warmings-terrify ing-new-math-20120719; John Fullerton, "Big Choice," *The Future of Finance* (blog), Capital Institute, July 19, 2011, http://www.capitalinstitute.org/blog /big-choice-0.

17. John Fullerton, "Freedom in the Anthropocene," *The Future of Finance* (blog), Capital Institute, June 4, 2012, http://www.capitalinstitute.org/blog/freedom -anthropocene.

18. Patrick C. Doherty, "A New U.S. Grand Strategy," New America Foundation, January 9, 2013, http://www.prnewswire.com/news-releases/michael-r-bloom berg-and-mary-schapiro-appointed-to-sasbs-board-leadership-257486101.ht ml.
19. Richard Rosen, "How Should the Economy Be Regulated?" Paper presented at the Second Summit on the Future of the Corporation, Corporation 20/20, Boston, MA, June 2009, http://www.corporation2020.org/corporation2020/do cuments/Papers/2nd-Summit-Paper-Series.pdf.
20. http://www.gabv.org/our-news/report-shows-sustainable-banks-outperform -big-banks#.VC8IXSldXgo.
21. Jaromir Benes and Michael Kumhof, "The Chicago Plan Revisited," IMF Working Paper, 2012, https://www.imf.org/external/pubs/ft/wp/2012/wp12202 .pdf.
22. H. C. Simons, *Economic Policy for a Free Society* (Chicago: University of Chicago Press, 1948). The author is grateful to Gar Alperovitz for drawing attention to Simons's views on nationalization in his *New York Times* op-ed, Gar Alperovitz, "Wall Street Is Too Big to Regulate," *New York Times*, July 22, 2012.
23. Peter Brown and Geoffrey Garver, *Right Relationship, Building a Whole Earth Economy* (San Francisco: Berrett-Koehler, 2009).

PART IX

THE FINANCE AGREEMENTS

INTRODUCTION

John G. Taft

My father spent his entire professional career as a professor of physics at Yale University, serving also for a decade as dean of Yale College, which I attended as well. As a result, one thing that's always been on my bucket list has been to honor his legacy by teaching at Yale. Vikram Mansharamani made that happen. On a snowy March morning in New Haven, Connecticut, I followed up on Vikram's invitation to guest teach a class for his course, "Adventures in Business Ethics," at Yale. The topic: ethical decision making in the financial services industry.

My appearance in a Yale classroom was the quid pro quo for Vikram's agreement, which I secured at a CFA Institute symposium we both attended in Washington, D.C., to serve as the cleanup batter for this book. Vikram agreed to distill, summarize and connect the disparate messages running through the 20 contributed essays.

He does so in his own unique style, by drawing on the work of Mexican philosopher don Miguel Ruiz to postulate four "agreements" between society and finance, agreements that form a basis for finance to contribute, in a more consistently positive way, to social good.

Mansharamani's proposed agreements are aligned with what is, or should be, the stewardship mission of finance: be authentic, serve as a means to greater ends, be transparent and focus on delivering the outcomes clients and society want. Ultimately, success in meeting these goals is how the social utility of finance will be judged.

Norman Mailer once wrote that "writing is of use to the psyche only if the writer discovers something he did not know he knew in the act itself of writing."[1] I believe that. I believe the act of writing is a journey that ultimately brings the author back to where he or she started, but with the added ability to see their starting point anew, through fresh and different lenses, with more insight and wisdom than they started with. The most effective writing shares that journey with its readers.

My hope is that having come this far in reading *A Force for Good*, Mansharamani's essay will resonate for readers more than it would have at the outset of the book. That together we will have discovered something about the purpose and goals of finance that we didn't know before. That we will be inspired to reflect on those discoveries in our own professional pursuits and personal lives.

NOTE

1. Norman Mailer, *The Presidential Papers* (New York: G. P. Putnam's Sons, 1963), 219.

CHAPTER 20

THE FINANCE AGREEMENTS

A WORKING PHILOSOPHY FOR THE FUTURE

Vikram Mansharamani

Lecturer, Yale University,
Program on Ethics, Politics and Economics

In thinking about the future of finance, I have turned to Toltec wisdom for inspiration. I've chosen to use this ancient Mexican philosophy as a guide not as a fashionably esoteric application of a yoga-inspired, holistic self-help tradition, but rather because of its profound pertinence.

Don Miguel Ruiz, a medical surgeon turned shaman, shared the key insights of the Toltec tradition in *The Four Agreements: A Toltec Wisdom Book.*[1] Although pitched as a "practical guide to personal freedom," the framework he presents has stunning relevance for our current attempt to reset finance. It is a book about how to live, and in this regard, its message for financiers, both as individuals and as an industry, is profound.

In many ways, the spirit of his work echoes the essays you've just read. Consider some of the key topics discussed within these pages: authenticity, trust, stewardship, governance, sustainability, fiduciary principles, responsibility, et cetera. Even the mere title of Ruiz's work suggests a social contract in which one chooses to engage with the world under certain terms or, to use his word, "agreements." Below are the four agreements that I believe finance needs to make with society.

But before we begin, let me clarify what I mean by the terms *finance* and *financiers*. Finance is the ecosystem of activities focused on the movement, management and measurement of money. It is filled with practitioners ranging from M&A lawyers, accountants, mortgage bankers, hedge fund managers, mutual fund marketers, investment advisors, consultants, corporate treasurers, portfolio managers, community bankers and endowment chiefs (to name a few). I thus use the term *finance* to refer to the entire industry and *financiers* to describe all operating in the "money business."

AGREEMENT 1—FINANCE AGREES TO BE IMPECCABLE: A CALL FOR AUTHENTICITY

The first agreement described by Ruiz is for individuals to "be impeccable with your word."[2] The word *impeccable* literally means "without sin." Is this not a call for authenticity and transparency? Reconsider Donald Trone's piece on trust and authenticity—a true call for finance to be impeccable in its word.

Finance tends to attract ambitious and intelligent people who are, for the most part, honest and hardworking. A few bad actors, however, can rapidly destroy the trust that is so essential for finance to function effectively. Consider two names that loom large in public opinion and recollection: Bernard Madoff and Allen Stanford. These two individuals, we would all agree, were not impeccable in any capacity, and misled hundreds of investors. While their misconduct was brazen, the lack of transparency in other forms of asset management is equally problematic.

Consider a proposition I give to my students each year, which, although presented as genuine, is merely a lesson in understanding the complexities of finance. I offer to fund a start-up in which the students will write 256 different investment newsletters. Half of the newsletters will be bullish, half will be bearish. After one year, I claim, our start-up will have 128 newsletters that "called" the market correctly. We stop writing the 128 that were wrong in their market prediction but again repeat the exercise; 64 bullish, 64 bearish. At the end of two years, we will have 64 newsletters that have been right two years in a row. Repeat, repeat, repeat. At the end of the five years, we will have eight newsletters that have accurately called the market's direction for five years in a row, a truly impressive accomplishment that will be adequate, I believe, to attract capital to launch a small fund around the "proven" track record of market navigation. Let's suppose we then raise $100 million in each of the eight funds we launch. Again, half are positioned for a rising market, half are more bearish. At the end of year 1, four funds have been accurate. Repeat, repeat. At the end of year 3, we have a fund with a three-year proven investment track record of successful market performance following five years of proven and documented accuracy in market predictions.

I then suggest to my students that such a fund would be highly likely to attract significant capital (let's say $3 billion), demand a three-year lockup, and have a 1.5 percent management fee and 20 percent incentive fee.

Assuming the fund merely performs "in line" with the market (let's assume 8 percent), the firm will generate approximately $270 million in revenues over three years. I then calculate that extravagant offices, reasonable base salaries and all appropriate research-oriented accoutrements necessary to generate market average returns will cost the firm $5 million per year for a total of $15 million, which I round up to $20 million to be conservative. The net expected payout from this 11-year endeavor would be about $250 million.

I then ask the graduating students in my class if they are willing to participate. I remind them that they will have a great life for five years as the workload will be minimal compared to that of their investment banking peers, but that they will be earning a modest base salary that I have agreed to pay. They will then again endure an additional three years of lean pay during the "launch phase" while the firm establishes its auditable three-year track record.

I conclude my pitch by suggesting I'm only willing to support five "partners" in this endeavor for the first eight years, and that each will get 10 percent of the equity in return for their participation. As the investor and funding source behind the start-up, I tell them I will retain 50 percent of the equity. The highly probable outcome I offer is then made blunt: "Those who join me will likely have a $25 million payday before the age of 33, while retaining a better life during your twenties than many of your Wall Street–bound peers who may never earn as much." To make the lesson as true as possible, I reiterate several times that I am quite serious about starting this endeavor and that I have been looking for partners to join me in this project.

While it should not shock anyone that several students jump at the chance to join me in this (fictional) endeavor, most have a deep discomfort with the business and are not ready to commit. They sense it seems "unfair" and "fraudulent" and "sketchy." I assure them we will not break the law and will not in any way misrepresent the truth. "We will, in fact, actually have written the newsletter that produced a five-year perfect prediction pattern that launched and proved its model in the markets with a small fund over three years before we raise the big money." I'm happy to report that most remain uncomfortable.

I then turn the discussion to the modern mutual fund business, and inquire if our business plan is materially different from those pursued by the large asset management firms running most mutual funds. How many investors in mutual funds realize that many big complexes regularly seed new funds with the hopes that some generate sellable track records? Are mutual funds being impeccable? The most common question asked by my students is "Will we disclose that we started with 256 newsletters?" A valid question indeed. How many funds has the typical mutual fund complex started in the past 11 years?

Finance needs to hold itself to a higher standard than mere compliance with regulatory and legal requirements. The first Finance Agreement, I believe, should therefore be: *Individuals and entities in the financial services industry agree to be honest and authentic, not merely compliant.*

AGREEMENT 2—FINANCE AGREES NOT TO BE ABOUT FINANCE: IT'S ABOUT CLIENTS

The second agreement proposed by Ruiz is "Don't take anything personally,"[3] which I loosely interpret as "it's not about you." Effectively, this is a call to move away from the self-centeredness that dominates our world toward an interpretation of events as not being about you—that is, a call for humbleness.

When I first read *The Four Agreements*, it reminded me of the 2005 Kenyon College commencement speech[4] given by the MacArthur "Genius Grant"–winning English professor and writer David Foster Wallace. After welcoming the graduating students and their guests, he dove immediately into a simple yet powerful parable: "There are these two young fish swimming along and they happen to meet an older fish swimming the other way, who nods at them and says 'Morning, boys. How's the water?' And the two young fish swim on for a bit, and then eventually one of them looks over at the other and asks, 'What the hell is water?'"

The point of the fish story, Wallace suggests, is to highlight that "the most obvious, important realities are often the ones that are hardest to see." This, I submit to you, is one of the chief problems facing finance today. And just as the fish in the Wallace speech are comically unaware of their environment and their dependence upon an unseen, yet essential, reality, so too is finance (even today) remarkably lacking in self-awareness. This needs to change.

Wallace pinpoints this natural self-centeredness as one of the "hardwired default settings" we should seek to adjust. He highlights how each of us experiences the world through our own lens, our feelings and our own interactions. Finance, with the many intelligent, ambitious and hardworking professionals it attracts, is not immune from this sense of self-importance; indeed, it may be especially susceptible. Analysts are recruited from leading universities. Many analysts turn into associates, then vice presidents, directors and eventually managing directors. They are handsomely compensated. They do important work—"God's work," as Goldman Sachs chief Lloyd Blankfein put it in 2009. Is it shocking, then, that they believe finance is the absolute center of the world?

The blunt reality is that finance is an enabler, not an end unto itself, and is entirely dependent upon the "real" world. Recall the piece by Roger L.

Martin that articulates the difference between the real world and the expectations world. Just as fish cannot exist without water, so too is the expectations world dependent upon the existence of the real world. And with finance so heavily focused on the expectations world, an axiomatic and stark reality becomes obvious: finance is not the center of the world. In fact, it may not even be the center of the business world.

The movement of capital from those with to those in need is a noble, worthy and indeed essential endeavor, but let us not fool ourselves into believing that it centers on finance. Robert J. Shiller's earlier chapter, "Finance and the Good Society," persuasively reminds us of the positive impact finance has and continues to have on the progress of mankind and society. But let us not forget that finance is about those operating in the real world. Simply put, it's just not about us. And just as Wallace reminds us to regularly recall the obvious defaults ("This is water. . . . This is water."), so too must finance be reminded of the very simple, profound and rarely discussed fact that finance is not about the financiers. Finance is a supporting actor in a movie starring businesses, households and governments and, as such, needs to reinterpret its purpose and sense of self. Mary Schapiro's piece on the importance of equity markets and the availability of risk financing supports this point by suggesting that equity financing funds the innovation that drives economic progress and prosperity. Equity markets do not exist to serve equity traders, institutional saleswomen or even the investment bankers that populate those markets with securities.

"This is finance . . ."

"This is finance . . ."

This obvious default setting that has become so engrained in finance thinking needs to be reset, and doing so is not going to be easy. Any reader of *What It Takes: Seven Secrets of Success from the World's Greatest Professional Services Firm* by Charles D. Ellis will appreciate the complexities of corporate culture and how it replicates and reinforces an organization's values over time. Culture translates an organization's mission into what Ellis calls "specific, often idiosyncratic practices" and in so doing converts colleagues into a tribe.[5] Changing cultures in finance is essential, yet it remains a monumental task.

The outcome of a financial world that does not put itself at the center is beginning to take shape, and John Rogers provides us a glimpse into what it may look like in his piece on fiduciary capitalism. Client interests come first, and participants acknowledge that lower standards simply dilute what should be an uncontroversial reality: that finance exists to fulfill the needs of its clients. It's a service function.

Think of the role that housing finance can and should play, rather than the one it *did* play during 2007. Given the critical role of housing as an economic driver and its significance as a financial asset for most Americans, the importance of housing finance services cannot be overstated. As Jeremy Diamond suggests in his piece on designing a new system of housing finance, perhaps the waterfall of risks in housing needs to be reconsidered. Banks and others involved in the mortgage market need to be more client-oriented. Does this loan make sense? Does this banker care whether it's viable?

What if we celebrated client success instead of financial superstars? *Alpha* magazine regularly publishes its "Hedge Fund Rich List" that ranks the highest-paid hedge fund managers in the world—not by the returns they generated for clients, but rather by the amount they themselves have made. The 2014 list, which calculated 2013 compensation, had the top 25 individuals earning more than $21 billion for themselves![6] Granted, many of these dollars were due to gains on investments rather than fees charged to clients, but let's not forget that many private equity professionals also regularly extract hundreds of millions of dollars in fees each year for themselves. What if we instead celebrated client success? What if we spoke of the several hundred billion dollars of gains made by the sovereign wealth or pension fund communities? Or the endowment that pioneered a way into outsized returns to support educational objectives? (Oh wait, that's what Yale's chief investment officer, David Swensen, has done!)

Such a reorientation may in fact also support the piece by Dominic Barton and Mark Wiseman that suggested large owners of assets were the ones most likely to effect changes in finance. It's at least conceivable that such support for "Focusing Capital on the Long Term" would diminish the plague of myopia that seems to dominate corporate managers.

This leads me to my second recommended Finance Agreement: *Financiers agree to acknowledge, accept and embrace the priority of client interests.*

"This is finance . . ."

"This is finance . . ."

AGREEMENT 3—FINANCE AGREES TO BE CLEAR: TIME TO DISCLOSE INCENTIVES

The third agreement described by Ruiz is "don't make assumptions" and suggests greater communication and transparency in one's interactions. The finance equivalent, I believe, is a call for transparency and a clear articulation of potential conflicts of interest and the incentives financiers face.

Consider the now-infamous actions of Fabrice Tourre, the Goldman Sachs investment banker who peddled investments to clients that apparently neither he nor Goldman believed were worthwhile investments. As *Time* magazine reported,

Tourre became the object of ridicule over an email he sent to his girlfriend in which he boasted that he sold toxic mortgage bonds to "widows and orphans that I ran into at the airport." He also referred to the financial products he created as "pure intellectual masturbation." In another email, Tourre wrote, "The whole building is about to collapse anytime now," adding "Only potential survivor, the fabulous Fab . . . standing in the middle of all these complex, highly leveraged, exotic trades he created without necessarily understanding all the implications of those monstrosities!!!"[7]

Hardly the spirit of clear communication embodied in the idea of transparency or, to harken back to my second proposed finance agreement, the prioritization of client interests . . .

The urgent need for transparency and clear articulation of potential conflicts of interest becomes alarmingly clear when one considers the intensity of the principal-agent problem in business and finance today. Unlike the times when the CEO was the founder and majority owner of a business, today's managers are professionals hired to manage the business. The investors in their businesses are not capital owners, but rather agents hired to help manage the asset owners, who themselves are often agents of the underlying beneficiaries of a pension fund or other benefit plan. Most people are playing with other people's money.

The effective death of the owner-manager in corporate America has created a dynamic in which short-term incentives have focused executives on Martin's "expectations market." Dispensing with the nuances he so wonderfully articulates, I am going to suggest that his expectations market is effectively the financial market, the one dominated by Wall Street and the investment community. The expectations market sits in contrast to the real market, which remains focused not on quarterly results but on the underlying economic value being generated.

As Martin writes, the fact that "superior performance in the expectations market trumps better absolute performance in the real market" is convincing evidence that the stock-based, compensation-incentive structures designed to overcome the inherent agent nature of professional management is flawed. In our quest to create principal-like behavior, we've created an expectations-oriented monster. We need to rethink executive compensation programs in the context of behavioral implications. Who bears the loss for bad decisions that aren't revealed as bad until years later? Are there incentives to transact, irrelevant of the merits of those transactions? Who is earning money if proposed mergers, positions, allocations or transactions are pursued? There may be great insight in unpacking the incentive structures of the disproportionately powerful agents that are, by many analysts, merely dismissed as necessary friction and transaction costs borne by principals. This friction may in fact be driving the decisions of the principal actors and is therefore enormously important in the grand scheme of who is motivated to do what and why.

Finance also needs to consider one of the (if not *the*) most intractable problems in effective decision making today: career risk. Corporate executives and investors alike remain focused on not getting fired, an incentive structure that contributes to managerial myopia, as well as investors knowingly investing in overvalued securities because they are components of a benchmark index against which they are compared. Career risk creates groupthink on steroids and drives otherwise reasonable professionals into a lemminglike march. Merely discussing such career risk generates thoughts of Keynes's advice that "it is better for reputation to fail conventionally than to succeed unconventionally."[8] The result, not surprisingly, has been a mass conventional failing of finance's ability to meet the needs of clients.

Consider also the principal-agent problem that arises from proprietary trading. While I'm not in a position to disentangle the nuances of market making and the technicalities of principal and agent roles in the domain of trading, I do think transparency is unlikely to harm investors here. After all, if financiers do in fact have "one master," as noted by John Bogle, then making that clear can't be bad!

All of this leads to my third proposed Finance Agreement: *Finance agrees to be transparent about potential conflicts of interest.*

AGREEMENT 4—FINANCE NEEDS TO DO BETTER: "SATISFICING" VERSUS MAXIMIZING

The fourth agreement presented by Ruiz is to "always do your best."[9] I interpret this as acknowledgment that, while we will never be perfect, we should try to get as close as possible. Applying this concept can be tough in the domain of finance, where investors, intermediaries and other ambitious participants in the industry strive to outdo each other and claim recognition as the best ____, the highest ____ and the most important ____.

Such a spirit of entitlement has plagued America for a while, claims David McCullough Jr. in his recent book *You Are Not Special: . . . and Other Encouragements.* In it, McCullough notes, "We have of late, we Americans, to our detriment, come to love accolades more than genuine achievement. We have come to see them as the point—and we're happy to compromise standards, or ignore reality, if we suspect that's the quickest way, or only way, to have something to put on the mantelpiece, something to pose with, crow about, something with which to leverage ourselves into a better spot on the social totem pole."[10]

Finance is as guilty as America in this regard. Consider the spirit of self-prioritization in Tourre's self-referential "Fabulous Fab" nickname. This utter self-aggrandizement is in direct conflict with that of putting clients first in an authentic and transparent way. What if finance transformed itself to be a destination for the service-minded and ambitious, for those wanting to help others and for those seeking to leave the world a better place? The suggestion of finance as a destination for such do-gooders is laughable today, but it need not remain that way. Finance can and should become such a place.

If financiers found professional fulfillment in the nature of their work and approached it with an honesty and pride corresponding to such satisfaction, the industry would be impeccable. If financiers focused on the meaningfulness of their work and the impact they were having on the world, then our second agreement about prioritizing client interests would naturally follow. If financiers thought about satisfaction in their career and accepted the quiet nobility of earning a great living helping others, then transparency and conflict disclosure would not be seen as a grave threat to profitability and compensation. And finally, if financiers were upholding these first three agreements, they might be more likely to focus on client objectives rather than their own.

Consider the newly booming field of goals-based investing. In a recent talk I attended by Nobel laureate Robert Merton, he laid out the case for investment management that was oriented not toward maximizing returns but toward maximizing the probability of achieving an objective.[11]

The concept is fairly straightforward. Most investment advisors focus on a client's risk tolerance (i.e., how much capital loss is acceptable) and then maximize returns. This can best be thought of as purchasing a put, and comes with a cost. But what if we understood that a client was seeking a specific objective, such as having $250,000 for a child's education in 12 years . . . and genuinely did not care about having a penny more? Not surprisingly given his intellectual focus, Merton thinks about this dynamic as effectively selling a call option on portfolio gains above $250,000. Such an option, with a 12-year life, under almost any volatility assumption, would be worth a substantial sum of money. This option premium might equate to 25 to 30 percent of the targeted returns over the time frame and would therefore materially increase the probabilities of having the client achieve her objective. By shifting one's perspective, Merton noted, it is genuinely possible to improve client results.

The fundamental principle that needs to be reevaluated is that more is better, that one should seek to maximize within a constraint. What if this root objective is false? What if clients seek, as noted by Nobel laureate Herbert Simon, to "satisfice"[12] rather than "maximize" returns? It is possible today to effectively shrink both the left and right tails of a return distribution and concentrate the frequency of outcomes (and therefore increase the probability of success) on a narrow range immediately adjacent to the client's objectives.

This goals-based investing logic leads me to the fourth Finance Agreement: *Finance agrees to focus on understanding client objectives and increase the odds of achieving them.*

THE FOUR FINANCE AGREEMENTS
1. Individuals and entities in the financial services industry agree to be honest and authentic, not merely compliant.
2. Financiers agree to acknowledge, accept and embrace the priority of client interests.
3. Finance agrees to be transparent about potential conflicts of interest.
4. Finance agrees to focus on understanding client objectives and increase the odds of achieving them.

Given that we may conceive of this time, and indeed this book, as the beginning of new agreements between finance and society, I felt it appropriate to revisit wisdom offered in commencement speeches. Consider the following quote, taken from a Yale University commencement speech: "It is true—and of high importance—that the prosperity of this country depends on the assurance that all major elements within it will live up to their responsibilities. If business were to neglect its obligations to the public, if labor were blind to all public responsibility, above all, if government were to abandon its obvious—and statutory—duty of watchful concern for our economic health—if any of these things should happen, then confidence might well be weakened and the danger of stagnation would increase."[13]

This quote is from the 1962 commencement speech given by John F. Kennedy immediately upon being granted an honorary degree while an in-office U.S. president. As eerily relevant as it sounds today, it does suggest the time has come for us to reconsider the function of finance in the spirit of public service.

Cognizant of the responsibility granted to those in positions of power and privilege, it is telling that the speech made by Yale president Peter Salovey at a recent commencement did not announce that degrees admitted graduates to the "rights and privileges" thereof (as is conventional in such speeches), but rather that the degrees earned were accompanied by the "rights and responsibilities" thereof. The seemingly minor change is enormous in its implications and embodies the sense of service and duty so needed by finance today.

The future of finance is beginning now. Let it commence with our Four Finance Agreements in mind, and a philosophy that emphasizes responsibility rather than privilege.

NOTES

1. Miguel Ruiz, *The Four Agreements: A Toltec Wisdom Book* (San Rafael, CA: Amber-Allen Publishing, 1997).
2. Ibid., 27.
3. Ibid., 51.
4. David Foster Wallace, *This Is Water: Some Thoughts, Delivered on a Significant Occasion, about Living a Compassionate Life* (New York: Little, Brown & Company, 2009), 3–4.
5. Charles D. Ellis, *What It Takes: Seven Secrets of Success from the World's Greatest Professional Services Firm* (Hoboken, NJ: John Wiley & Sons, 2013), xiii.
6. Stephen Taub, "The Rich List: The Highest-Earning Hedge Fund Managers of the Past Year," *Institutional Investor's Alpha*, May 6, 2014, http://www.institutionalinvestorsalpha.com/Article/3337321/The-Rich-List-The-Highest-Earning-Hedge-Fund-Managers-of-the-Past-Year.html.
7. Sam Gustin, "Not So 'Fabulous' Fab: Ex-Goldman Sachs Trader Fabrice Tourre Found Liable for Fraud," *Time*, August 1, 2013, http://business.time.com/2013/08/01/not-so-fabulous-fab-ex-goldman-sachs-trader-found-liable-for-fraud/.
8. John Maynard Keynes, *The General Theory of Employment, Interest, & Money* (New York: Harcourt, Brace & World, 1965), 67.
9. Ruiz, *Four Agreements*, 85.
10. David McCullough, *You Are Not Special: And Other Encouragements* (New York: HarperCollins, 2014), 309.
11. Robert Merton, comments delivered at the MIT Sloan School of Management conference entitled "Financial Systems 2.0" at the Mandarin Oriental Hotel, Boston, MA, May 16, 2014.
12. Herbert A. Simon, "Rational Choice and the Structure of the Environment," *Psychological Review* 63, no. 2 (1956): 129–138.
13. "John F. Kennedy, Yale University Commencement (June 11, 1962)," *Miller Center at University of Virginia*, http://millercenter.org/president/speeches/speech-3370.

ACKNOWLEDGMENTS

A *Force for Good* grows out of the opportunity I had, as a member of the CFA Institute's Future of Finance Initiative advisory council, to participate in discussions with industry colleagues about many of the topics addressed in this book. In my opinion, the CFA Institute has done as much or more than any organization—from its Integrity List to its Code of Ethics to its Research Foundation—to address the question of what the financial services industry can and needs to do to contribute more consistently to positive social outcomes. I am grateful to the CFA Institute for including me, and I am honored to have been a part of its efforts.

I am also grateful to my agent and editor, Leah Spiro, whose knowledge, professionalism and insights have helped me develop a voice compelling enough to be heard amid the clutter and noise of business media. My colleague at RBC Wealth Management, Sally Schreiber, expertly handled the administrative tasks that attends any publishing project, and handled an increasing share of the editing responsibilities as well.

I appreciate the efforts of the team at Palgrave Macmillan—Karen Wolny, Emily Carleton, Michelle Fitzgerald and Lauren Dwyer-Janiec—and want to thank my colleague at RBC, George Lewis, who has for years allowed me to step outside the lines that usually constrain the activities of financial services professionals to advocate first for "responsible" finance and now, in this book, for "enlightened finance."

Finally, I want to thank my wife, Laura, the love of my life, who despite all my faults and flaws continues to encourage me to be an advocate for and example of responsibility and stewardship values, not just in the world of finance, but in my personal life as well; values which she embodies and personifies more completely than anyone I have ever known.

INDEX